HEROES AND VILLAINS ENTER

presents

TRACKER ™

written by:
Jonathan Lincoln

line art by:
Francis Tsai, Derec Donovan
and Abhishek Malsuni

colors by:
Francis Tsai and Shashank Mishra

letters by:
Troy Peteri

published by
Top Cow Productions, Inc.
Los Angeles

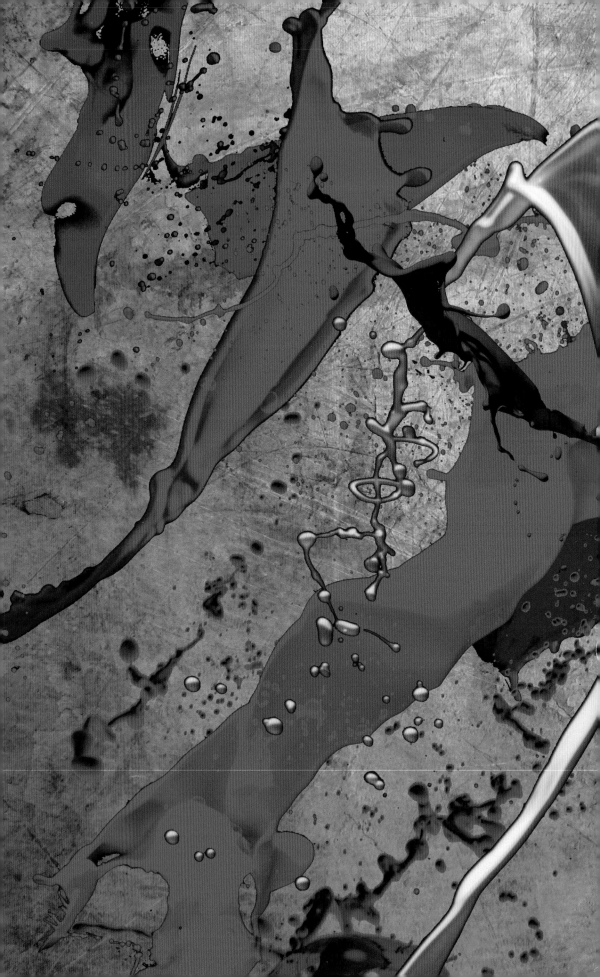

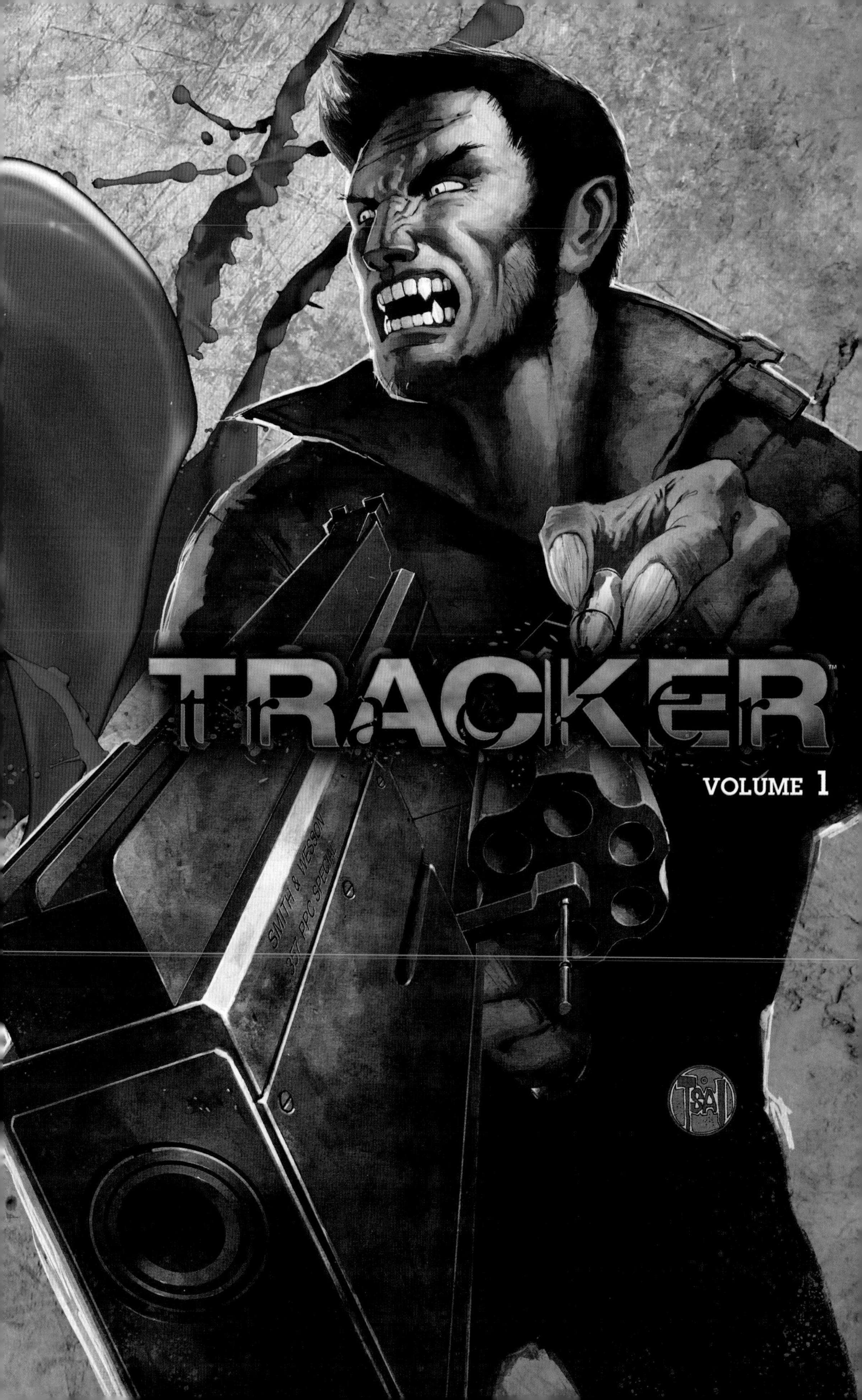
TRACKER™
VOLUME 1
SMITH & WESSON
357 PPC SPECIAL

For Top Cow Productions, Inc.:
Marc Silvestri - Chief Executive Officer
Matt Hawkins - President and Chief Operating Officer
Filip Sablik - Publisher
Phil Smith - Managing Editor
Atom Freeman - Director of Sales & Marketing
Bryan Rountree - Assistant to the Publisher
Christine Dinh - Marketing Assistant
Mark Haynes - Webmaster
Anthony McAfee and **Ernesto Gomez** - Interns

For Heroes and Villains Entertainment
Markus Goerg, Dick Hillenbrand,
& Mikhail Nayfeld

For rights inquiries contact
Heroes and Villains Entertainment: 323 850 2990
INFO@HEROESANDVILLAINS-ENT.COM

M MATURE AUDIENCE
GRAPHIC CONTENT
SOME MATERIAL MAY NOT
BE SUITABLE FOR CHILDREN

for *image* comics
publisher:
Eric Stephenson

COMIC SHOP LOCATOR SERVICE
888-COMICBOOK
888-266-4226

to find the comic shop
nearest you call:
1-888-COMICBOOK

Want more info? check out:
www.topcow.com and **www.thetopcowstore.com**
for news and exclusive Top Cow merchandise!

For this edition Cover Art by:	For this edition	Original editions edited by:
Francis Tsai	Book Design and Layout by: Phil Smith	Filip Sablik & Phil Smith

Tracker volume 1 Trade Paperback
December 2010. FIRST PRINTING, ISBN: 978-1-60706-197-7
Published by Image Comics Inc.. Office of Publication: 2134 Allston Way, 2nd Floor Berkeley, CA 94704, $19.99 U.S.D.. Originally published in single magazine form as Tracker volume 1 issue #0-5. TRACKER © 2010 Top Cow Productions, Inc. and Heroes and Villains Entertainment. "Tracker," the Tracker logos, and the likeness of all featured characters are trademarks of Top Cow Productions, Inc. and Heroes and Villains Entertainment. All rights reserved. Image Comics and the Image Comics logo are trademarks of Image Comics, Inc. The characters, events, and stories in this publication are entirely fictional. Any resemblance to actual persons (living or dead), events, institutions, or locales, without satiric intent, is coincidental. No portion of this publication may be reproduced or transmitted, in any form or by any means, without the express written permission of Top Cow Productions, Inc..
PRINTED IN KOREA.

TABLE OF CONTENTS

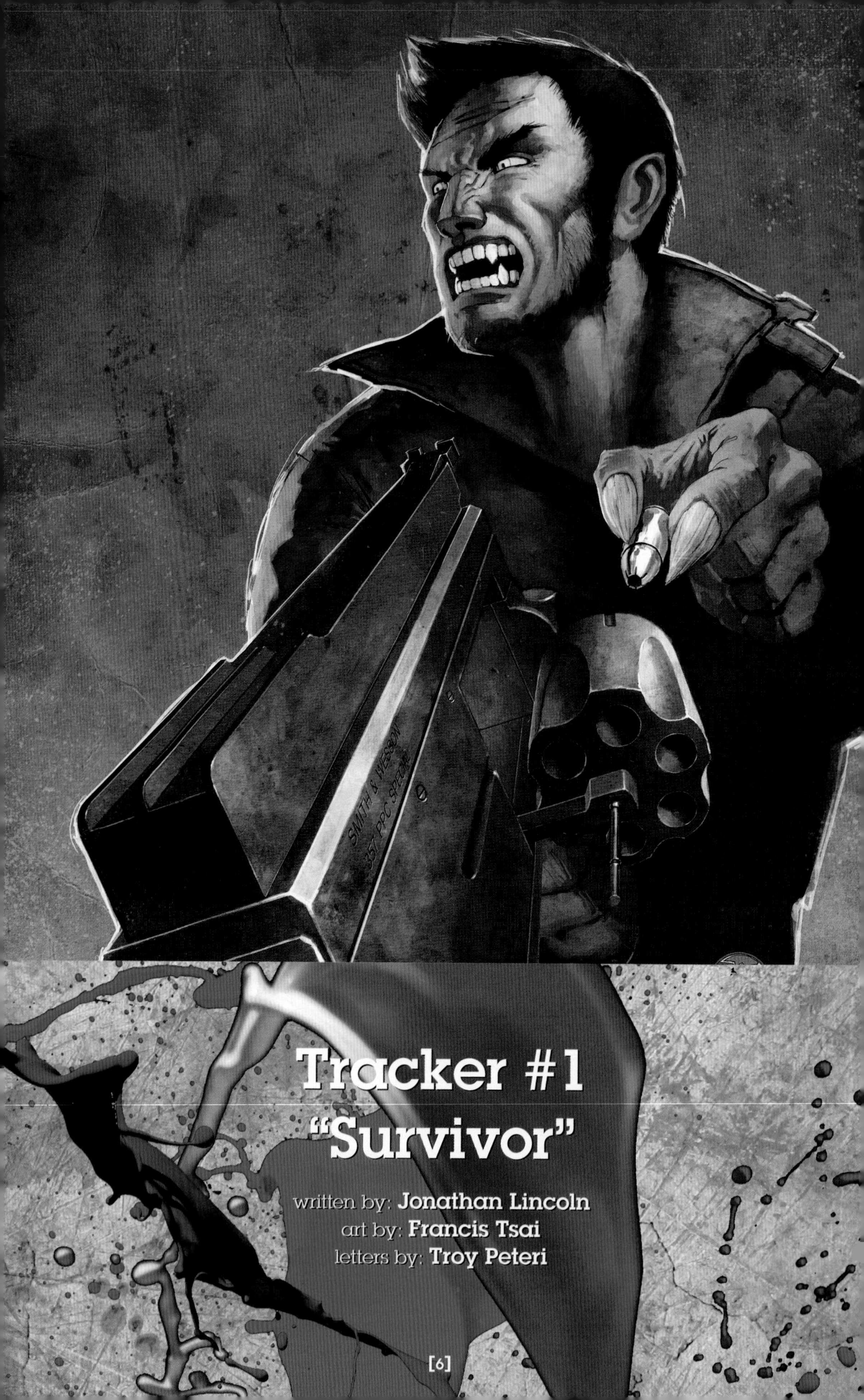
SMITH & WESSON
357 PPC SPECIAL

Tracker #1
"Survivor"

written by: **Jonathan Lincoln**
art by: **Francis Tsai**
letters by: **Troy Peteri**

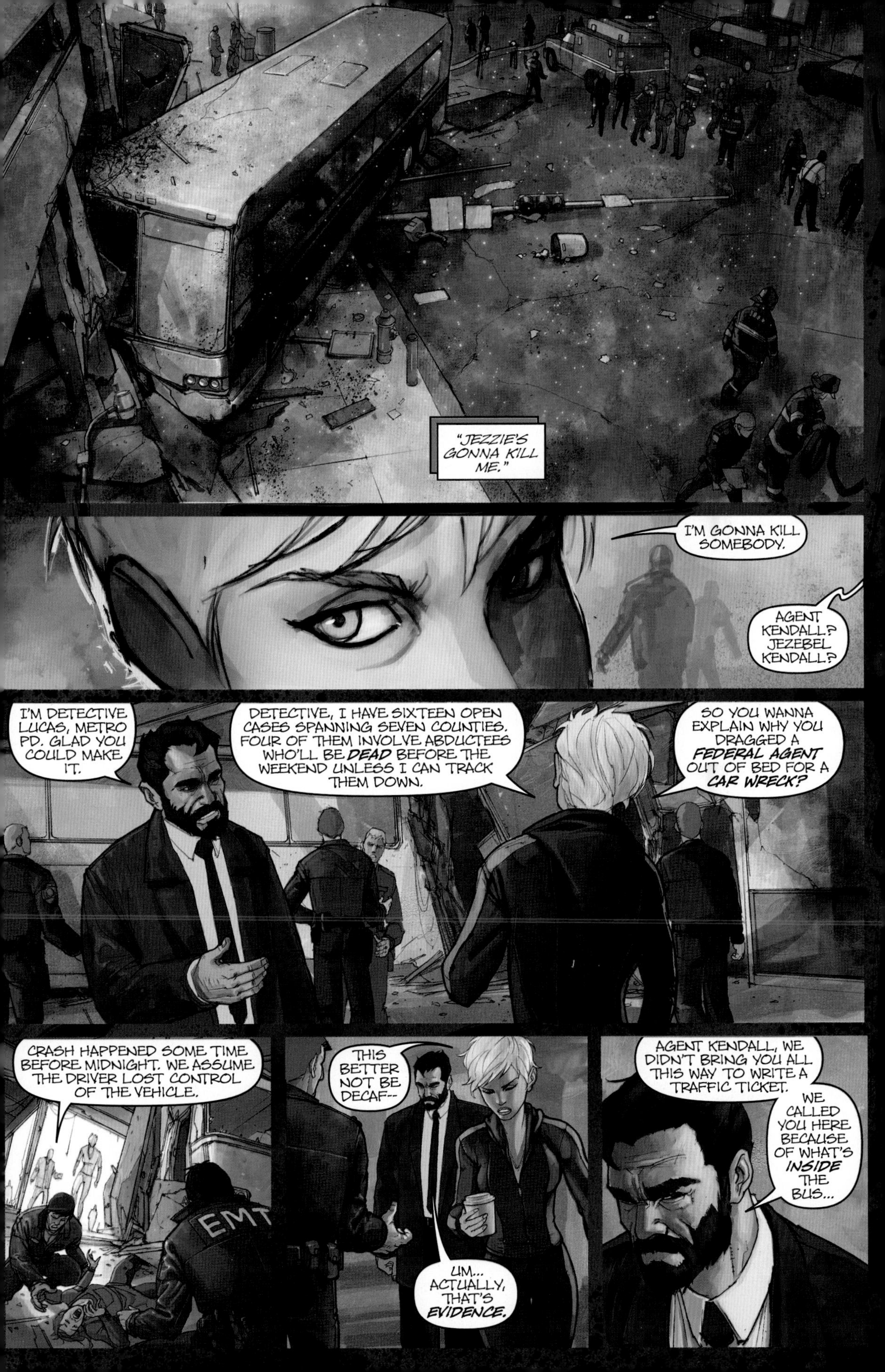
"JEZZIE'S GONNA KILL ME."
I'M GONNA KILL SOMEBODY.
AGENT KENDALL? JEZEBEL KENDALL?
I'M DETECTIVE LUCAS, METRO PD. GLAD YOU COULD MAKE IT.
DETECTIVE, I HAVE SIXTEEN OPEN CASES SPANNING SEVEN COUNTIES. FOUR OF THEM INVOLVE ABDUCTEES WHO'LL BE *DEAD* BEFORE THE WEEKEND UNLESS I CAN TRACK THEM DOWN.
SO YOU WANNA EXPLAIN WHY YOU DRAGGED A *FEDERAL AGENT* OUT OF BED FOR A *CAR WRECK?*
CRASH HAPPENED SOME TIME BEFORE MIDNIGHT. WE ASSUME THE DRIVER LOST CONTROL OF THE VEHICLE.
EMT
THIS BETTER NOT BE DECAF--
UM... ACTUALLY, THAT'S *EVIDENCE.*
AGENT KENDALL, WE DIDN'T BRING YOU ALL THIS WAY TO WRITE A TRAFFIC TICKET.
WE CALLED YOU HERE BECAUSE OF WHAT'S *INSIDE* THE BUS...

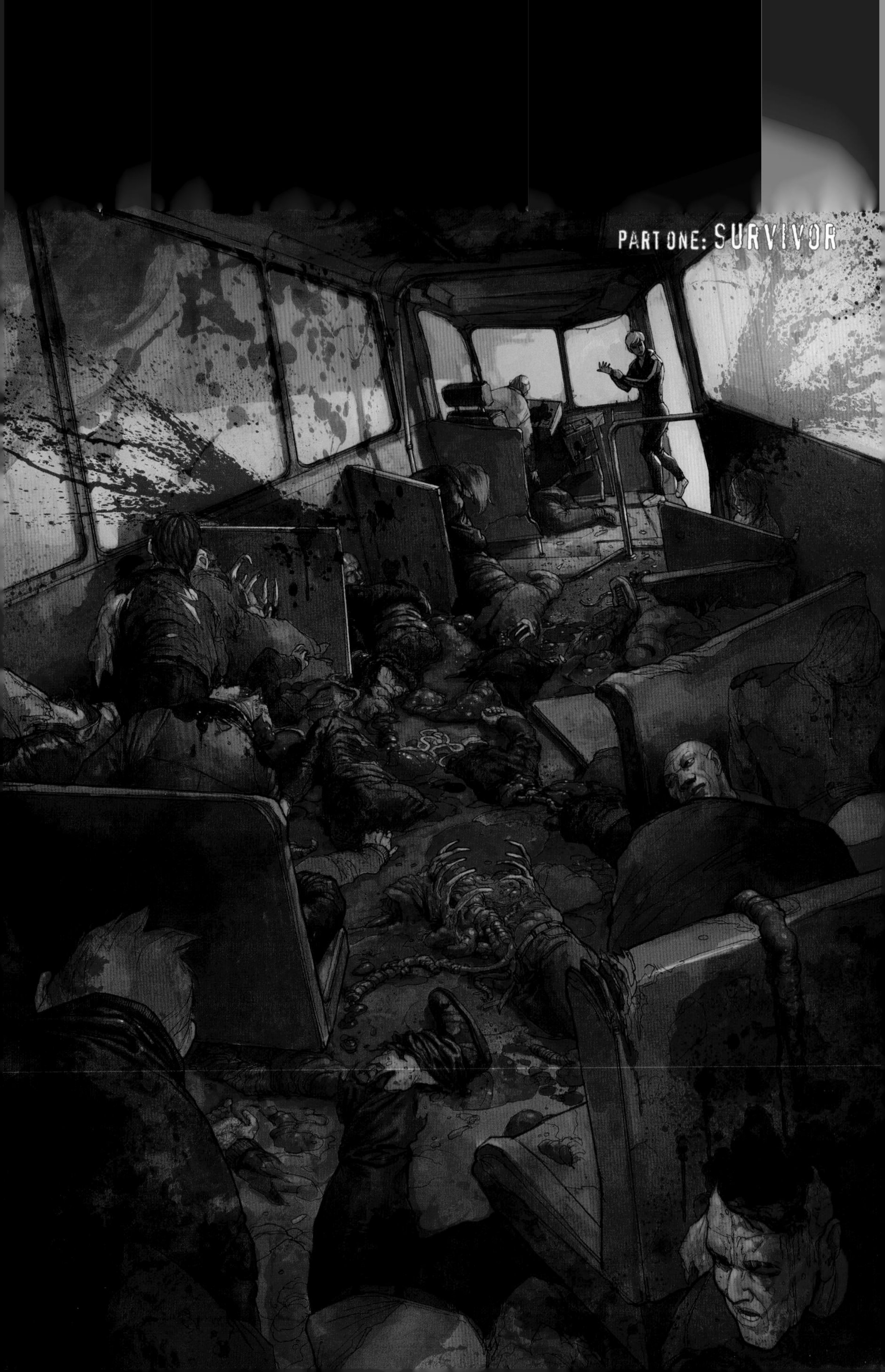
PART ONE: SURVIVOR

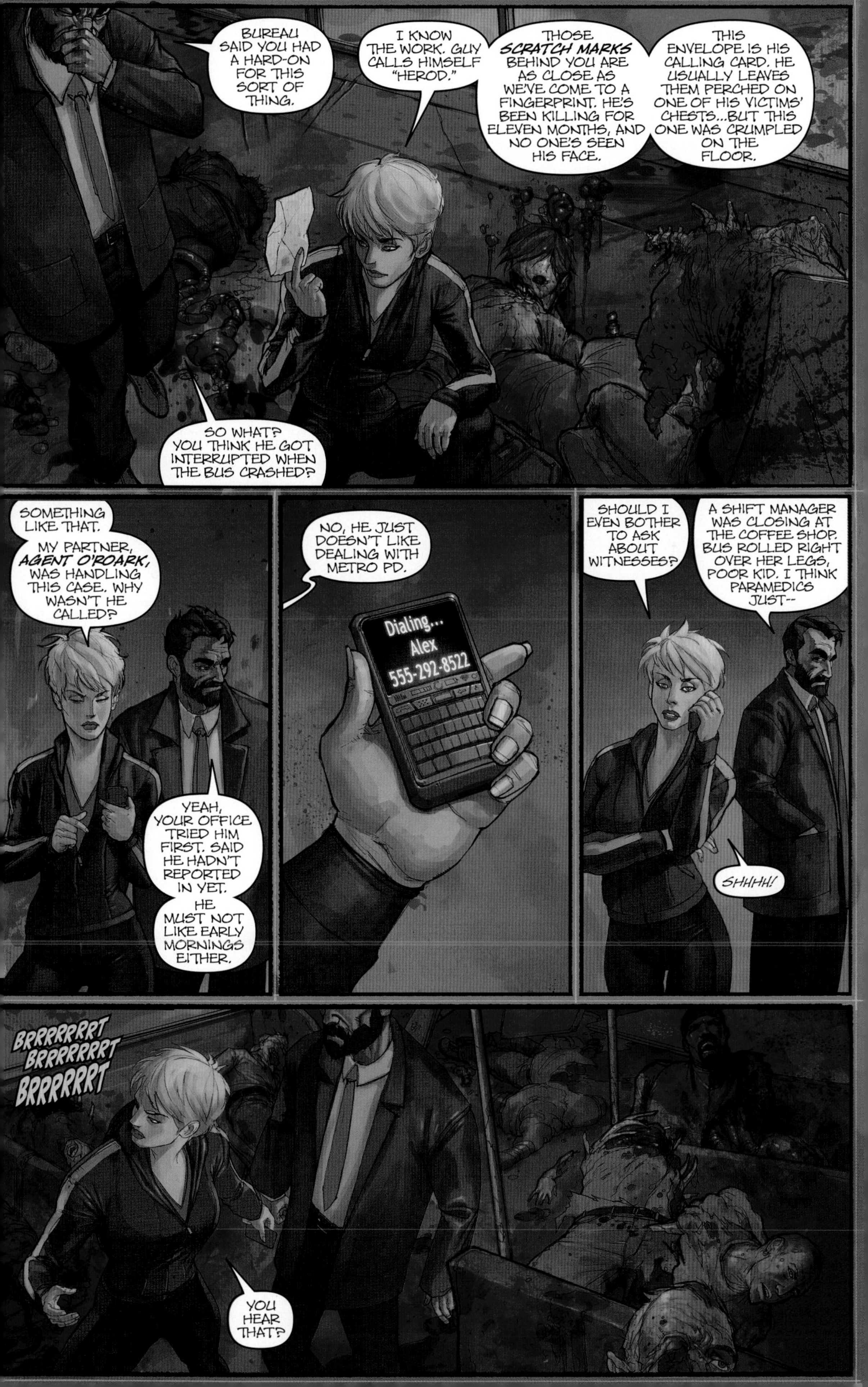
BUREAU SAID YOU HAD A HARD-ON FOR THIS SORT OF THING.
I KNOW THE WORK. GUY CALLS HIMSELF "HEROD."
THOSE *SCRATCH MARKS* BEHIND YOU ARE AS CLOSE AS WE'VE COME TO A FINGERPRINT. HE'S BEEN KILLING FOR ELEVEN MONTHS, AND NO ONE'S SEEN HIS FACE.
THIS ENVELOPE IS HIS CALLING CARD. HE USUALLY LEAVES THEM PERCHED ON ONE OF HIS VICTIMS' CHESTS...BUT THIS ONE WAS CRUMPLED ON THE FLOOR.
SO WHAT? YOU THINK HE GOT INTERRUPTED WHEN THE BUS CRASHED?
SOMETHING LIKE THAT.
MY PARTNER, *AGENT O'ROARK,* WAS HANDLING THIS CASE. WHY WASN'T HE CALLED?
YEAH, YOUR OFFICE TRIED HIM FIRST. SAID HE HADN'T REPORTED IN YET.
HE MUST NOT LIKE EARLY MORNINGS EITHER.
NO, HE JUST DOESN'T LIKE DEALING WITH METRO PD.
Dialing... Alex 555-292-8522
SHOULD I EVEN BOTHER TO ASK ABOUT WITNESSES?
A SHIFT MANAGER WAS CLOSING AT THE COFFEE SHOP. BUS ROLLED RIGHT OVER HER LEGS, POOR KID. I THINK PARAMEDICS JUST--
SHHHH!
BRRRRRRT BRRRRRRRT BRRRRRRT
YOU HEAR THAT?

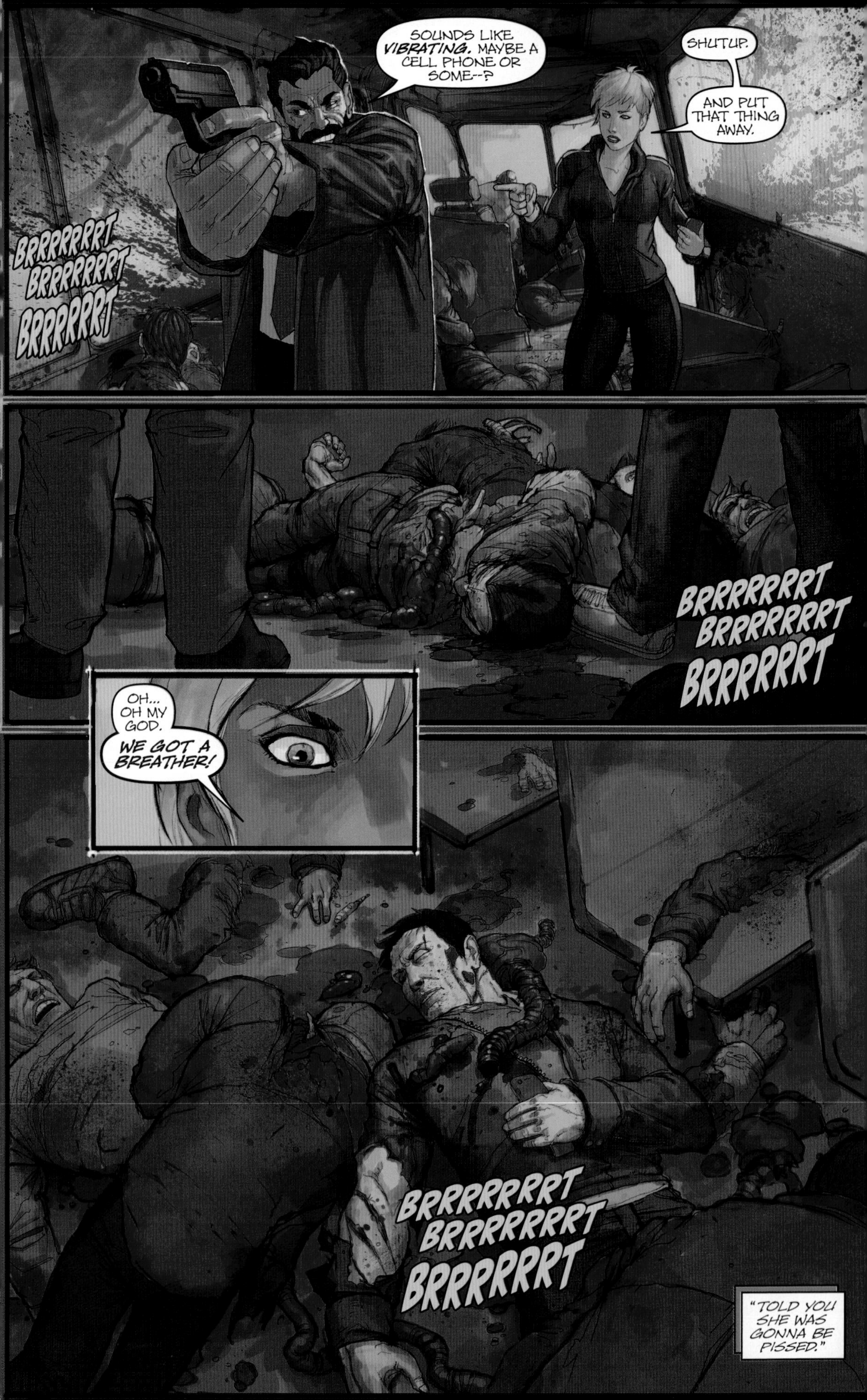
SOUNDS LIKE VIBRATING. MAYBE A CELL PHONE OR SOME--?
SHUTUP.
AND PUT THAT THING AWAY.
BRRRRRRT BRRRRRRRT BRRRRRRT
BRRRRRRRT BRRRRRRRT BRRRRRRT
OH... OH MY GOD. WE GOT A BREATHER!
BRRRRRRRT BRRRRRRRT BRRRRRRT
"TOLD YOU SHE WAS GONNA BE PISSED."

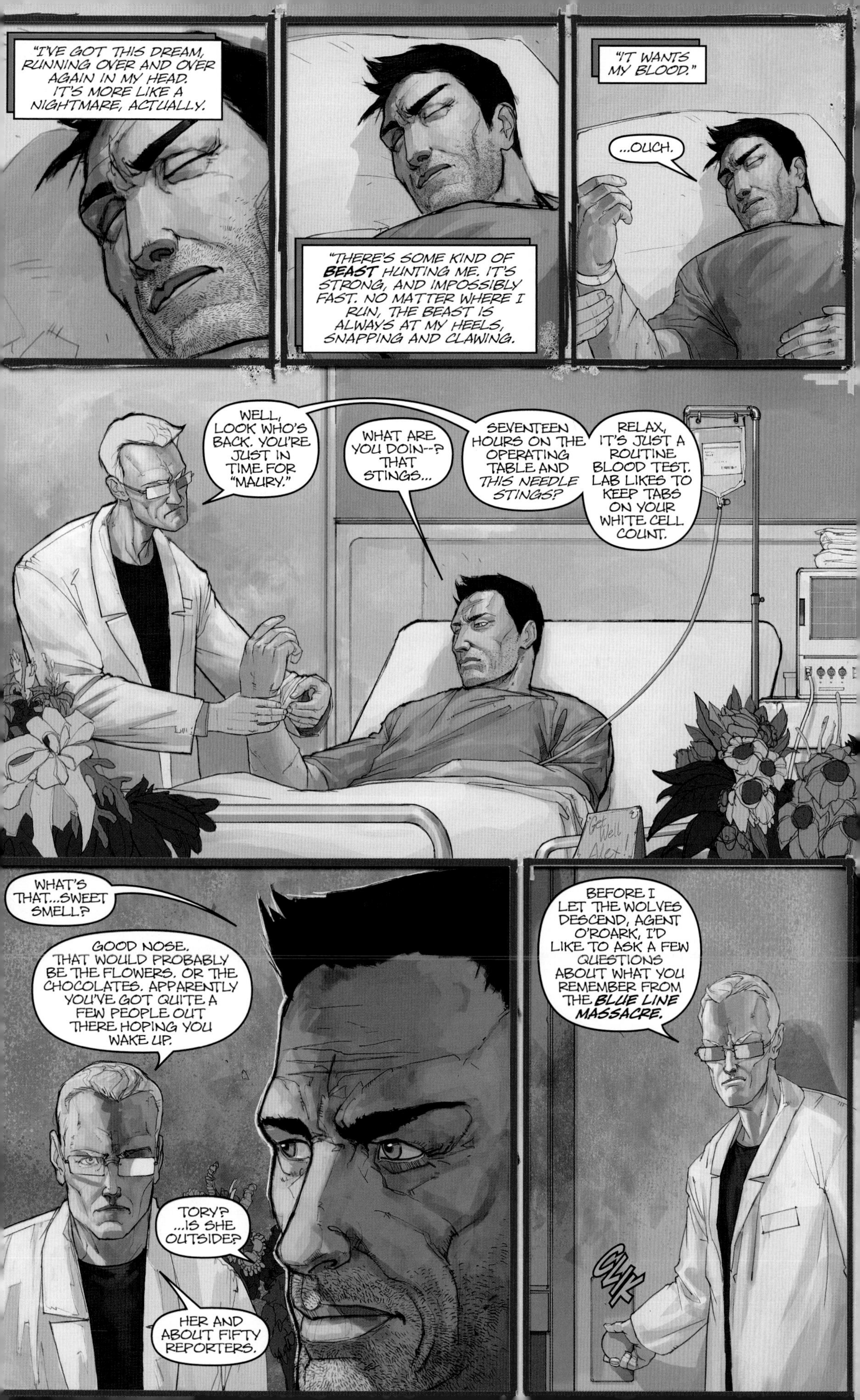
"I'VE GOT THIS DREAM, RUNNING OVER AND OVER AGAIN IN MY HEAD. IT'S MORE LIKE A NIGHTMARE, ACTUALLY.
"THERE'S SOME KIND OF BEAST HUNTING ME. IT'S STRONG, AND IMPOSSIBLY FAST. NO MATTER WHERE I RUN, THE BEAST IS ALWAYS AT MY HEELS, SNAPPING AND CLAWING.
"IT WANTS MY BLOOD."
...OUCH.
WELL, LOOK WHO'S BACK. YOU'RE JUST IN TIME FOR "MAURY."
WHAT ARE YOU DOIN--? THAT STINGS...
SEVENTEEN HOURS ON THE OPERATING TABLE AND THIS NEEDLE STINGS?
RELAX, IT'S JUST A ROUTINE BLOOD TEST. LAB LIKES TO KEEP TABS ON YOUR WHITE CELL COUNT.
Get Well Alex!
WHAT'S THAT...SWEET SMELL?
GOOD NOSE. THAT WOULD PROBABLY BE THE FLOWERS. OR THE CHOCOLATES. APPARENTLY YOU'VE GOT QUITE A FEW PEOPLE OUT THERE HOPING YOU WAKE UP.
TORY? ...IS SHE OUTSIDE?
HER AND ABOUT FIFTY REPORTERS.
BEFORE I LET THE WOLVES DESCEND, AGENT O'ROARK, I'D LIKE TO ASK A FEW QUESTIONS ABOUT WHAT YOU REMEMBER FROM THE BLUE LINE MASSACRE.
CLIK

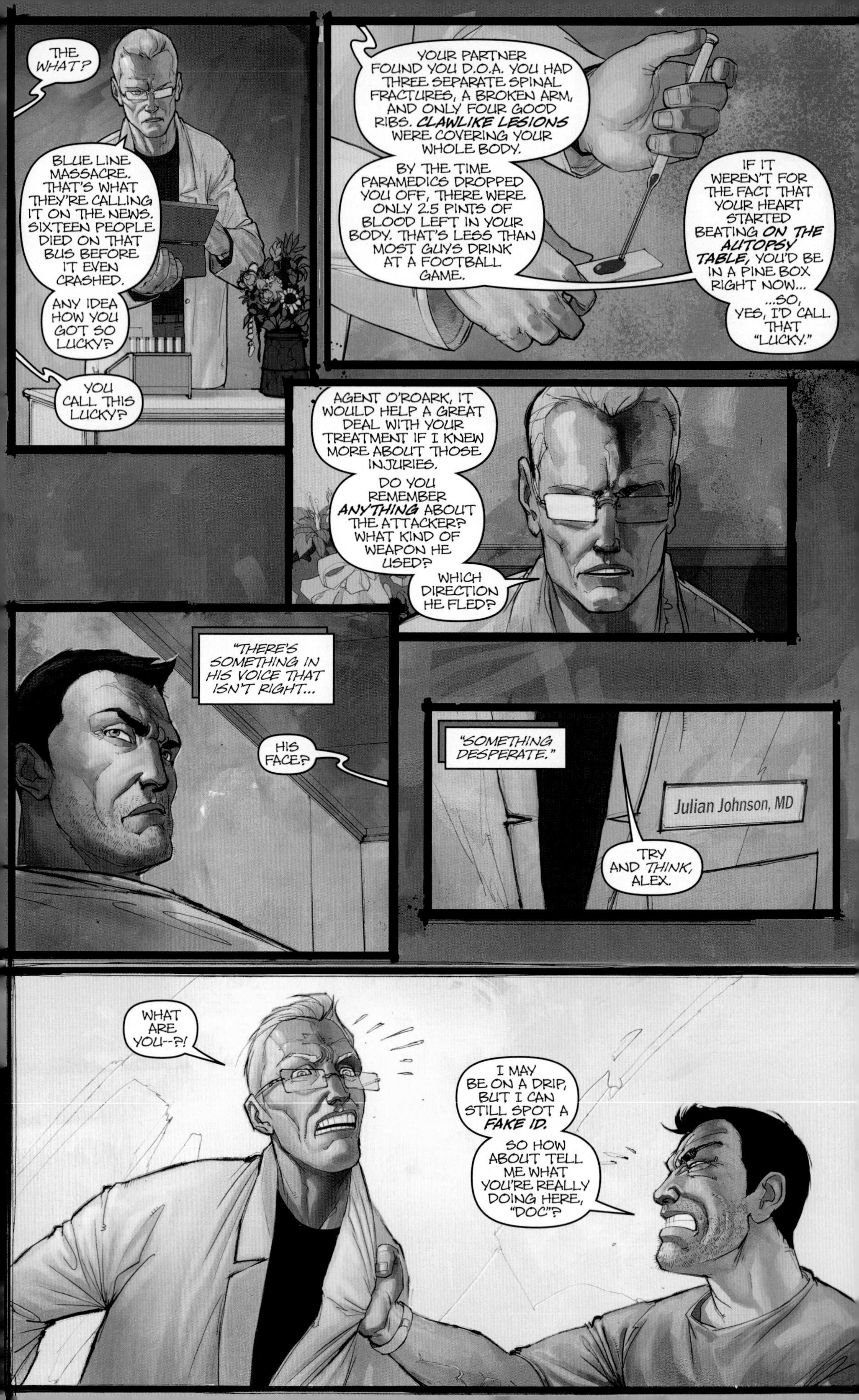
THE WHAT?
YOUR PARTNER FOUND YOU D.O.A. YOU HAD THREE SEPARATE SPINAL FRACTURES, A BROKEN ARM, AND ONLY FOUR GOOD RIBS. CLAWLIKE LESIONS WERE COVERING YOUR WHOLE BODY.
BY THE TIME PARAMEDICS DROPPED YOU OFF, THERE WERE ONLY 2.5 PINTS OF BLOOD LEFT IN YOUR BODY. THAT'S LESS THAN MOST GUYS DRINK AT A FOOTBALL GAME.
IF IT WEREN'T FOR THE FACT THAT YOUR HEART STARTED BEATING ON THE AUTOPSY TABLE, YOU'D BE IN A PINE BOX RIGHT NOW...
...SO, YES, I'D CALL THAT "LUCKY."
BLUE LINE MASSACRE. THAT'S WHAT THEY'RE CALLING IT ON THE NEWS. SIXTEEN PEOPLE DIED ON THAT BUS BEFORE IT EVEN CRASHED.
ANY IDEA HOW YOU GOT SO LUCKY?
YOU CALL THIS LUCKY?
AGENT O'ROARK, IT WOULD HELP A GREAT DEAL WITH YOUR TREATMENT IF I KNEW MORE ABOUT THOSE INJURIES.
DO YOU REMEMBER ANYTHING ABOUT THE ATTACKER? WHAT KIND OF WEAPON HE USED?
WHICH DIRECTION HE FLED?
"THERE'S SOMETHING IN HIS VOICE THAT ISN'T RIGHT...
HIS FACE?
"SOMETHING DESPERATE."
Julian Johnson, MD
TRY AND THINK, ALEX.
WHAT ARE YOU--?!
I MAY BE ON A DRIP, BUT I CAN STILL SPOT A FAKE ID.
SO HOW ABOUT TELL ME WHAT YOU'RE REALLY DOING HERE, "DOC"?

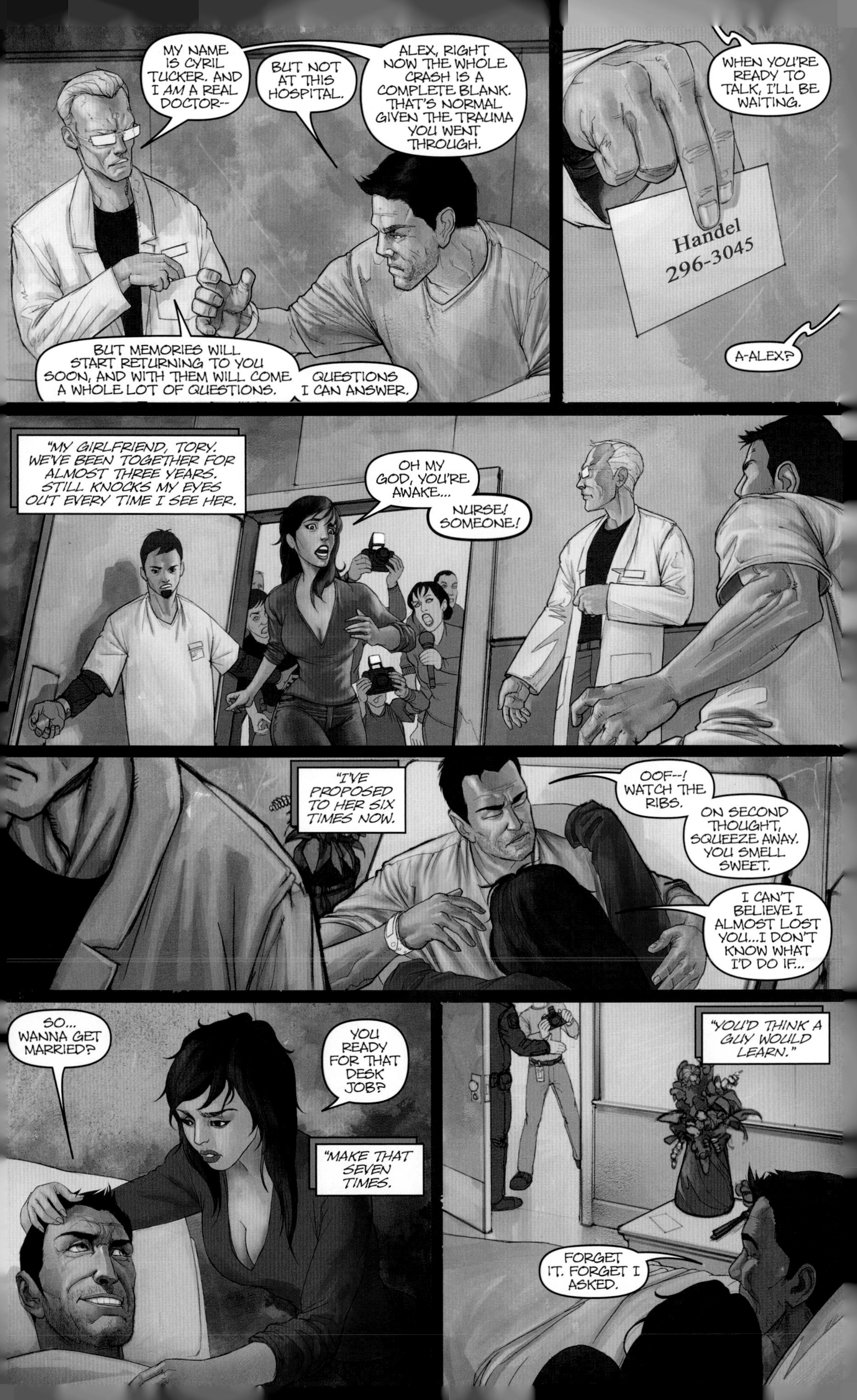

MY NAME IS CYRIL TUCKER. AND I AM A REAL DOCTOR--
BUT NOT AT THIS HOSPITAL.
ALEX, RIGHT NOW THE WHOLE CRASH IS A COMPLETE BLANK. THAT'S NORMAL GIVEN THE TRAUMA YOU WENT THROUGH.
BUT MEMORIES WILL START RETURNING TO YOU SOON, AND WITH THEM WILL COME A WHOLE LOT OF QUESTIONS.
QUESTIONS I CAN ANSWER.
WHEN YOU'RE READY TO TALK, I'LL BE WAITING.
Handel
296-3045
A-ALEX?
"MY GIRLFRIEND, TORY. WE'VE BEEN TOGETHER FOR ALMOST THREE YEARS. STILL KNOCKS MY EYES OUT EVERY TIME I SEE HER.
OH MY GOD, YOU'RE AWAKE...
NURSE! SOMEONE!
"I'VE PROPOSED TO HER SIX TIMES NOW.
OOF--! WATCH THE RIBS.
ON SECOND THOUGHT, SQUEEZE AWAY. YOU SMELL SWEET.
I CAN'T BELIEVE I ALMOST LOST YOU...I DON'T KNOW WHAT I'D DO IF...
SO... WANNA GET MARRIED?
YOU READY FOR THAT DESK JOB?
"MAKE THAT SEVEN TIMES.
"YOU'D THINK A GUY WOULD LEARN."
FORGET IT. FORGET I ASKED.

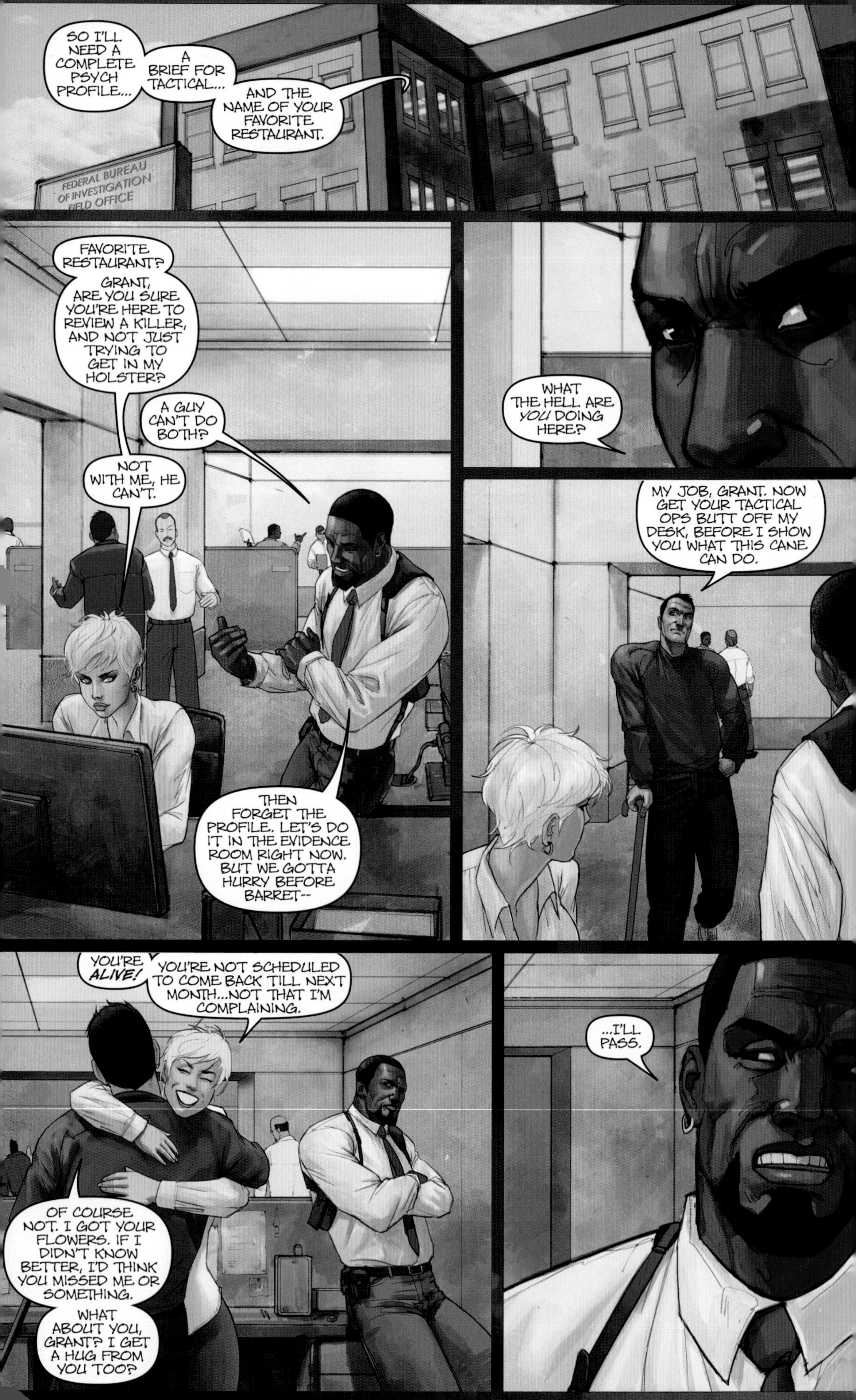
SO I'LL NEED A COMPLETE PSYCH PROFILE...
A BRIEF FOR TACTICAL...
AND THE NAME OF YOUR FAVORITE RESTAURANT.
FEDERAL BUREAU OF INVESTIGATION FIELD OFFICE
FAVORITE RESTAURANT?
GRANT, ARE YOU SURE YOU'RE HERE TO REVIEW A KILLER, AND NOT JUST TRYING TO GET IN MY HOLSTER?
A GUY CAN'T DO BOTH?
NOT WITH ME, HE CAN'T.
THEN FORGET THE PROFILE. LET'S DO IT IN THE EVIDENCE ROOM RIGHT NOW. BUT WE GOTTA HURRY BEFORE BARRET--
WHAT THE HELL ARE *YOU* DOING HERE?
MY JOB, GRANT. NOW GET YOUR TACTICAL OPS BUTT OFF MY DESK, BEFORE I SHOW YOU WHAT THIS CANE CAN DO.
YOU'RE *ALIVE!*
YOU'RE NOT SCHEDULED TO COME BACK TILL NEXT MONTH...NOT THAT I'M COMPLAINING.
OF COURSE NOT. I GOT YOUR FLOWERS. IF I DIDN'T KNOW BETTER, I'D THINK YOU MISSED ME OR SOMETHING.
WHAT ABOUT YOU, GRANT? I GET A HUG FROM YOU TOO?
...I'LL PASS.

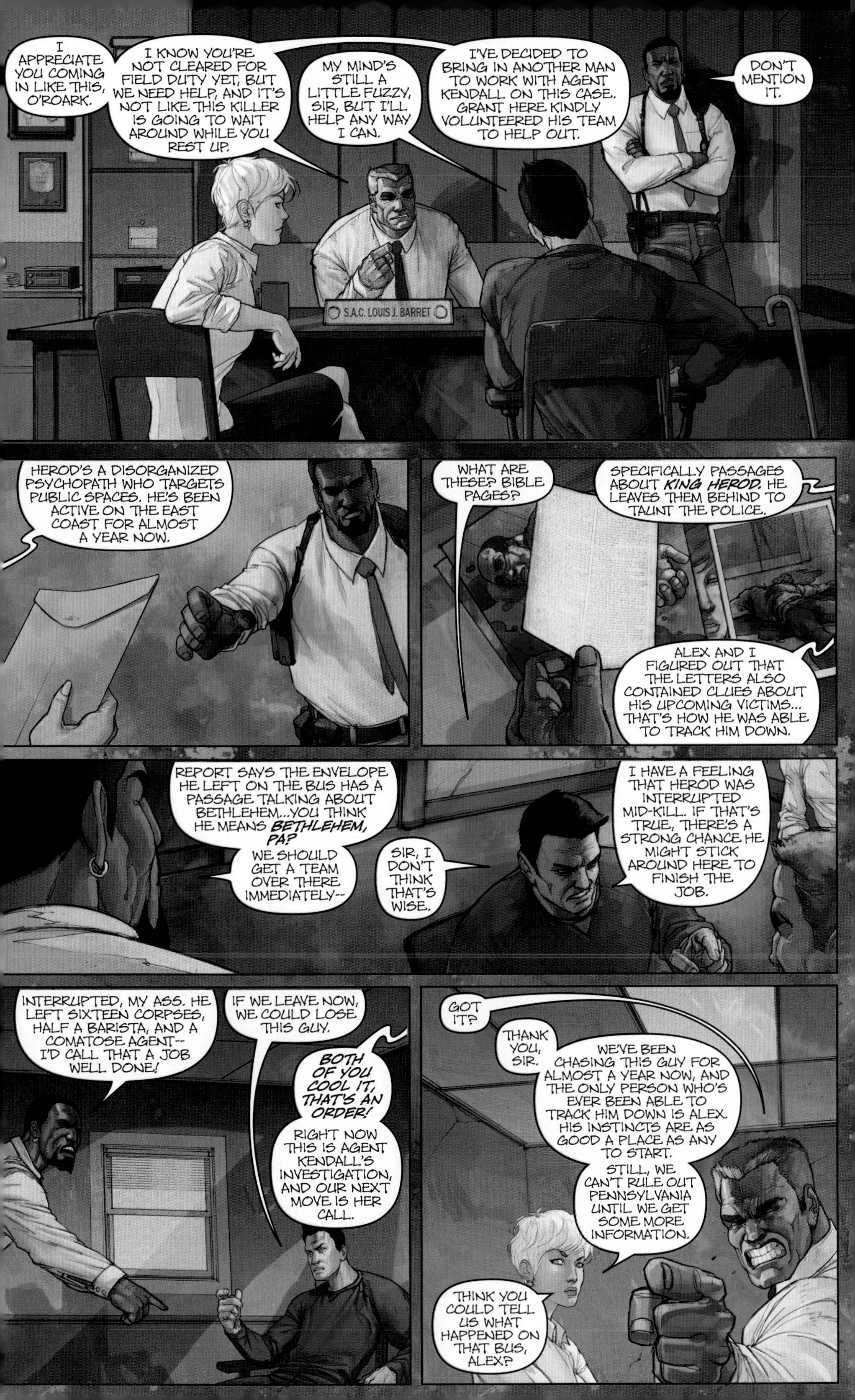
I APPRECIATE YOU COMING IN LIKE THIS, O'ROARK.
I KNOW YOU'RE NOT CLEARED FOR FIELD DUTY YET, BUT WE NEED HELP, AND IT'S NOT LIKE THIS KILLER IS GOING TO WAIT AROUND WHILE YOU REST UP.
MY MIND'S STILL A LITTLE FUZZY, SIR, BUT I'LL HELP ANY WAY I CAN.
I'VE DECIDED TO BRING IN ANOTHER MAN TO WORK WITH AGENT KENDALL ON THIS CASE. GRANT HERE KINDLY VOLUNTEERED HIS TEAM TO HELP OUT.
DON'T MENTION IT.
S.A.C. LOUIS J. BARRET
HEROD'S A DISORGANIZED PSYCHOPATH WHO TARGETS PUBLIC SPACES. HE'S BEEN ACTIVE ON THE EAST COAST FOR ALMOST A YEAR NOW.
WHAT ARE THESE? BIBLE PAGES?
SPECIFICALLY PASSAGES ABOUT **KING HEROD.** HE LEAVES THEM BEHIND TO TAUNT THE POLICE.
ALEX AND I FIGURED OUT THAT THE LETTERS ALSO CONTAINED CLUES ABOUT HIS UPCOMING VICTIMS... THAT'S HOW HE WAS ABLE TO TRACK HIM DOWN.
REPORT SAYS THE ENVELOPE HE LEFT ON THE BUS HAS A PASSAGE TALKING ABOUT BETHLEHEM...YOU THINK HE MEANS **BETHLEHEM, PA?**
WE SHOULD GET A TEAM OVER THERE IMMEDIATELY--
SIR, I DON'T THINK THAT'S WISE.
I HAVE A FEELING THAT HEROD WAS INTERRUPTED MID-KILL. IF THAT'S TRUE, THERE'S A STRONG CHANCE HE MIGHT STICK AROUND HERE TO FINISH THE JOB.
INTERRUPTED, MY ASS. HE LEFT SIXTEEN CORPSES, HALF A BARISTA, AND A COMATOSE AGENT-- I'D CALL THAT A JOB WELL DONE!
IF WE LEAVE NOW, WE COULD LOSE THIS GUY.
BOTH OF YOU COOL IT, THAT'S AN ORDER!
RIGHT NOW THIS IS AGENT KENDALL'S INVESTIGATION, AND OUR NEXT MOVE IS HER CALL.
GOT IT?
THANK YOU, SIR.
WE'VE BEEN CHASING THIS GUY FOR ALMOST A YEAR NOW, AND THE ONLY PERSON WHO'S EVER BEEN ABLE TO TRACK HIM DOWN IS ALEX. HIS INSTINCTS ARE AS GOOD A PLACE AS ANY TO START.
STILL, WE CAN'T RULE OUT PENNSYLVANIA UNTIL WE GET SOME MORE INFORMATION.
THINK YOU COULD TELL US WHAT HAPPENED ON THAT BUS, ALEX?

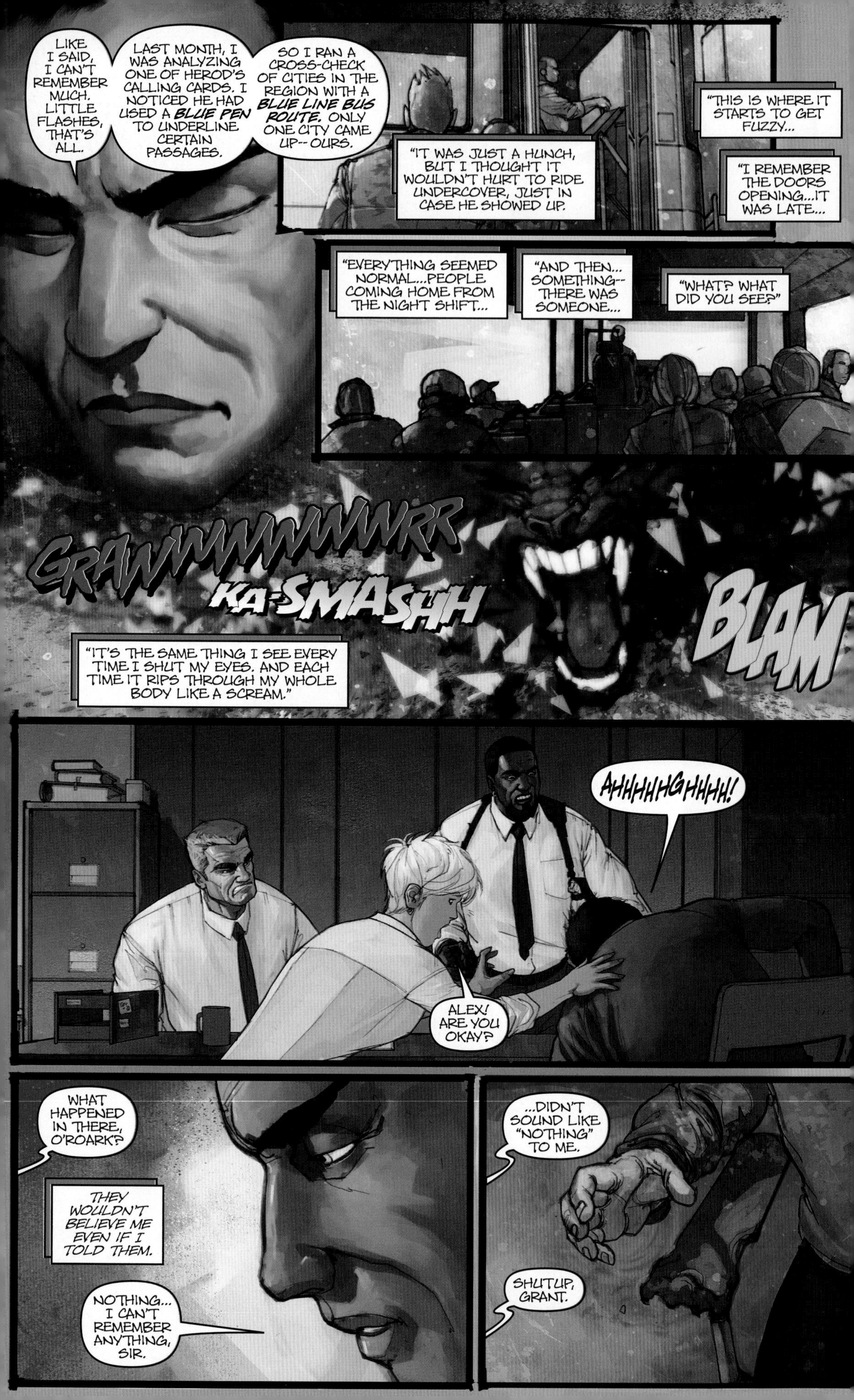
LIKE I SAID, I CAN'T REMEMBER MUCH. LITTLE FLASHES, THAT'S ALL.
LAST MONTH, I WAS ANALYZING ONE OF HEROD'S CALLING CARDS. I NOTICED HE HAD USED A BLUE PEN TO UNDERLINE CERTAIN PASSAGES.
SO I RAN A CROSS-CHECK OF CITIES IN THE REGION WITH A BLUE LINE BUS ROUTE. ONLY ONE CITY CAME UP-- OURS.
"IT WAS JUST A HUNCH, BUT I THOUGHT IT WOULDN'T HURT TO RIDE UNDERCOVER, JUST IN CASE HE SHOWED UP.
"THIS IS WHERE IT STARTS TO GET FUZZY...
"I REMEMBER THE DOORS OPENING...IT WAS LATE...
"EVERYTHING SEEMED NORMAL...PEOPLE COMING HOME FROM THE NIGHT SHIFT...
"AND THEN... SOMETHING-- THERE WAS SOMEONE...
"WHAT? WHAT DID YOU SEE?"
GRAWWWWWWRR
KA-SMASHH
BLAM
"IT'S THE SAME THING I SEE EVERY TIME I SHUT MY EYES. AND EACH TIME IT RIPS THROUGH MY WHOLE BODY LIKE A SCREAM."
AHHHHGHHHH!
ALEX! ARE YOU OKAY?
WHAT HAPPENED IN THERE, O'ROARK?
THEY WOULDN'T BELIEVE ME EVEN IF I TOLD THEM.
NOTHING... I CAN'T REMEMBER ANYTHING, SIR.
...DIDN'T SOUND LIKE "NOTHING" TO ME.
SHUTUP, GRANT.

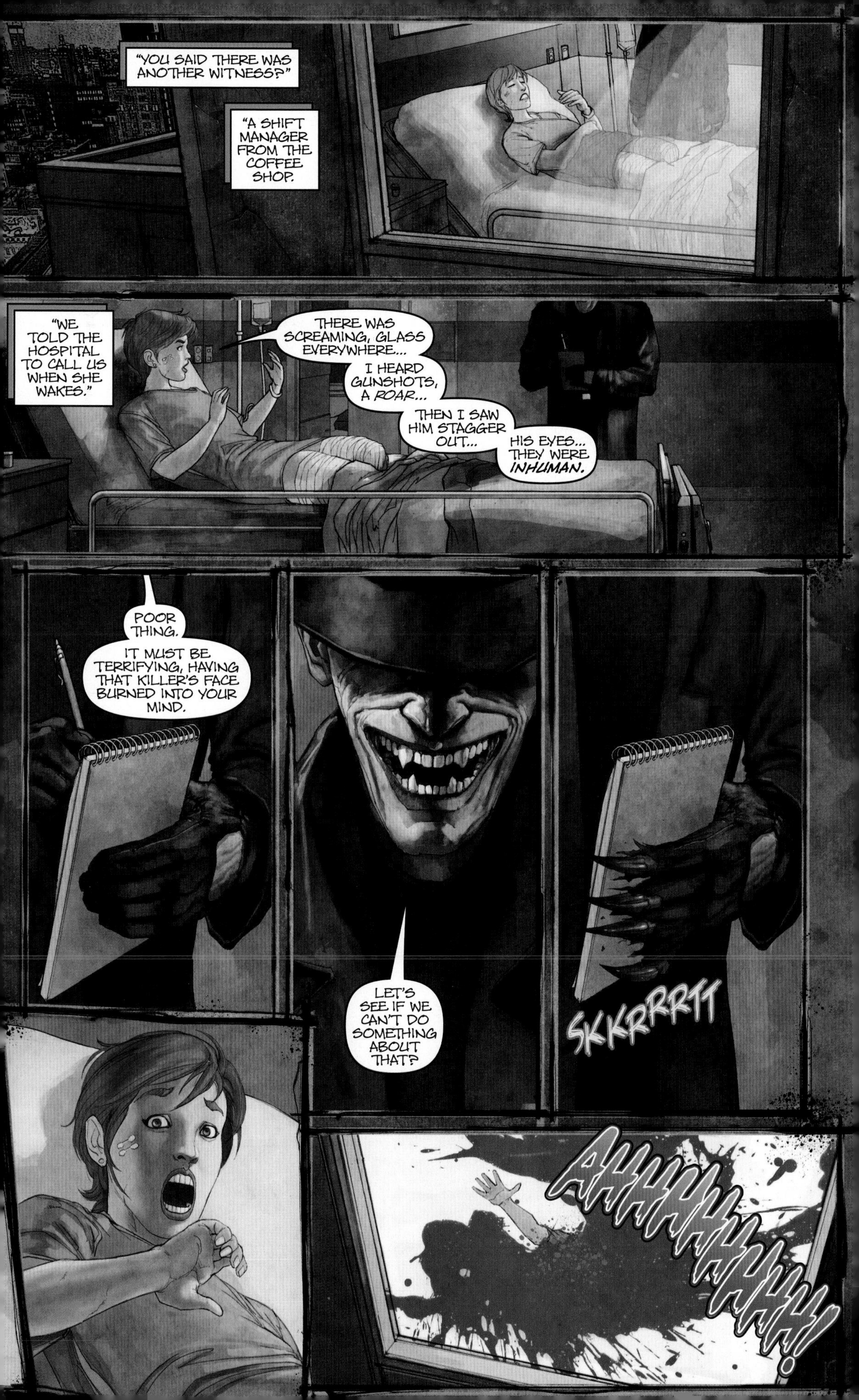
"YOU SAID THERE WAS ANOTHER WITNESS?"
"A SHIFT MANAGER FROM THE COFFEE SHOP.
"WE TOLD THE HOSPITAL TO CALL US WHEN SHE WAKES."
THERE WAS SCREAMING, GLASS EVERYWHERE...
I HEARD GUNSHOTS, A *ROAR*...
THEN I SAW HIM STAGGER OUT...
HIS EYES... THEY WERE ***INHUMAN.***
POOR THING.
IT MUST BE TERRIFYING, HAVING THAT KILLER'S FACE BURNED INTO YOUR MIND.
LET'S SEE IF WE CAN'T DO SOMETHING ABOUT THAT?
SKKRRRTT
AHHHHHHHH!

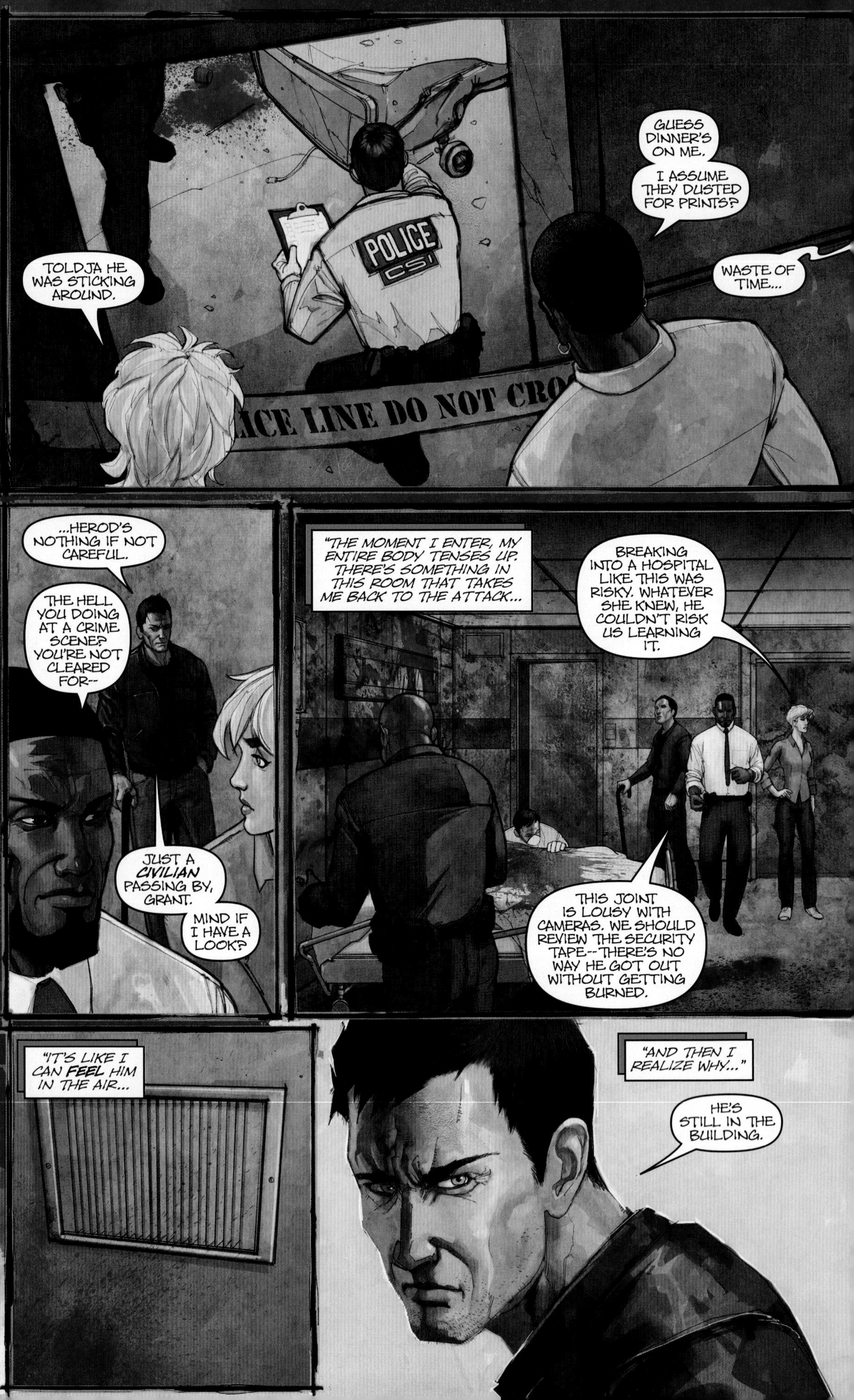
POLICE CSI
TOLDJA HE WAS STICKING AROUND.
GUESS DINNER'S ON ME.
I ASSUME THEY DUSTED FOR PRINTS?
WASTE OF TIME...
...ICE LINE DO NOT CRO...
...HEROD'S NOTHING IF NOT CAREFUL.
THE HELL YOU DOING AT A CRIME SCENE? YOU'RE NOT CLEARED FOR--
JUST A *CIVILIAN* PASSING BY, GRANT.
MIND IF I HAVE A LOOK?
"THE MOMENT I ENTER, MY ENTIRE BODY TENSES UP. THERE'S SOMETHING IN THIS ROOM THAT TAKES ME BACK TO THE ATTACK...
BREAKING INTO A HOSPITAL LIKE THIS WAS RISKY. WHATEVER SHE KNEW, HE COULDN'T RISK US LEARNING IT.
THIS JOINT IS LOUSY WITH CAMERAS. WE SHOULD REVIEW THE SECURITY TAPE--THERE'S NO WAY HE GOT OUT WITHOUT GETTING BURNED.
"IT'S LIKE I CAN **FEEL** HIM IN THE AIR...
"AND THEN I REALIZE WHY..."
HE'S STILL IN THE BUILDING.

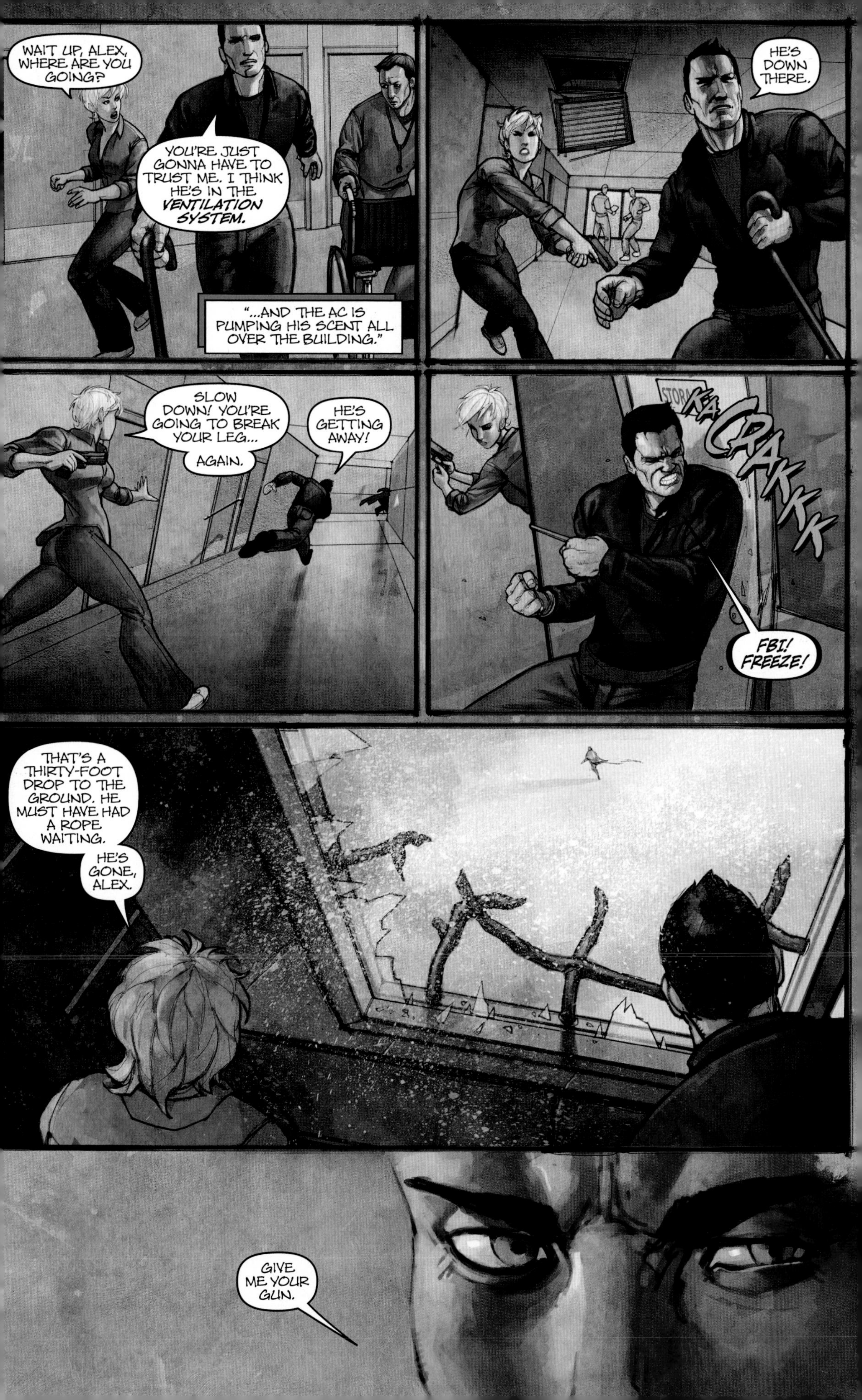
WAIT UP, ALEX, WHERE ARE YOU GOING?
YOU'RE JUST GONNA HAVE TO TRUST ME. I THINK HE'S IN THE VENTILATION SYSTEM.
"...AND THE AC IS PUMPING HIS SCENT ALL OVER THE BUILDING."
HE'S DOWN THERE.
SLOW DOWN! YOU'RE GOING TO BREAK YOUR LEG...
AGAIN.
HE'S GETTING AWAY!
KA-CRAKKK
FBI! FREEZE!
THAT'S A THIRTY-FOOT DROP TO THE GROUND. HE MUST HAVE HAD A ROPE WAITING.
HE'S GONE, ALEX.
GIVE ME YOUR GUN.

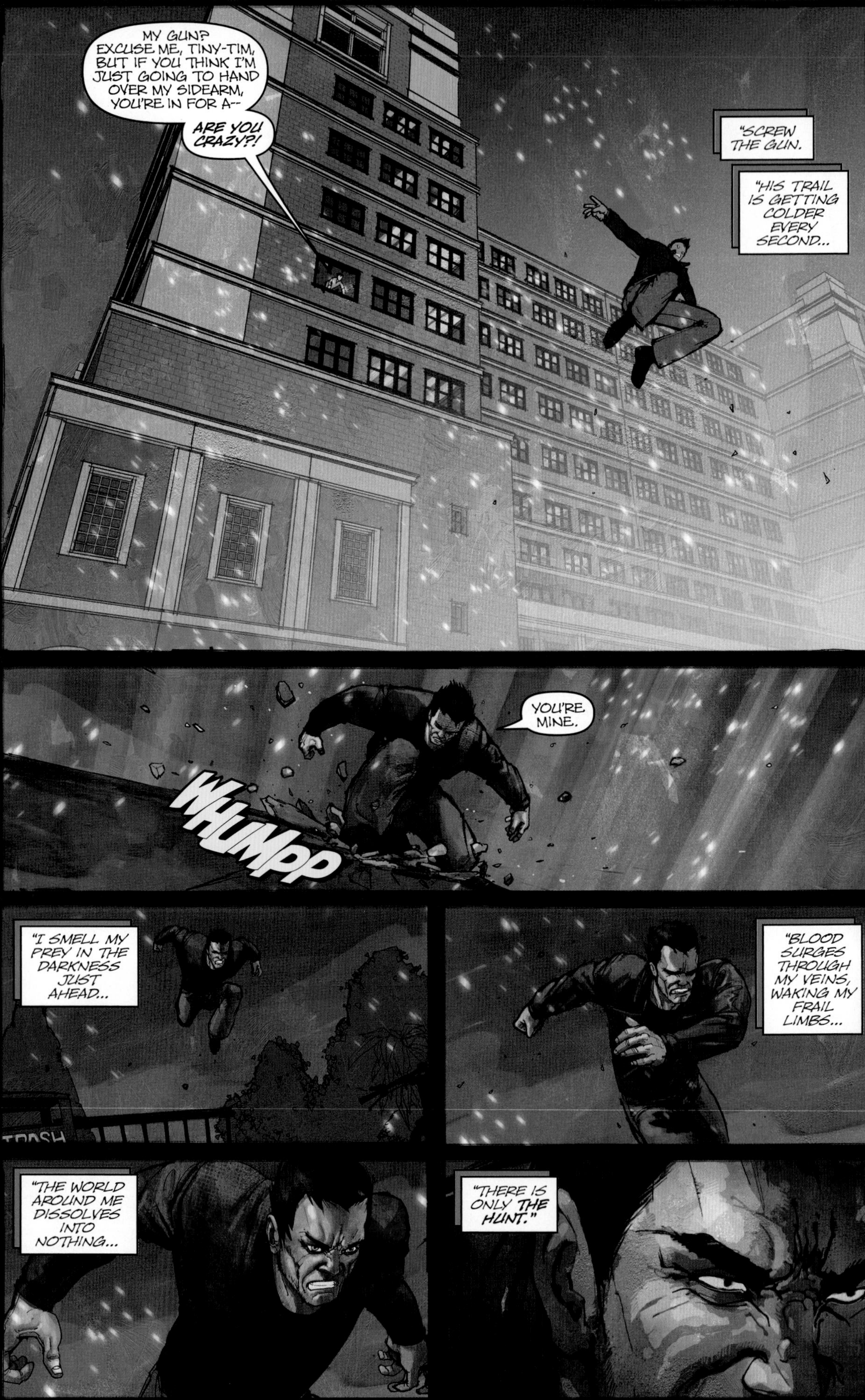
MY GUN? EXCUSE ME, TINY-TIM, BUT IF YOU THINK I'M JUST GOING TO HAND OVER MY SIDEARM, YOU'RE IN FOR A--
ARE YOU CRAZY?!
"SCREW THE GUN.
"HIS TRAIL IS GETTING COLDER EVERY SECOND...
YOU'RE MINE.
WHUMPP
"I SMELL MY PREY IN THE DARKNESS JUST AHEAD...
"BLOOD SURGES THROUGH MY VEINS, WAKING MY FRAIL LIMBS...
"THE WORLD AROUND ME DISSOLVES INTO NOTHING...
"THERE IS ONLY THE HUNT."

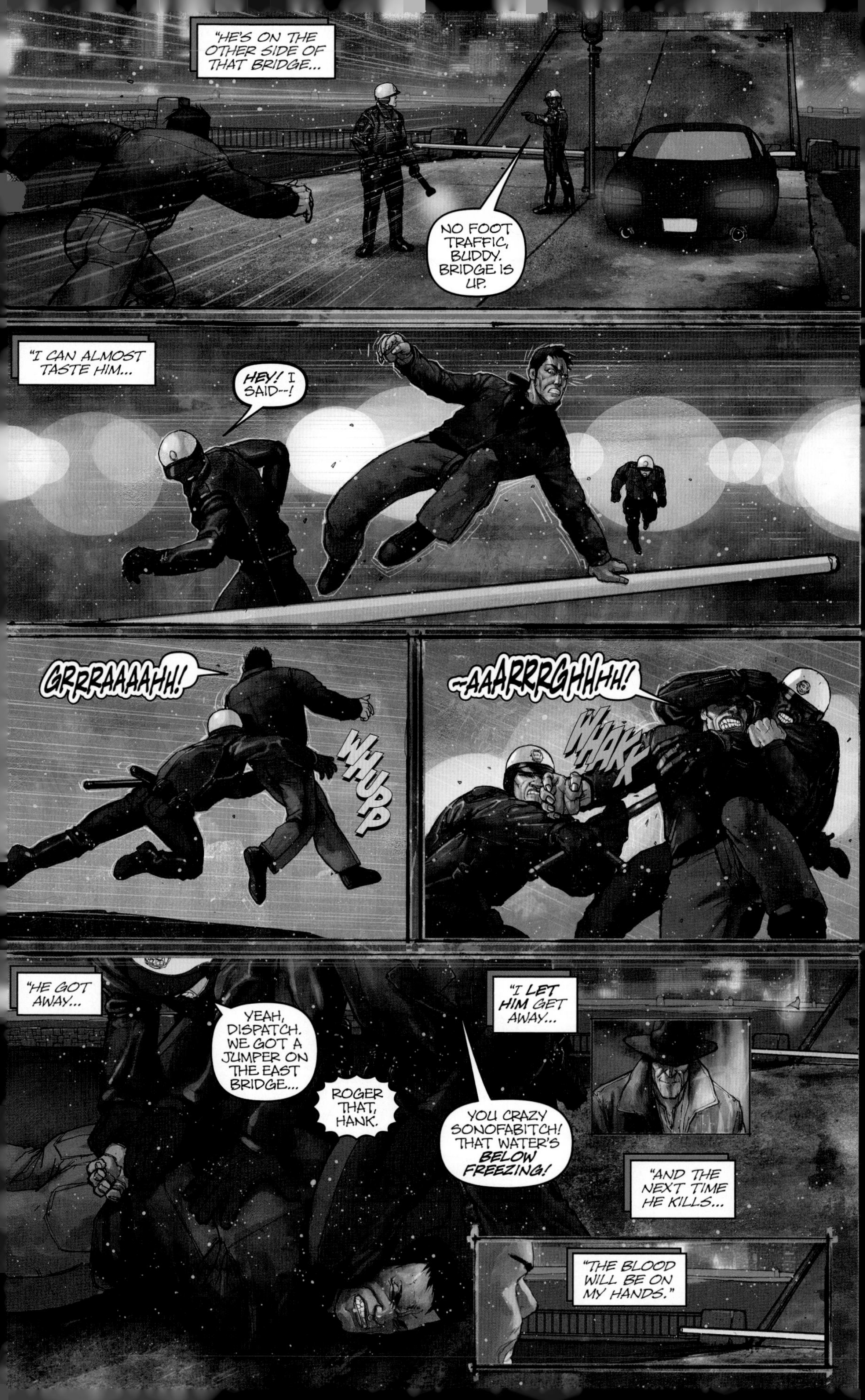
"HE'S ON THE OTHER SIDE OF THAT BRIDGE...
NO FOOT TRAFFIC, BUDDY. BRIDGE IS UP.
"I CAN ALMOST TASTE HIM...
HEY! I SAID--!
GRRRAAAAHH!
WHUPP
--AAARRRGHHHH!
WHAKK
"HE GOT AWAY...
YEAH, DISPATCH. WE GOT A JUMPER ON THE EAST BRIDGE...
ROGER THAT, HANK.
YOU CRAZY SONOFABITCH! THAT WATER'S BELOW FREEZING!
"I LET HIM GET AWAY...
"AND THE NEXT TIME HE KILLS...
"THE BLOOD WILL BE ON MY HANDS."

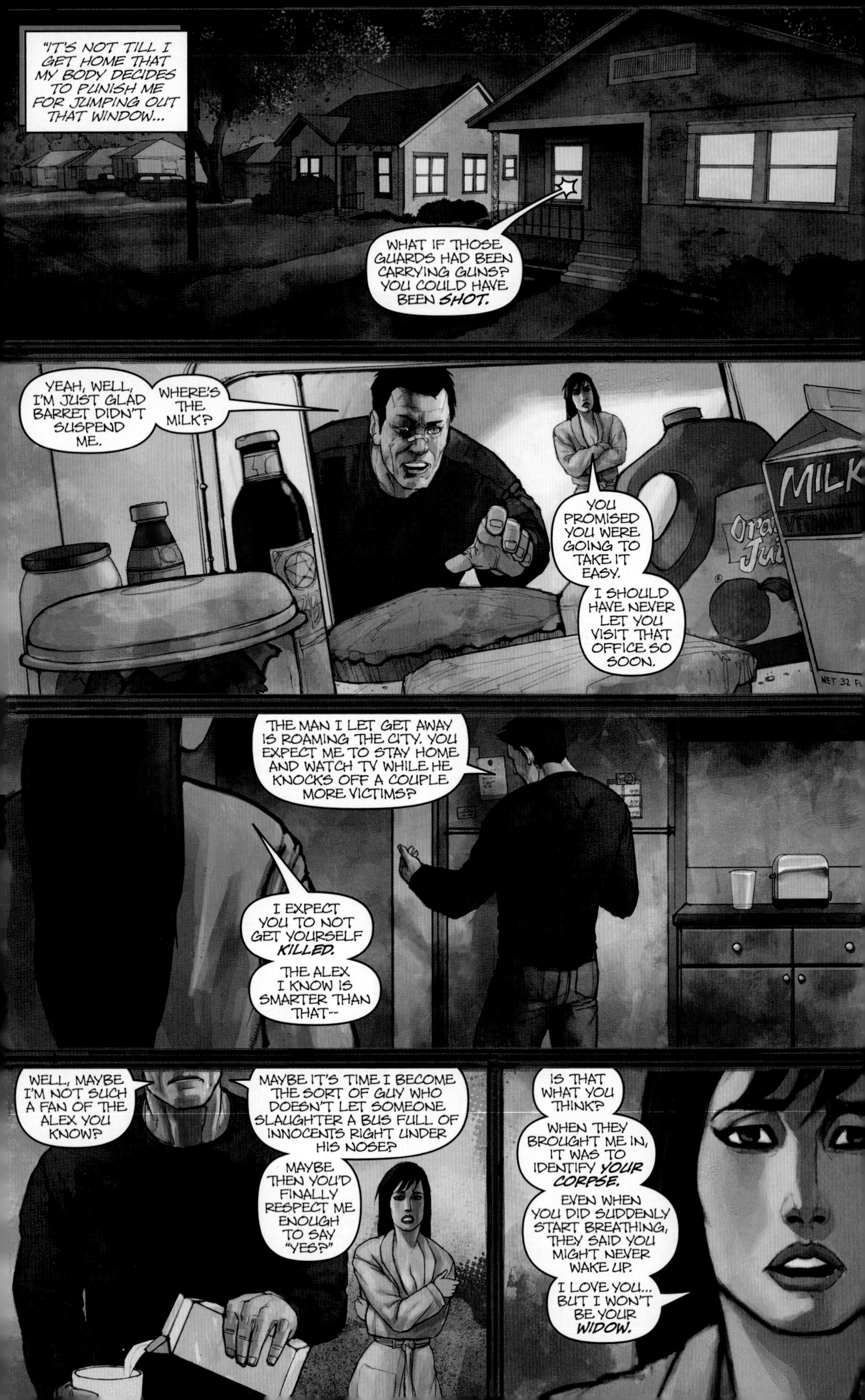
"IT'S NOT TILL I GET HOME THAT MY BODY DECIDES TO PUNISH ME FOR JUMPING OUT THAT WINDOW...
WHAT IF THOSE GUARDS HAD BEEN CARRYING GUNS? YOU COULD HAVE BEEN SHOT.
YEAH, WELL, I'M JUST GLAD BARRET DIDN'T SUSPEND ME.
WHERE'S THE MILK?
MILK
YOU PROMISED YOU WERE GOING TO TAKE IT EASY.
I SHOULD HAVE NEVER LET YOU VISIT THAT OFFICE SO SOON.
THE MAN I LET GET AWAY IS ROAMING THE CITY. YOU EXPECT ME TO STAY HOME AND WATCH TV WHILE HE KNOCKS OFF A COUPLE MORE VICTIMS?
I EXPECT YOU TO NOT GET YOURSELF KILLED.
THE ALEX I KNOW IS SMARTER THAN THAT--
WELL, MAYBE I'M NOT SUCH A FAN OF THE ALEX YOU KNOW?
MAYBE IT'S TIME I BECOME THE SORT OF GUY WHO DOESN'T LET SOMEONE SLAUGHTER A BUS FULL OF INNOCENTS RIGHT UNDER HIS NOSE?
MAYBE THEN YOU'D FINALLY RESPECT ME ENOUGH TO SAY "YES?"
IS THAT WHAT YOU THINK?
WHEN THEY BROUGHT ME IN, IT WAS TO IDENTIFY YOUR CORPSE.
EVEN WHEN YOU DID SUDDENLY START BREATHING, THEY SAID YOU MIGHT NEVER WAKE UP.
I LOVE YOU... BUT I WON'T BE YOUR WIDOW.

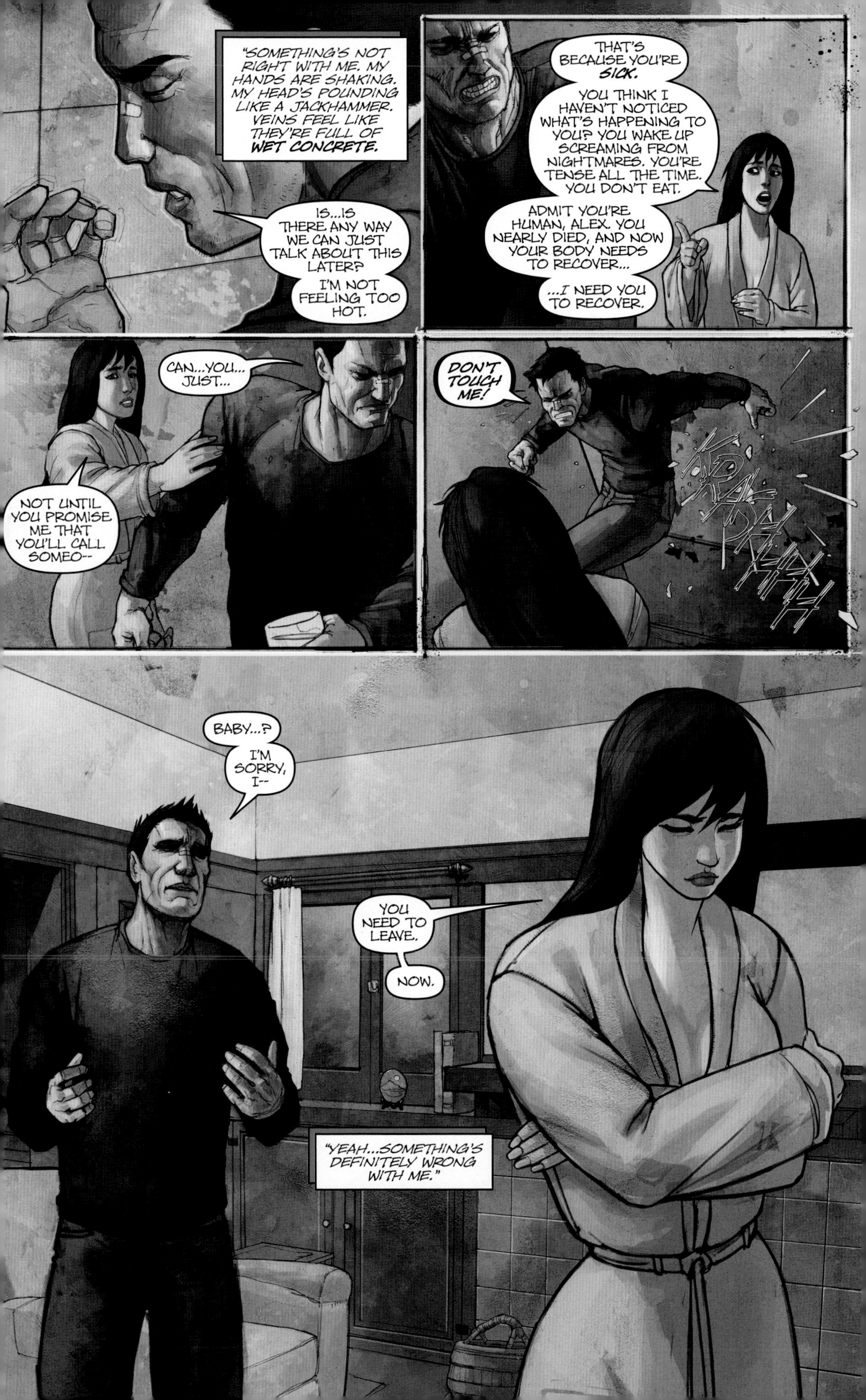
"SOMETHING'S NOT RIGHT WITH ME. MY HANDS ARE SHAKING. MY HEAD'S POUNDING LIKE A JACKHAMMER. VEINS FEEL LIKE THEY'RE FULL OF WET CONCRETE.
IS...IS THERE ANY WAY WE CAN JUST TALK ABOUT THIS LATER?
I'M NOT FEELING TOO HOT.
THAT'S BECAUSE YOU'RE SICK.
YOU THINK I HAVEN'T NOTICED WHAT'S HAPPENING TO YOU? YOU WAKE UP SCREAMING FROM NIGHTMARES. YOU'RE TENSE ALL THE TIME. YOU DON'T EAT.
ADMIT YOU'RE HUMAN, ALEX. YOU NEARLY DIED, AND NOW YOUR BODY NEEDS TO RECOVER...
...I NEED YOU TO RECOVER.
CAN...YOU... JUST...
NOT UNTIL YOU PROMISE ME THAT YOU'LL CALL SOMEO--
DON'T TOUCH ME!
BABY...?
I'M SORRY, I--
YOU NEED TO LEAVE.
NOW.
"YEAH...SOMETHING'S DEFINITELY WRONG WITH ME."

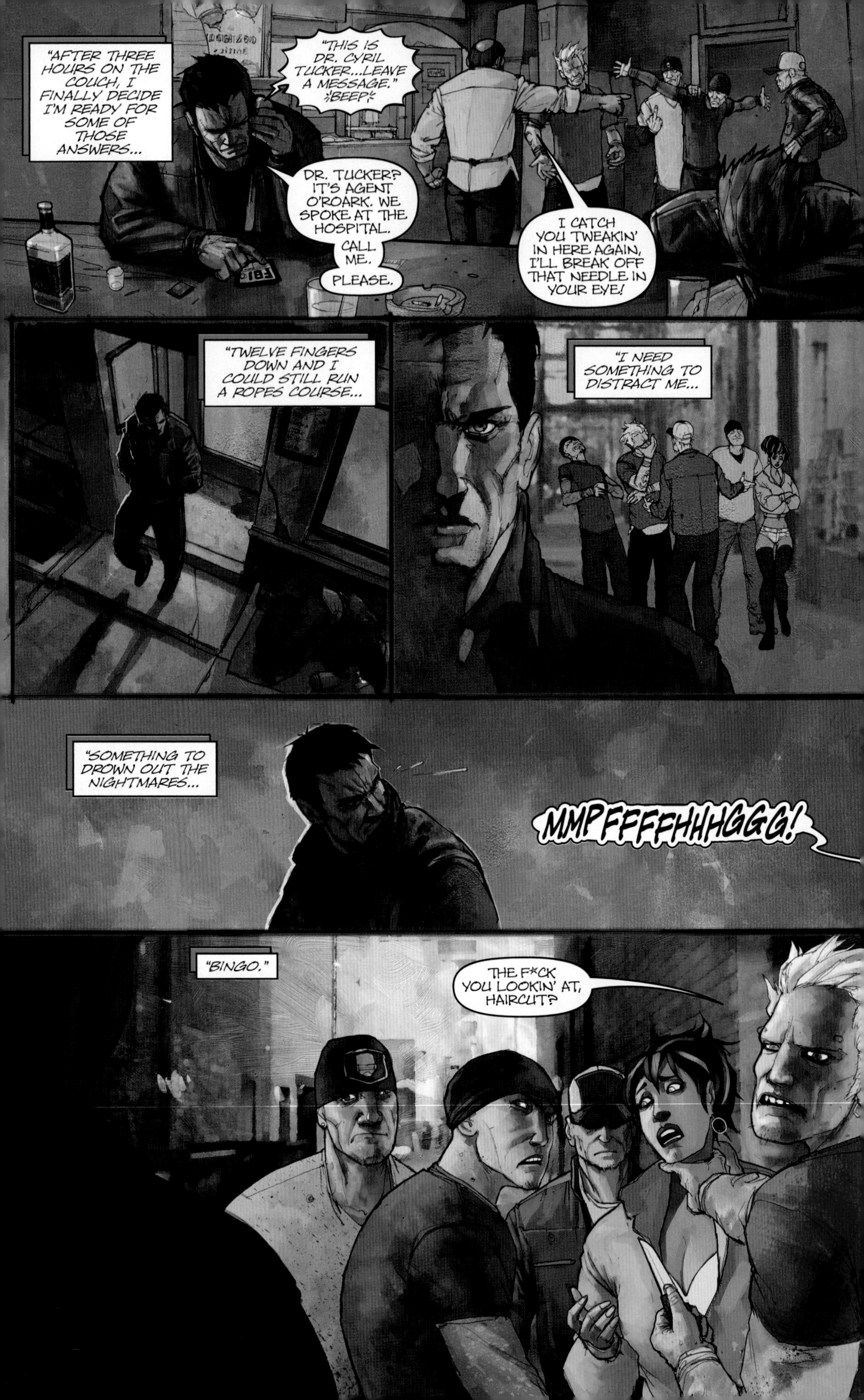
"AFTER THREE HOURS ON THE COUCH, I FINALLY DECIDE I'M READY FOR SOME OF THOSE ANSWERS...
"THIS IS DR. CYRIL TUCKER...LEAVE A MESSAGE." *BEEP*
DR. TUCKER? IT'S AGENT O'ROARK. WE SPOKE AT THE HOSPITAL.
CALL ME.
PLEASE.
I CATCH YOU TWEAKIN' IN HERE AGAIN, I'LL BREAK OFF THAT NEEDLE IN YOUR EYE!
"TWELVE FINGERS DOWN AND I COULD STILL RUN A ROPES COURSE...
"I NEED SOMETHING TO DISTRACT ME...
"SOMETHING TO DROWN OUT THE NIGHTMARES...
MMPFFFFHHHGGG!
"BINGO."
THE F*CK YOU LOOKIN' AT, HAIRCUT?

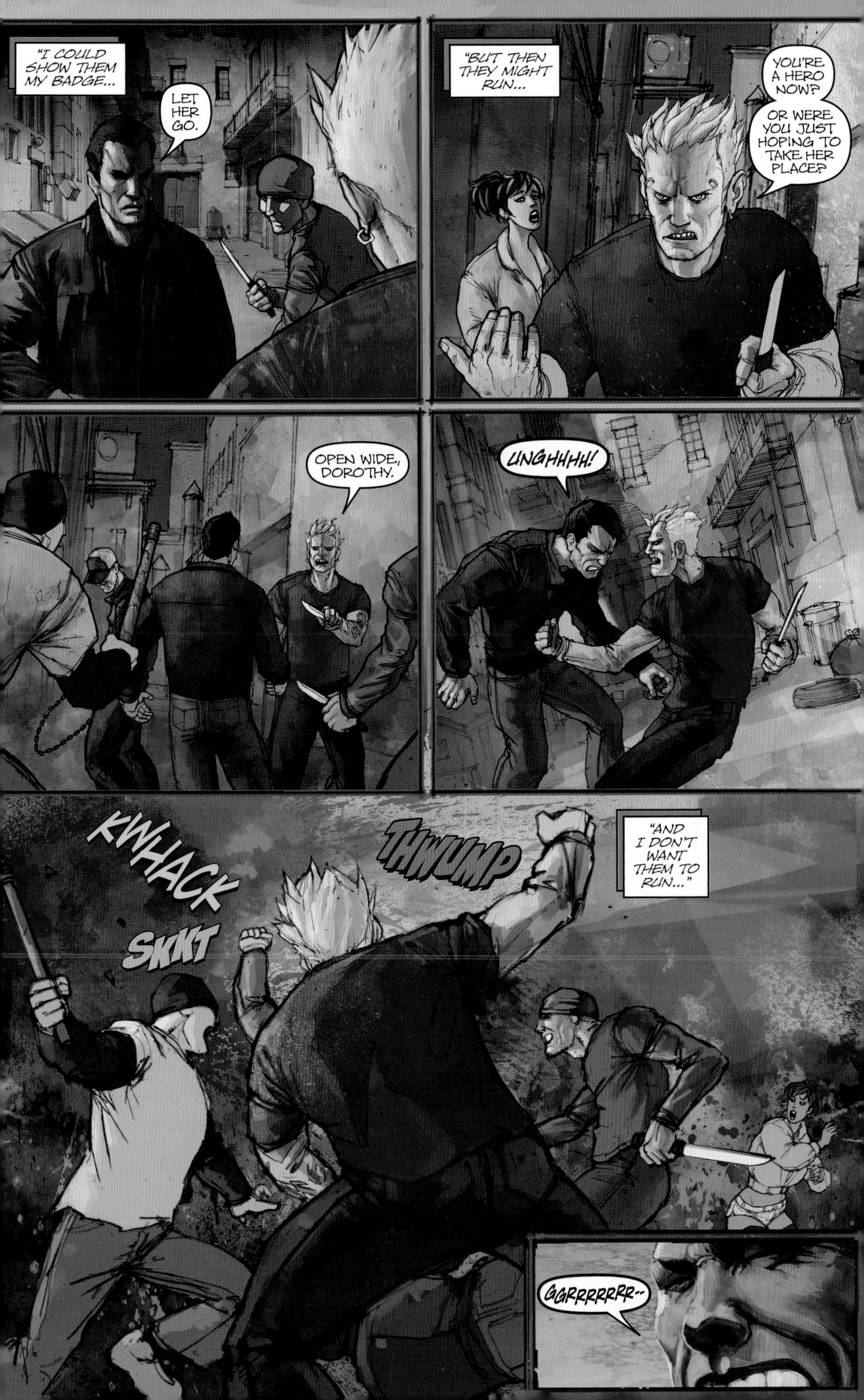
"I COULD SHOW THEM MY BADGE...
LET HER GO.
"BUT THEN THEY MIGHT RUN...
YOU'RE A HERO NOW?
OR WERE YOU JUST HOPING TO TAKE HER PLACE?
OPEN WIDE, DOROTHY.
UNGHHHH!
KWHACK
THWUMP
"AND I DON'T WANT THEM TO RUN..."
SKKT
GGRRRRRRR--

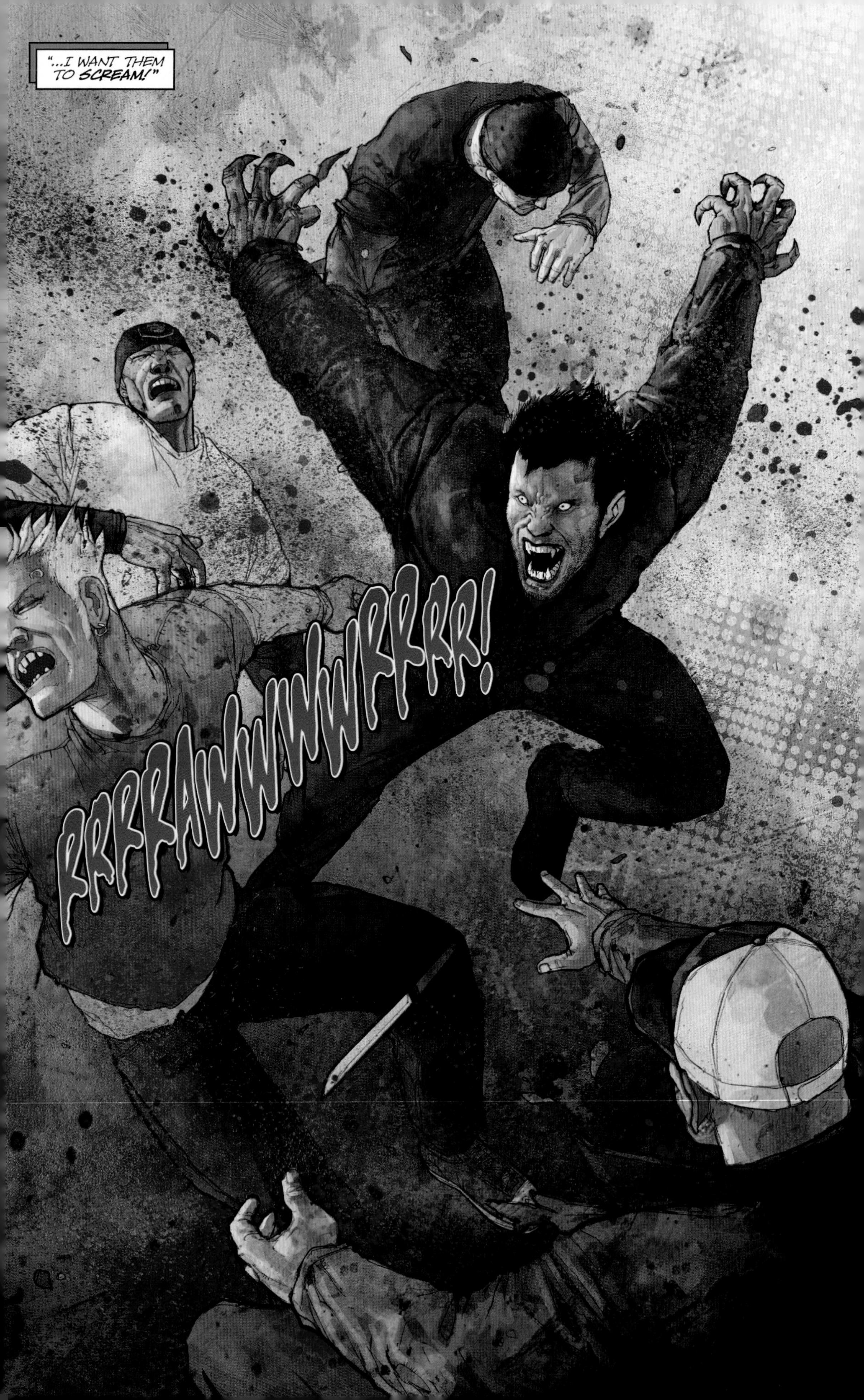
"...I WANT THEM TO SCREAM!"
RRRRAWWWWRRRR!

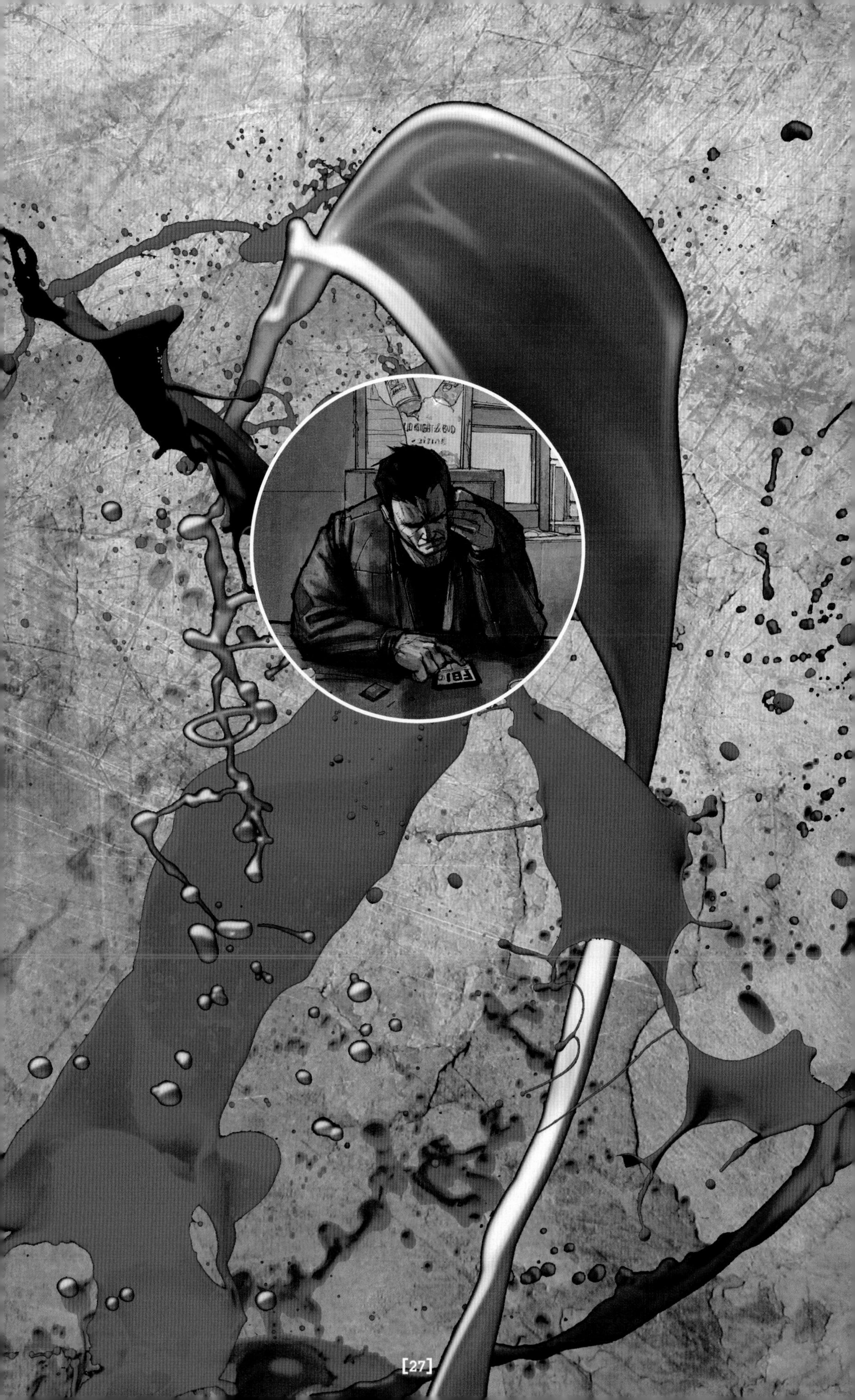
FBI

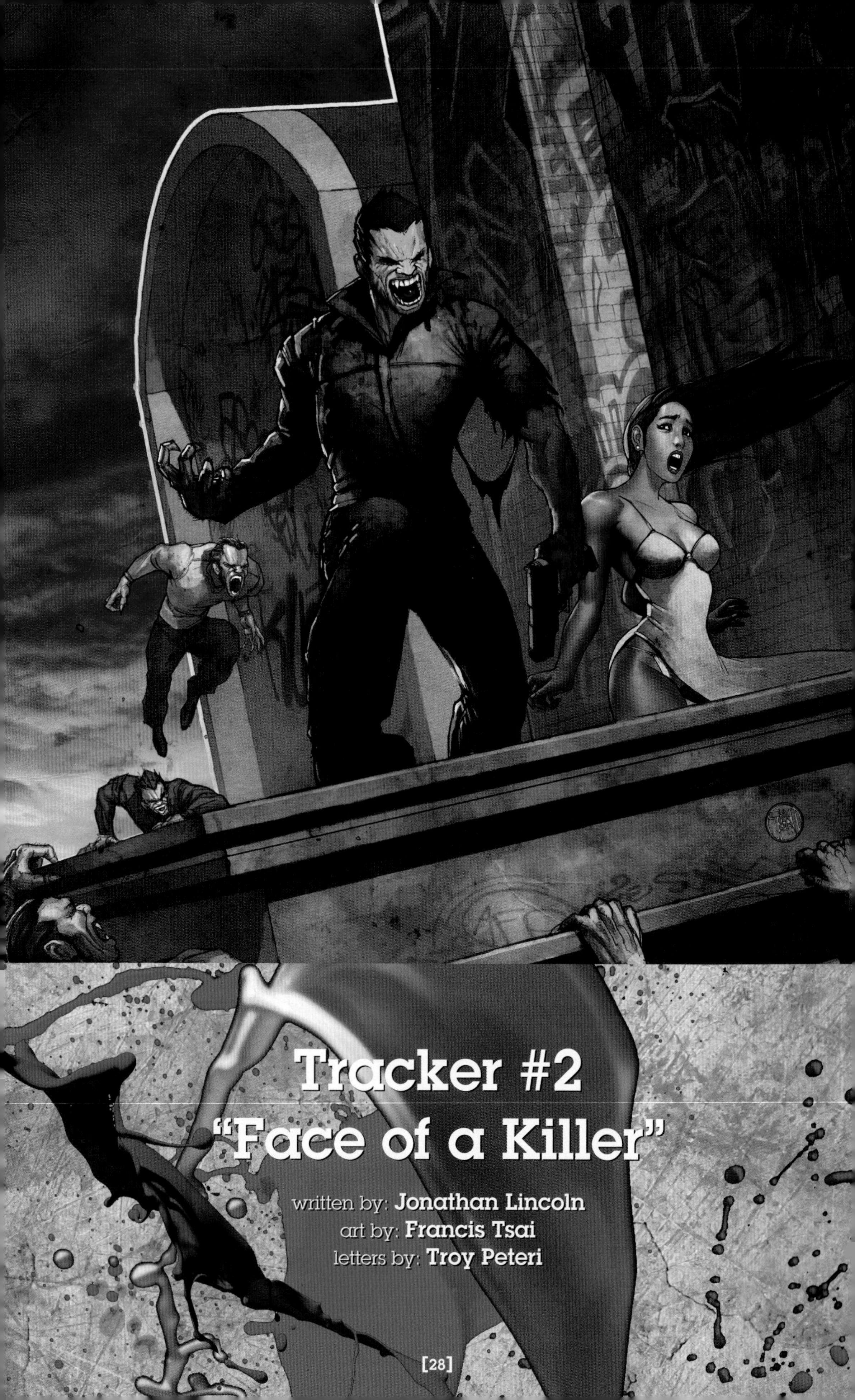

Tracker #2
"Face of a Killer"

written by: **Jonathan Lincoln**
art by: **Francis Tsai**
letters by: **Troy Peteri**

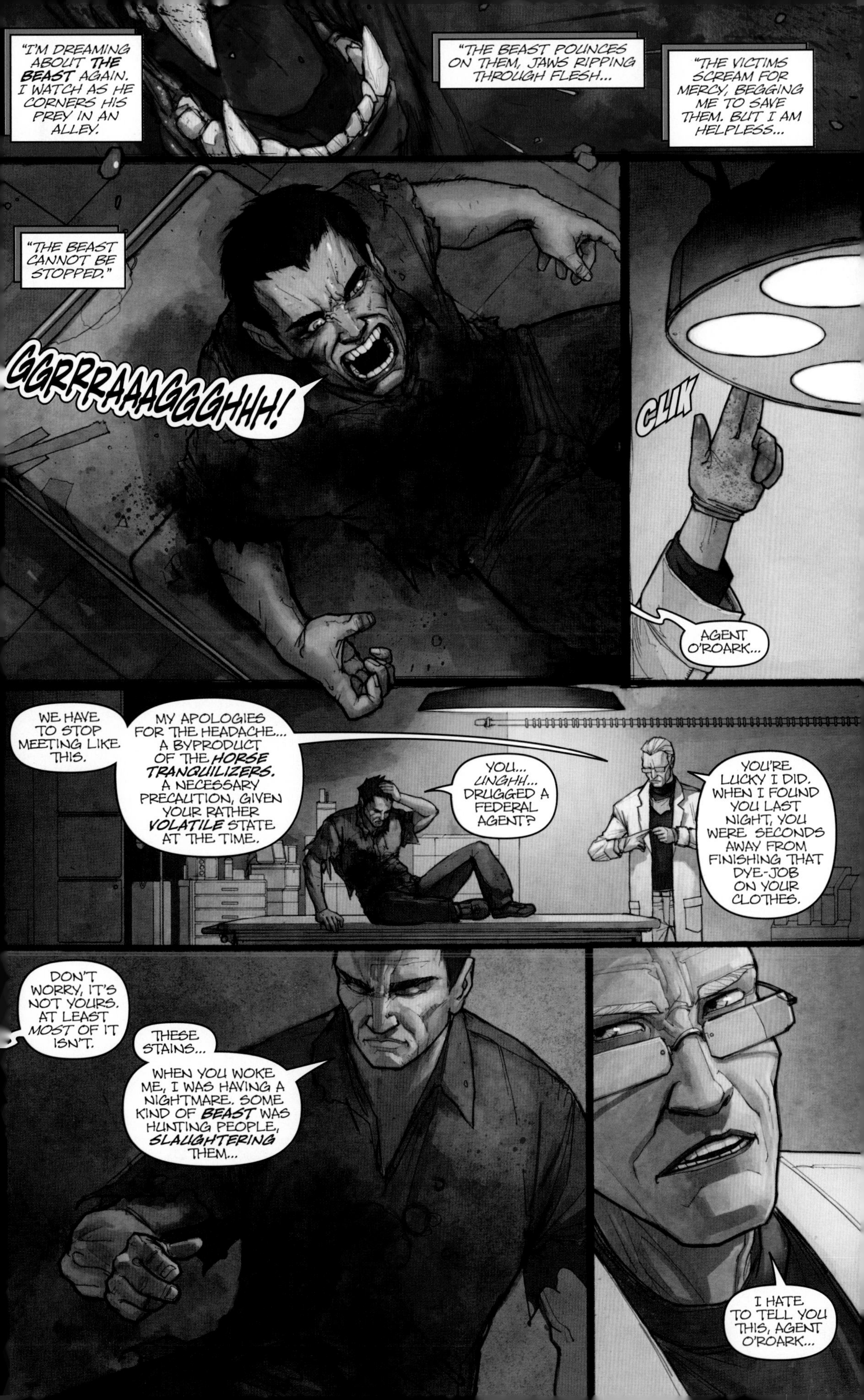
"I'M DREAMING ABOUT THE BEAST AGAIN. I WATCH AS HE CORNERS HIS PREY IN AN ALLEY.
"THE BEAST POUNCES ON THEM, JAWS RIPPING THROUGH FLESH...
"THE VICTIMS SCREAM FOR MERCY, BEGGING ME TO SAVE THEM. BUT I AM HELPLESS...
"THE BEAST CANNOT BE STOPPED."
GGRRRAAAGGGHHH!
CLIK
AGENT O'ROARK...
WE HAVE TO STOP MEETING LIKE THIS.
MY APOLOGIES FOR THE HEADACHE... A BYPRODUCT OF THE HORSE TRANQUILIZERS. A NECESSARY PRECAUTION, GIVEN YOUR RATHER VOLATILE STATE AT THE TIME.
YOU... UNGHH... DRUGGED A FEDERAL AGENT?
YOU'RE LUCKY I DID. WHEN I FOUND YOU LAST NIGHT, YOU WERE SECONDS AWAY FROM FINISHING THAT DYE-JOB ON YOUR CLOTHES.
THESE STAINS...
DON'T WORRY, IT'S NOT YOURS. AT LEAST MOST OF IT ISN'T.
WHEN YOU WOKE ME, I WAS HAVING A NIGHTMARE. SOME KIND OF BEAST WAS HUNTING PEOPLE, SLAUGHTERING THEM...
I HATE TO TELL YOU THIS, AGENT O'ROARK...

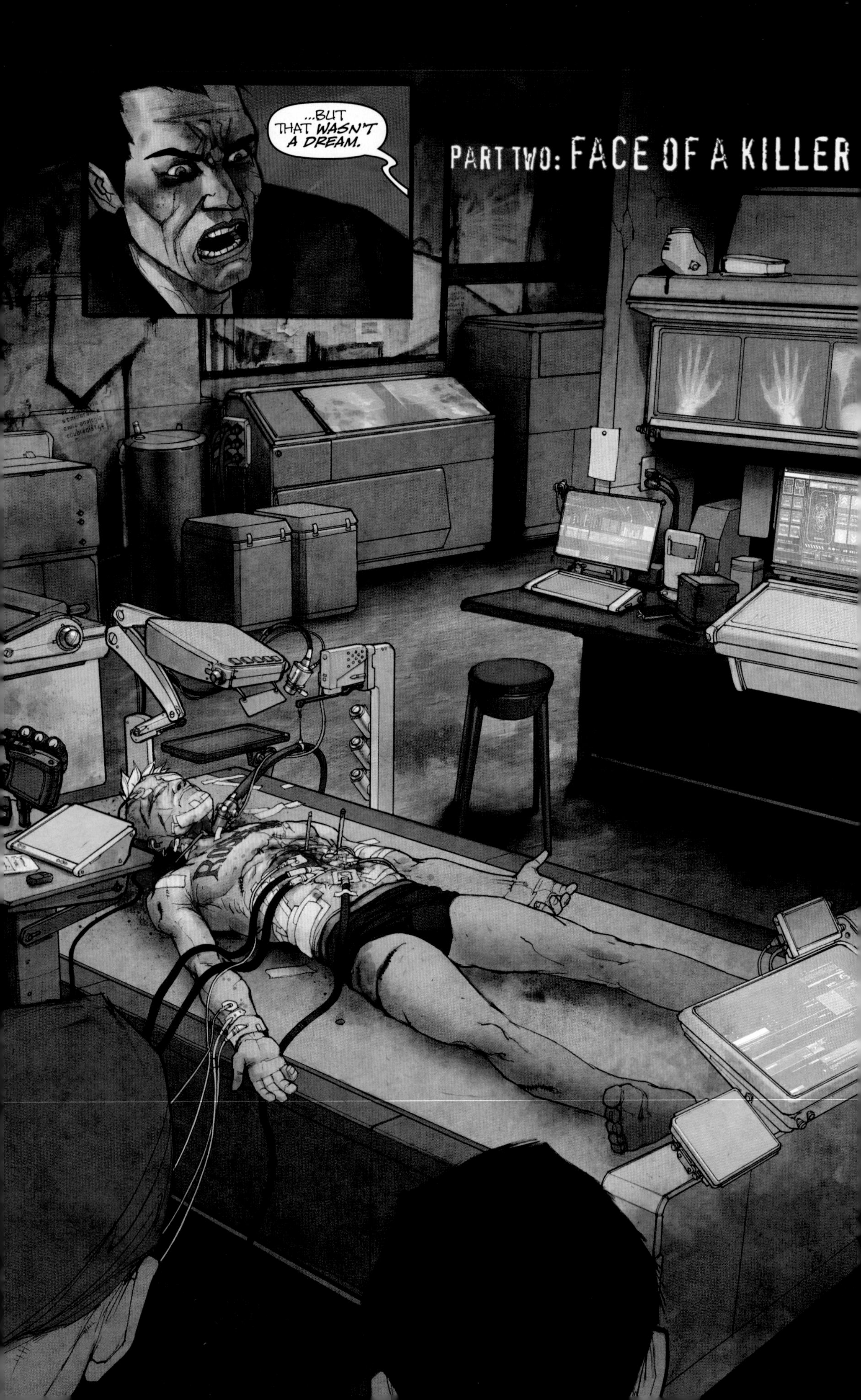
...BUT THAT WASN'T A DREAM.
PART TWO: FACE OF A KILLER

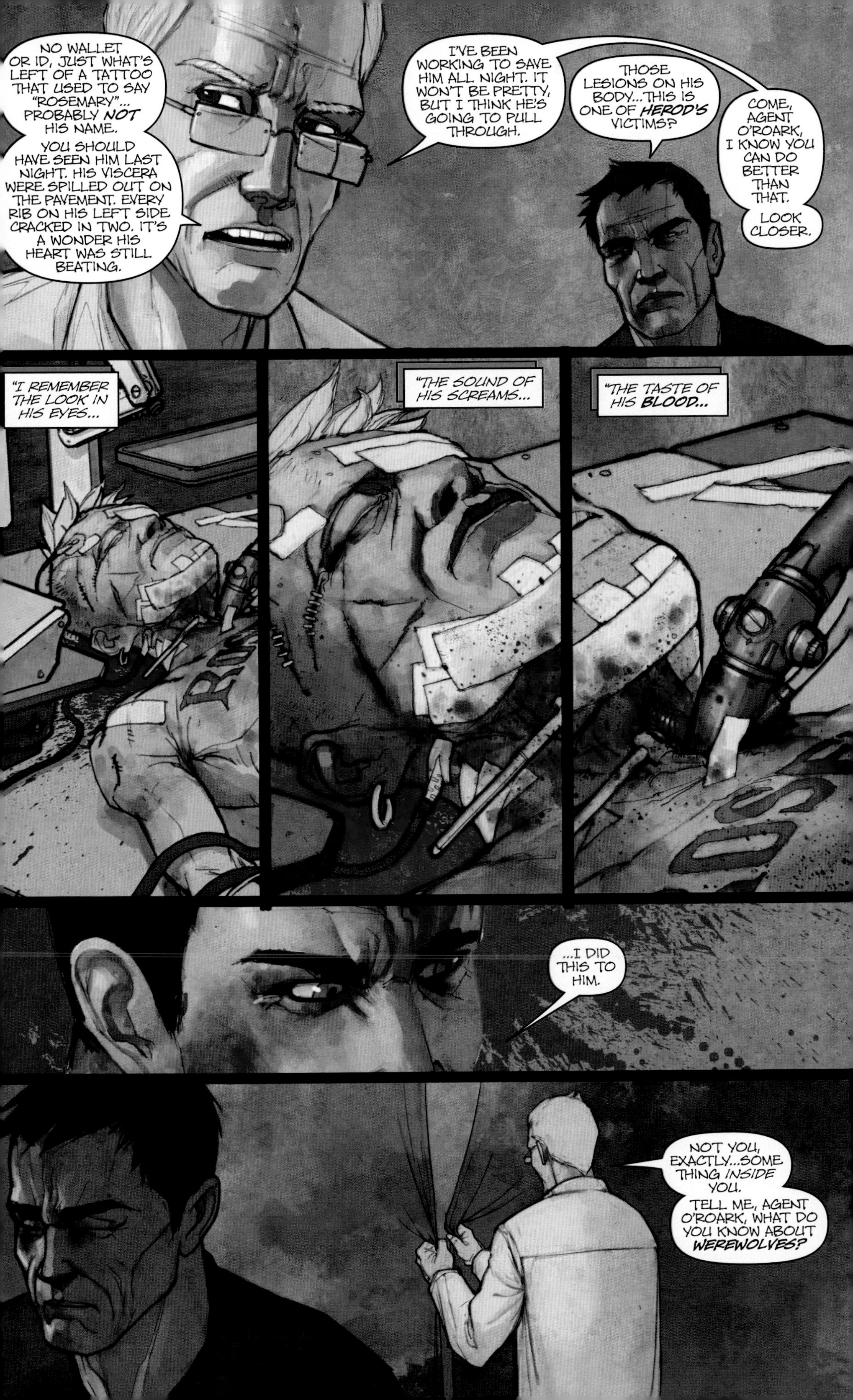
NO WALLET OR ID, JUST WHAT'S LEFT OF A TATTOO THAT USED TO SAY "ROSEMARY"... PROBABLY *NOT* HIS NAME.
YOU SHOULD HAVE SEEN HIM LAST NIGHT. HIS VISCERA WERE SPILLED OUT ON THE PAVEMENT. EVERY RIB ON HIS LEFT SIDE CRACKED IN TWO. IT'S A WONDER HIS HEART WAS STILL BEATING.
I'VE BEEN WORKING TO SAVE HIM ALL NIGHT. IT WON'T BE PRETTY, BUT I THINK HE'S GOING TO PULL THROUGH.
THOSE LESIONS ON HIS BODY...THIS IS ONE OF *HEROD'S* VICTIMS?
COME, AGENT O'ROARK, I KNOW YOU CAN DO BETTER THAN THAT.
LOOK CLOSER.
"I REMEMBER THE LOOK IN HIS EYES...
"THE SOUND OF HIS SCREAMS...
"THE TASTE OF HIS *BLOOD*...
...I DID THIS TO HIM.
NOT YOU, EXACTLY...SOME THING *INSIDE* YOU.
TELL ME, AGENT O'ROARK, WHAT DO YOU KNOW ABOUT *WEREWOLVES?*

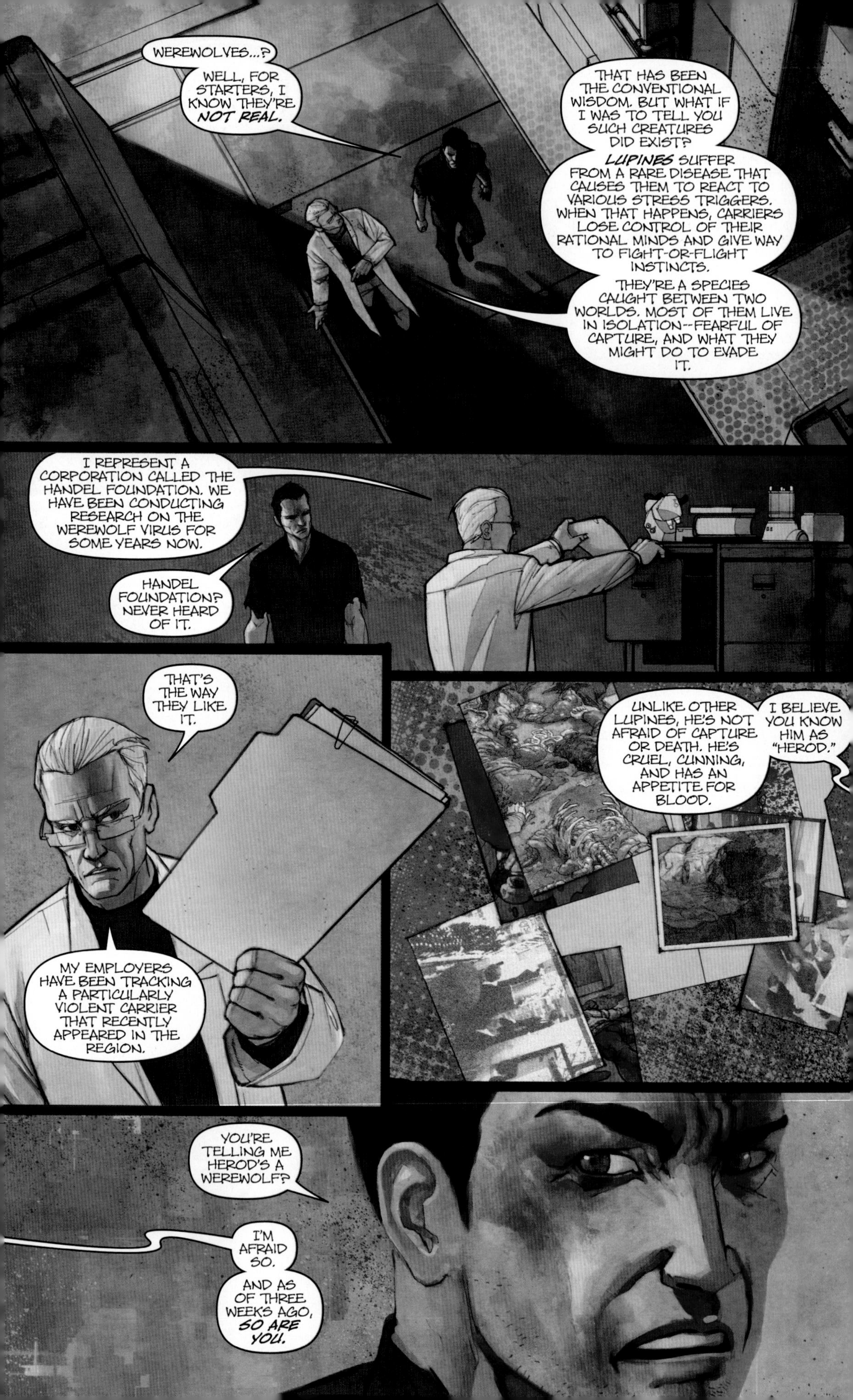
WEREWOLVES...?
WELL, FOR STARTERS, I KNOW THEY'RE ***NOT REAL.***
THAT HAS BEEN THE CONVENTIONAL WISDOM. BUT WHAT IF I WAS TO TELL YOU SUCH CREATURES DID EXIST?
LUPINES SUFFER FROM A RARE DISEASE THAT CAUSES THEM TO REACT TO VARIOUS STRESS TRIGGERS. WHEN THAT HAPPENS, CARRIERS LOSE CONTROL OF THEIR RATIONAL MINDS AND GIVE WAY TO FIGHT-OR-FLIGHT INSTINCTS.
THEY'RE A SPECIES CAUGHT BETWEEN TWO WORLDS. MOST OF THEM LIVE IN ISOLATION--FEARFUL OF CAPTURE, AND WHAT THEY MIGHT DO TO EVADE IT.
I REPRESENT A CORPORATION CALLED THE HANDEL FOUNDATION. WE HAVE BEEN CONDUCTING RESEARCH ON THE WEREWOLF VIRUS FOR SOME YEARS NOW.
HANDEL FOUNDATION? NEVER HEARD OF IT.
THAT'S THE WAY THEY LIKE IT.
MY EMPLOYERS HAVE BEEN TRACKING A PARTICULARLY VIOLENT CARRIER THAT RECENTLY APPEARED IN THE REGION.
UNLIKE OTHER LUPINES, HE'S NOT AFRAID OF CAPTURE OR DEATH. HE'S CRUEL, CUNNING, AND HAS AN APPETITE FOR BLOOD.
I BELIEVE YOU KNOW HIM AS "HEROD."
YOU'RE TELLING ME HEROD'S A WEREWOLF?
I'M AFRAID SO.
AND AS OF THREE WEEKS AGO, ***SO ARE YOU.***

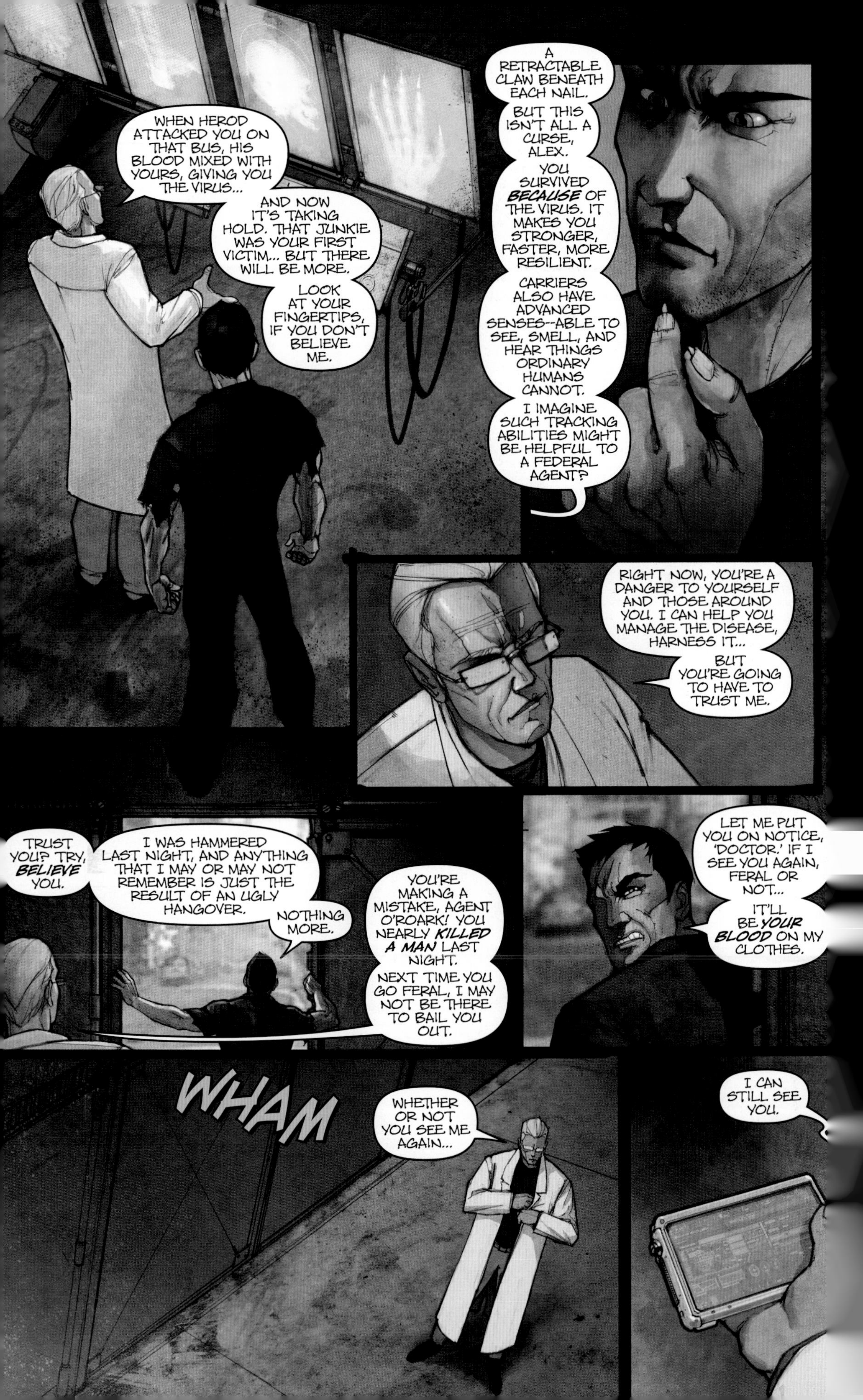
WHEN HEROD ATTACKED YOU ON THAT BUS, HIS BLOOD MIXED WITH YOURS, GIVING YOU THE VIRUS...
AND NOW IT'S TAKING HOLD. THAT JUNKIE WAS YOUR FIRST VICTIM... BUT THERE WILL BE MORE.
LOOK AT YOUR FINGERTIPS, IF YOU DON'T BELIEVE ME.
A RETRACTABLE CLAW BENEATH EACH NAIL.
BUT THIS ISN'T ALL A CURSE, ALEX.
YOU SURVIVED BECAUSE OF THE VIRUS. IT MAKES YOU STRONGER, FASTER, MORE RESILIENT.
CARRIERS ALSO HAVE ADVANCED SENSES--ABLE TO SEE, SMELL, AND HEAR THINGS ORDINARY HUMANS CANNOT.
I IMAGINE SUCH TRACKING ABILITIES MIGHT BE HELPFUL TO A FEDERAL AGENT?
RIGHT NOW, YOU'RE A DANGER TO YOURSELF AND THOSE AROUND YOU. I CAN HELP YOU MANAGE THE DISEASE, HARNESS IT...
BUT YOU'RE GOING TO HAVE TO TRUST ME.
TRUST YOU? TRY, BELIEVE YOU.
I WAS HAMMERED LAST NIGHT, AND ANYTHING THAT I MAY OR MAY NOT REMEMBER IS JUST THE RESULT OF AN UGLY HANGOVER.
NOTHING MORE.
YOU'RE MAKING A MISTAKE, AGENT O'ROARK! YOU NEARLY KILLED A MAN LAST NIGHT.
NEXT TIME YOU GO FERAL, I MAY NOT BE THERE TO BAIL YOU OUT.
LET ME PUT YOU ON NOTICE, 'DOCTOR.' IF I SEE YOU AGAIN, FERAL OR NOT...
IT'LL BE YOUR BLOOD ON MY CLOTHES.
WHAM
WHETHER OR NOT YOU SEE ME AGAIN...
I CAN STILL SEE YOU.

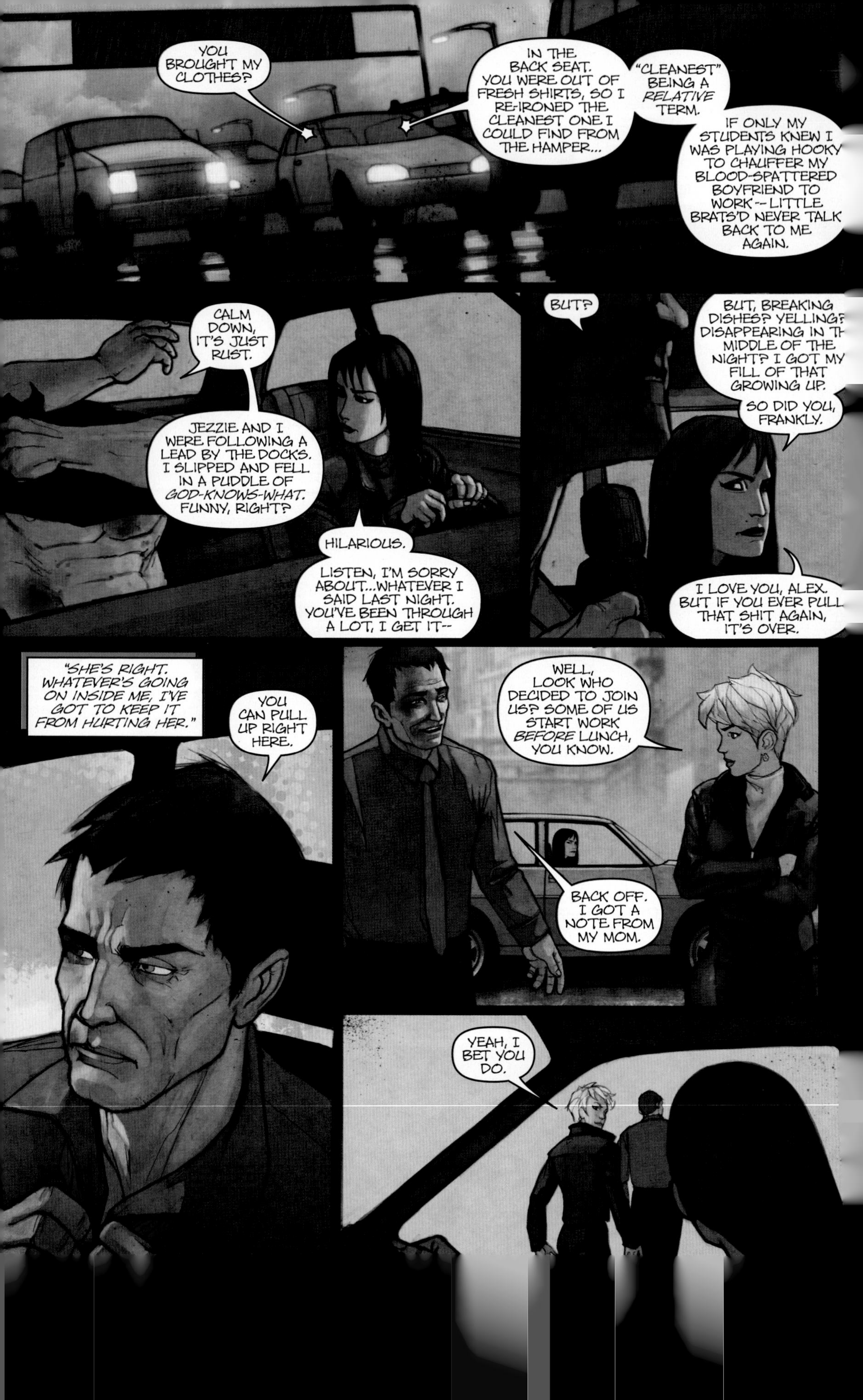
YOU BROUGHT MY CLOTHES?
IN THE BACK SEAT. YOU WERE OUT OF FRESH SHIRTS, SO I RE-IRONED THE CLEANEST ONE I COULD FIND FROM THE HAMPER...
"CLEANEST" BEING A RELATIVE TERM.
IF ONLY MY STUDENTS KNEW I WAS PLAYING HOOKY TO CHAUFFER MY BLOOD-SPATTERED BOYFRIEND TO WORK -- LITTLE BRATS'D NEVER TALK BACK TO ME AGAIN.
CALM DOWN, IT'S JUST RUST.
JEZZIE AND I WERE FOLLOWING A LEAD BY THE DOCKS. I SLIPPED AND FELL IN A PUDDLE OF GOD-KNOWS-WHAT. FUNNY, RIGHT?
HILARIOUS.
LISTEN, I'M SORRY ABOUT...WHATEVER I SAID LAST NIGHT. YOU'VE BEEN THROUGH A LOT, I GET IT--
BUT?
BUT, BREAKING DISHES? YELLING? DISAPPEARING IN TH MIDDLE OF THE NIGHT? I GOT MY FILL OF THAT GROWING UP.
SO DID YOU, FRANKLY.
I LOVE YOU, ALEX. BUT IF YOU EVER PULL THAT SHIT AGAIN, IT'S OVER.
"SHE'S RIGHT. WHATEVER'S GOING ON INSIDE ME, I'VE GOT TO KEEP IT FROM HURTING HER."
YOU CAN PULL UP RIGHT HERE.
WELL, LOOK WHO DECIDED TO JOIN US? SOME OF US START WORK BEFORE LUNCH, YOU KNOW.
BACK OFF. I GOT A NOTE FROM MY MOM.
YEAH, I BET YOU DO.

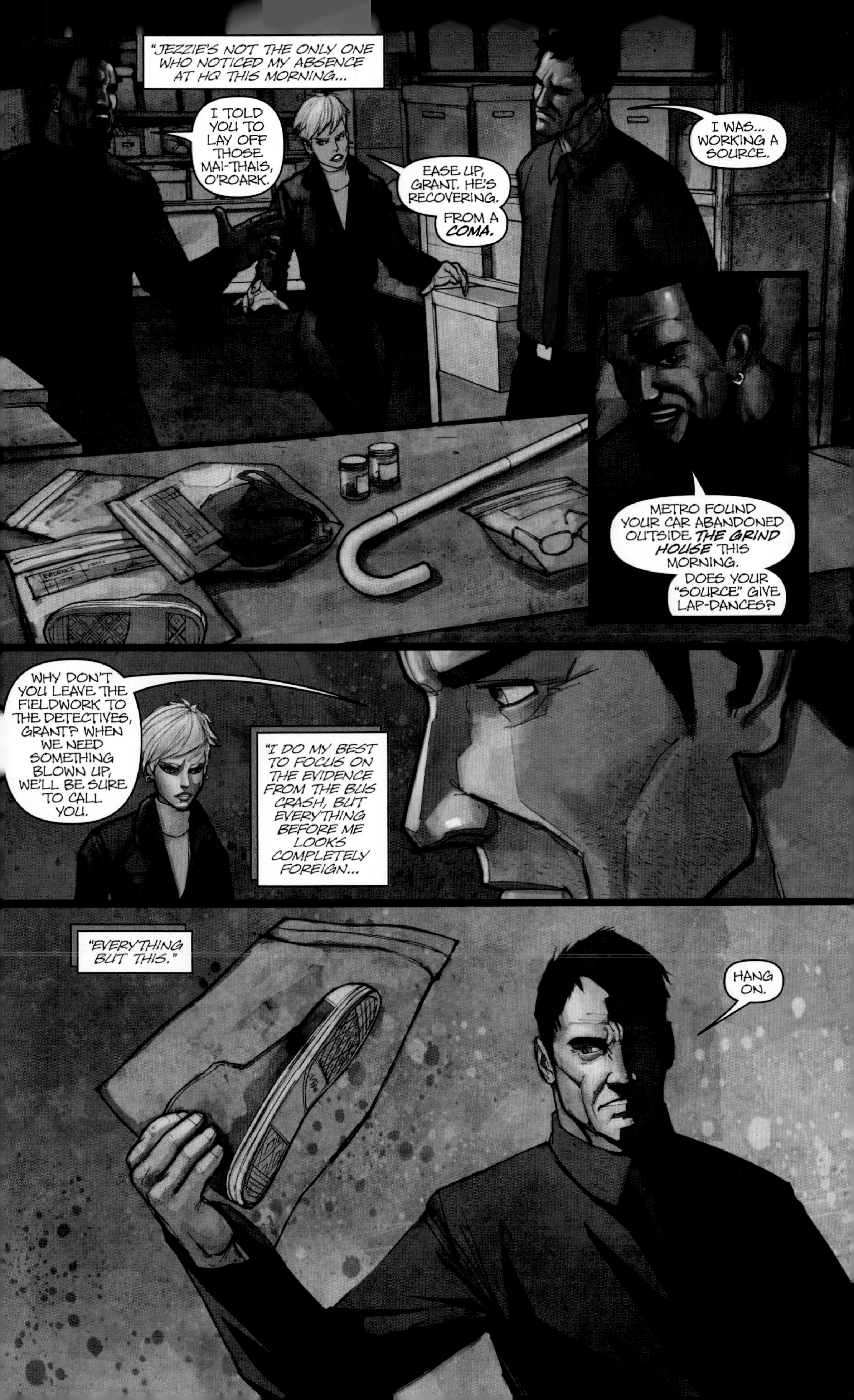
"JEZZIE'S NOT THE ONLY ONE WHO NOTICED MY ABSENCE AT HQ THIS MORNING...
I TOLD YOU TO LAY OFF THOSE MAI-THAIS, O'ROARK.
EASE UP, GRANT. HE'S RECOVERING.
FROM A **COMA.**
I WAS... WORKING A SOURCE.
METRO FOUND YOUR CAR ABANDONED OUTSIDE ***THE GRIND HOUSE*** THIS MORNING.
DOES YOUR "SOURCE" GIVE LAP-DANCES?
WHY DON'T YOU LEAVE THE FIELDWORK TO THE DETECTIVES, GRANT? WHEN WE NEED SOMETHING BLOWN UP, WE'LL BE SURE TO CALL YOU.
"I DO MY BEST TO FOCUS ON THE EVIDENCE FROM THE BUS CRASH, BUT EVERYTHING BEFORE ME LOOKS COMPLETELY FOREIGN...
"EVERYTHING BUT THIS."
HANG ON.

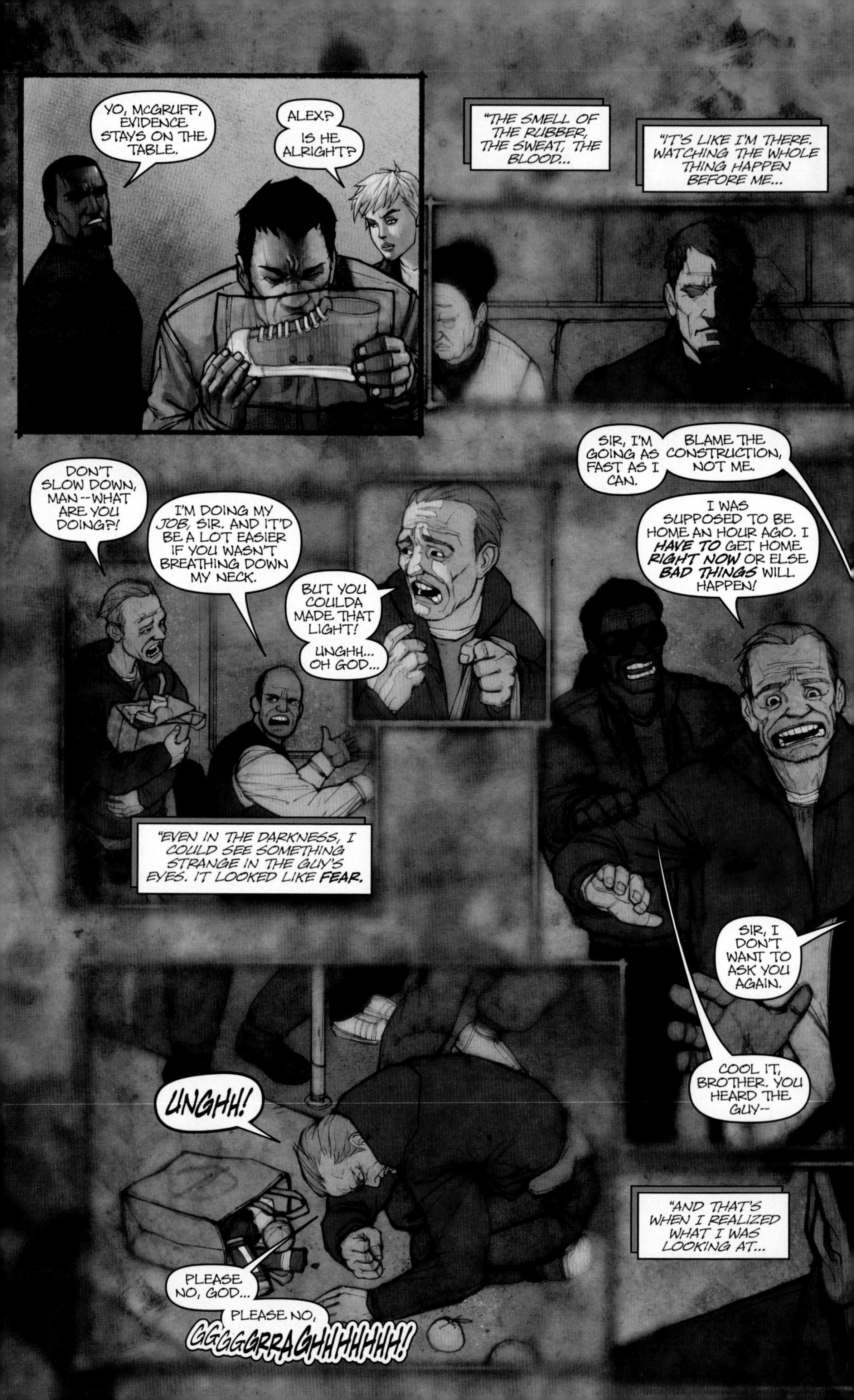
YO, MCGRUFF, EVIDENCE STAYS ON THE TABLE.
ALEX?
IS HE ALRIGHT?
"THE SMELL OF THE RUBBER, THE SWEAT, THE BLOOD...
"IT'S LIKE I'M THERE. WATCHING THE WHOLE THING HAPPEN BEFORE ME...
DON'T SLOW DOWN, MAN--WHAT ARE YOU DOING?!
I'M DOING MY JOB, SIR. AND IT'D BE A LOT EASIER IF YOU WASN'T BREATHING DOWN MY NECK.
BUT YOU COULDA MADE THAT LIGHT!
UNGHH... OH GOD...
SIR, I'M GOING AS FAST AS I CAN.
BLAME THE CONSTRUCTION, NOT ME.
I WAS SUPPOSED TO BE HOME AN HOUR AGO. I HAVE TO GET HOME RIGHT NOW OR ELSE BAD THINGS WILL HAPPEN!
"EVEN IN THE DARKNESS, I COULD SEE SOMETHING STRANGE IN THE GUY'S EYES. IT LOOKED LIKE FEAR.
SIR, I DON'T WANT TO ASK YOU AGAIN.
COOL IT, BROTHER. YOU HEARD THE GUY--
UNGHH!
"AND THAT'S WHEN I REALIZED WHAT I WAS LOOKING AT...
PLEASE NO, GOD...
PLEASE NO,
GGGGGRRAGHHHHHHH!

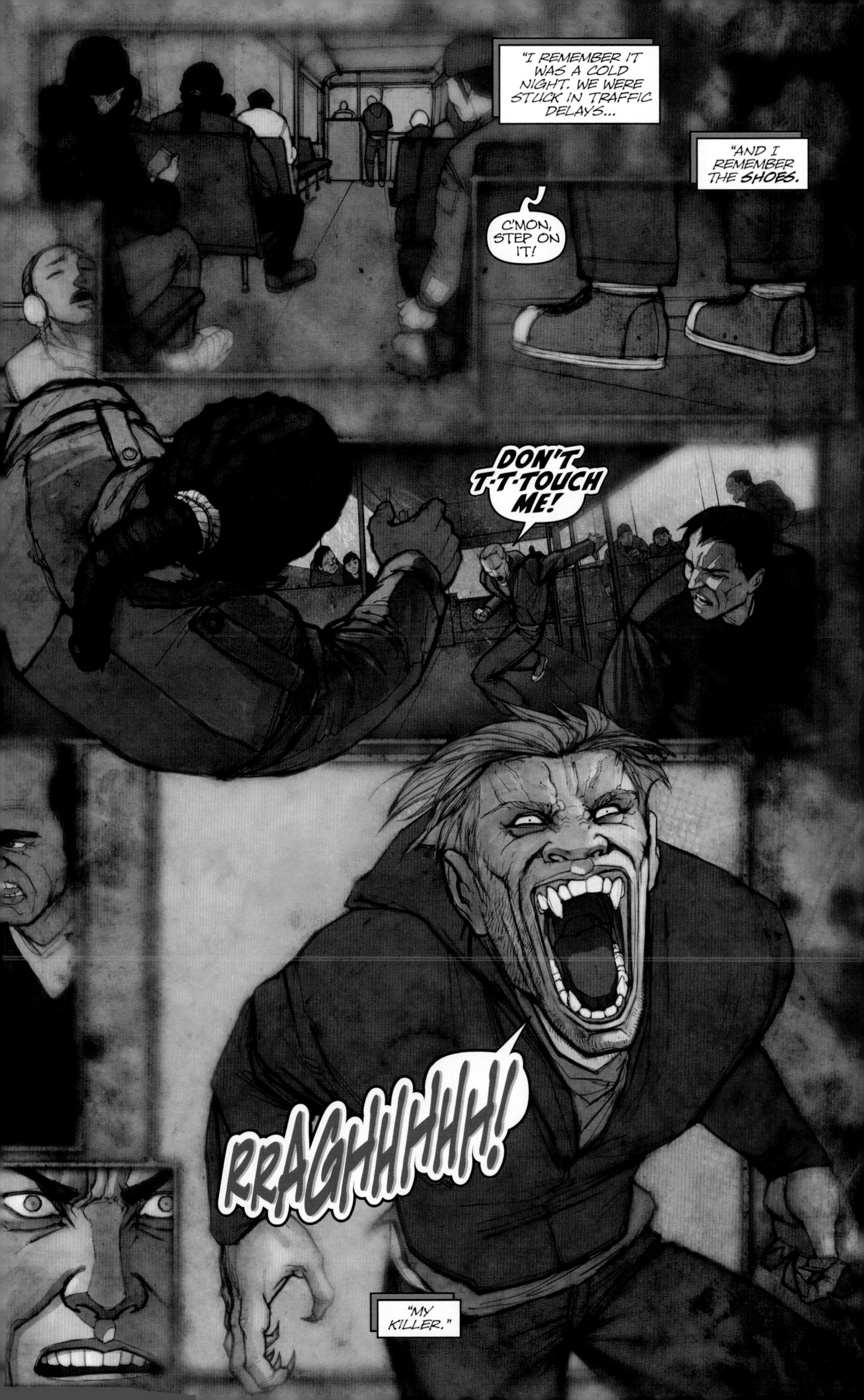
"I REMEMBER IT WAS A COLD NIGHT. WE WERE STUCK IN TRAFFIC DELAYS...
"AND I REMEMBER THE SHOES.
C'MON, STEP ON IT!
DON'T T-T-TOUCH ME!
RRAGHHHHH!
"MY KILLER."

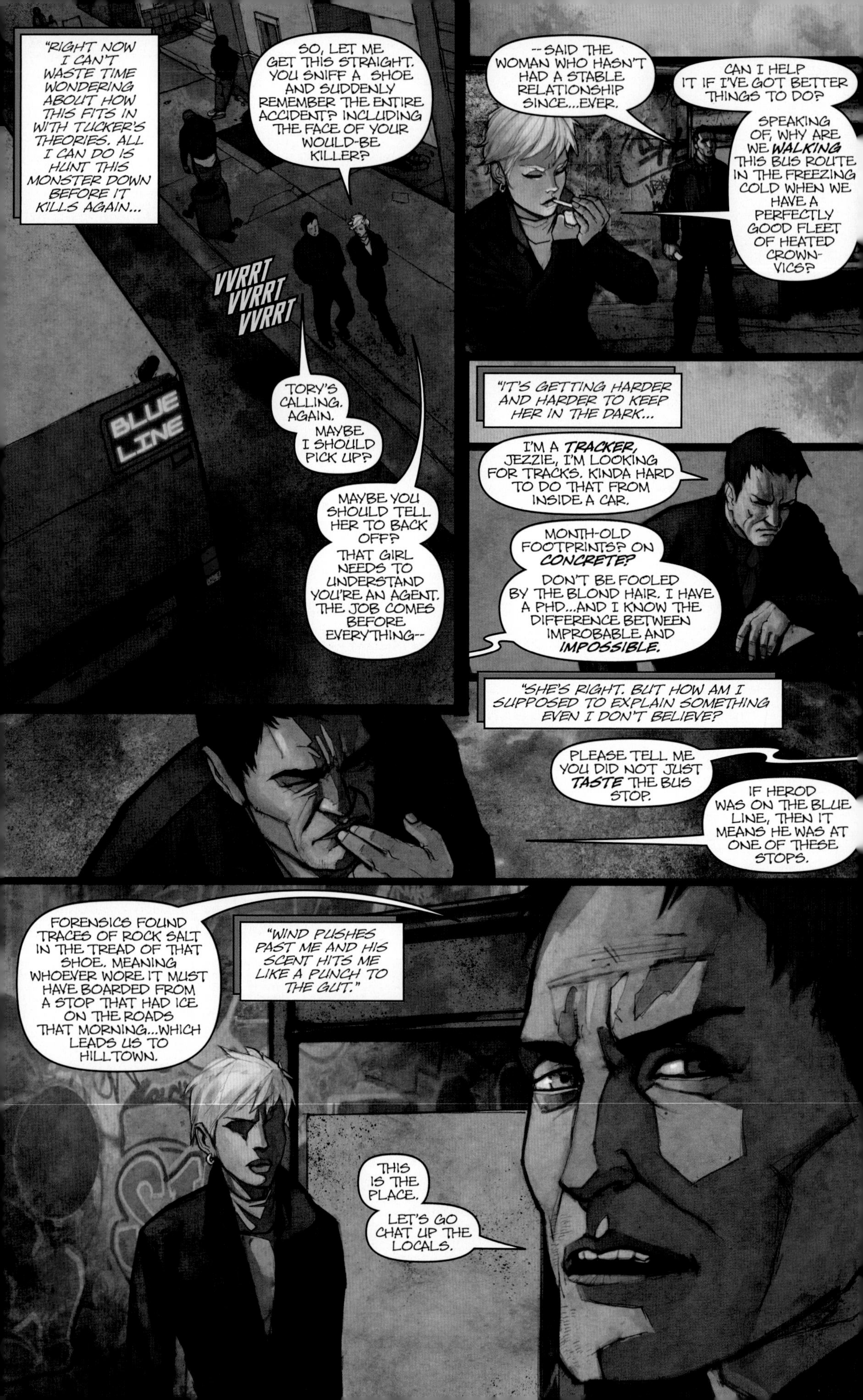
"RIGHT NOW I CAN'T WASTE TIME WONDERING ABOUT HOW THIS FITS IN WITH TUCKER'S THEORIES. ALL I CAN DO IS HUNT THIS MONSTER DOWN BEFORE IT KILLS AGAIN...
SO, LET ME GET THIS STRAIGHT. YOU SNIFF A SHOE AND SUDDENLY REMEMBER THE ENTIRE ACCIDENT? INCLUDING THE FACE OF YOUR WOULD-BE KILLER?
VVRRT VVRRT VVRRT
BLUE LINE
TORY'S CALLING. AGAIN.
MAYBE I SHOULD PICK UP?
MAYBE YOU SHOULD TELL HER TO BACK OFF?
THAT GIRL NEEDS TO UNDERSTAND YOU'RE AN AGENT. THE JOB COMES BEFORE EVERYTHING--
--SAID THE WOMAN WHO HASN'T HAD A STABLE RELATIONSHIP SINCE...EVER.
CAN I HELP IT IF I'VE GOT BETTER THINGS TO DO?
SPEAKING OF, WHY ARE WE WALKING THIS BUS ROUTE IN THE FREEZING COLD WHEN WE HAVE A PERFECTLY GOOD FLEET OF HEATED CROWN-VICS?
"IT'S GETTING HARDER AND HARDER TO KEEP HER IN THE DARK...
I'M A TRACKER, JEZZIE, I'M LOOKING FOR TRACKS. KINDA HARD TO DO THAT FROM INSIDE A CAR.
MONTH-OLD FOOTPRINTS? ON CONCRETE?
DON'T BE FOOLED BY THE BLOND HAIR. I HAVE A PHD...AND I KNOW THE DIFFERENCE BETWEEN IMPROBABLE AND IMPOSSIBLE.
"SHE'S RIGHT. BUT HOW AM I SUPPOSED TO EXPLAIN SOMETHING EVEN I DON'T BELIEVE?
PLEASE TELL ME YOU DID NOT JUST TASTE THE BUS STOP.
IF HEROD WAS ON THE BLUE LINE, THEN IT MEANS HE WAS AT ONE OF THESE STOPS.
FORENSICS FOUND TRACES OF ROCK SALT IN THE TREAD OF THAT SHOE. MEANING WHOEVER WORE IT MUST HAVE BOARDED FROM A STOP THAT HAD ICE ON THE ROADS THAT MORNING...WHICH LEADS US TO HILLTOWN.
"WIND PUSHES PAST ME AND HIS SCENT HITS ME LIKE A PUNCH TO THE GUT."
THIS IS THE PLACE.
LET'S GO CHAT UP THE LOCALS.

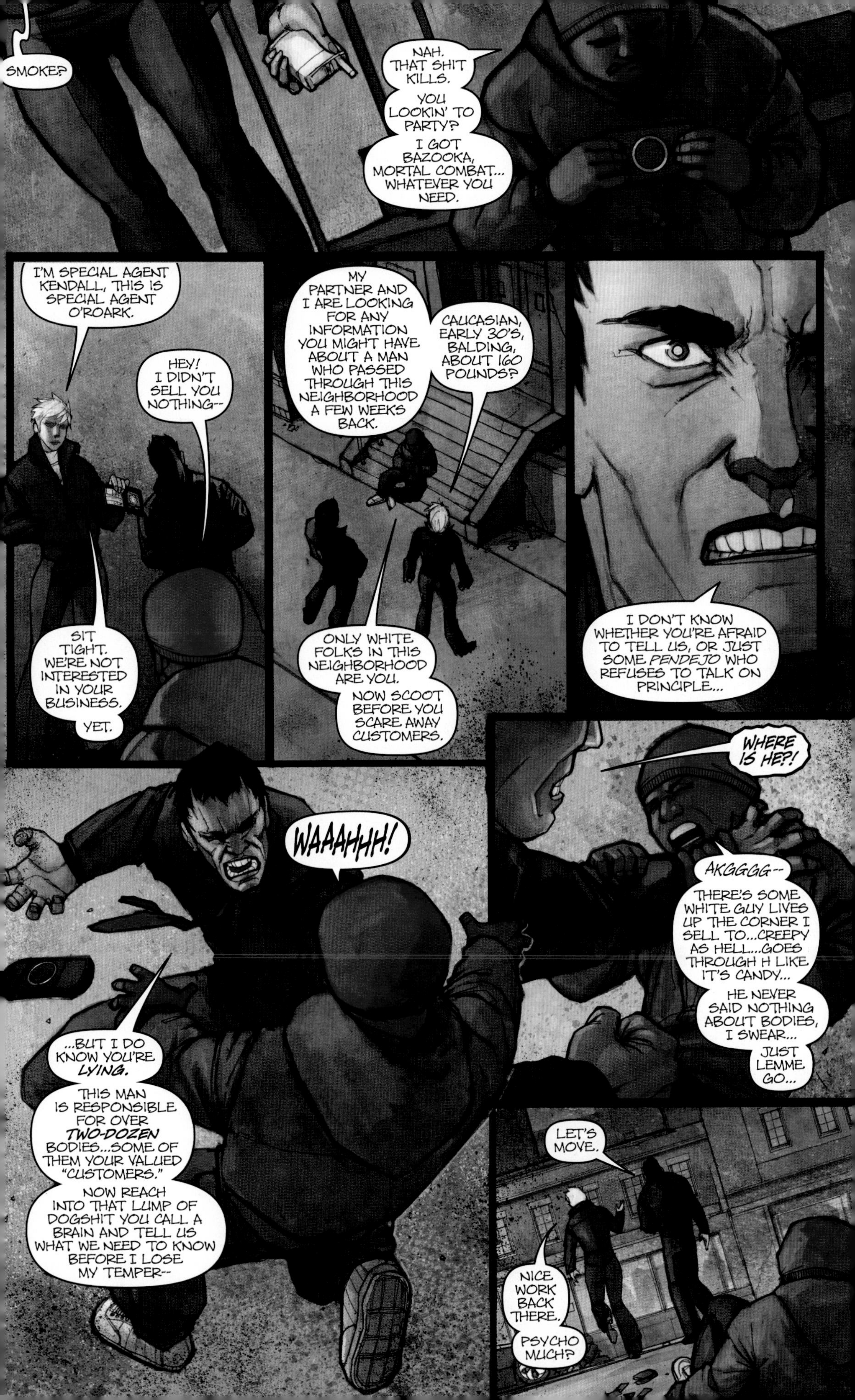
SMOKE?
NAH. THAT SHIT KILLS.
YOU LOOKIN' TO PARTY?
I GOT BAZOOKA, MORTAL COMBAT... WHATEVER YOU NEED.
I'M SPECIAL AGENT KENDALL, THIS IS SPECIAL AGENT O'ROARK.
HEY! I DIDN'T SELL YOU NOTHING--
SIT TIGHT. WE'RE NOT INTERESTED IN YOUR BUSINESS.
YET.
MY PARTNER AND I ARE LOOKING FOR ANY INFORMATION YOU MIGHT HAVE ABOUT A MAN WHO PASSED THROUGH THIS NEIGHBORHOOD A FEW WEEKS BACK.
CAUCASIAN, EARLY 30'S, BALDING, ABOUT 160 POUNDS?
ONLY WHITE FOLKS IN THIS NEIGHBORHOOD ARE YOU.
NOW SCOOT BEFORE YOU SCARE AWAY CUSTOMERS.
I DON'T KNOW WHETHER YOU'RE AFRAID TO TELL US, OR JUST SOME PENDEJO WHO REFUSES TO TALK ON PRINCIPLE...
WAAAHHH!
...BUT I DO KNOW YOU'RE LYING.
THIS MAN IS RESPONSIBLE FOR OVER TWO-DOZEN BODIES...SOME OF THEM YOUR VALUED "CUSTOMERS."
NOW REACH INTO THAT LUMP OF DOGSHIT YOU CALL A BRAIN AND TELL US WHAT WE NEED TO KNOW BEFORE I LOSE MY TEMPER--
WHERE IS HE?!
AKGGGG--
THERE'S SOME WHITE GUY LIVES UP THE CORNER I SELL TO...CREEPY AS HELL...GOES THROUGH H LIKE IT'S CANDY...
HE NEVER SAID NOTHING ABOUT BODIES, I SWEAR...
JUST LEMME GO...
LET'S MOVE.
NICE WORK BACK THERE.
PSYCHO MUCH?

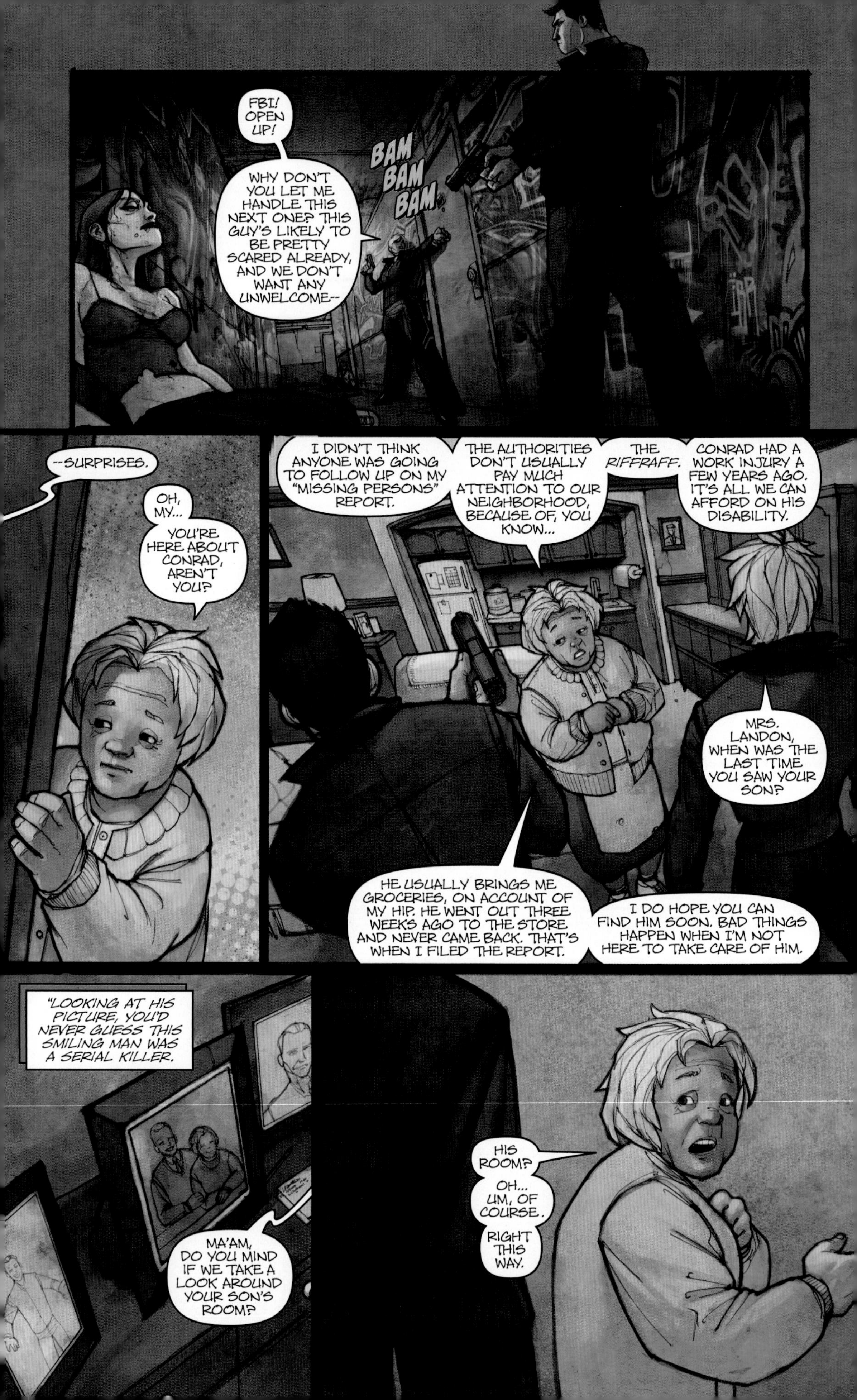

FBI! OPEN UP!
BAM BAM BAM
WHY DON'T YOU LET ME HANDLE THIS NEXT ONE? THIS GUY'S LIKELY TO BE PRETTY SCARED ALREADY, AND WE DON'T WANT ANY UNWELCOME--
--SURPRISES.
OH, MY...
YOU'RE HERE ABOUT CONRAD, AREN'T YOU?
I DIDN'T THINK ANYONE WAS GOING TO FOLLOW UP ON MY "MISSING PERSONS" REPORT.
THE AUTHORITIES DON'T USUALLY PAY MUCH ATTENTION TO OUR NEIGHBORHOOD, BECAUSE OF, YOU KNOW...
THE *RIFFRAFF.*
CONRAD HAD A WORK INJURY A FEW YEARS AGO. IT'S ALL WE CAN AFFORD ON HIS DISABILITY.
MRS. LANDON, WHEN WAS THE LAST TIME YOU SAW YOUR SON?
HE USUALLY BRINGS ME GROCERIES, ON ACCOUNT OF MY HIP. HE WENT OUT THREE WEEKS AGO TO THE STORE AND NEVER CAME BACK. THAT'S WHEN I FILED THE REPORT.
I DO HOPE YOU CAN FIND HIM SOON. BAD THINGS HAPPEN WHEN I'M NOT HERE TO TAKE CARE OF HIM.
"LOOKING AT HIS PICTURE, YOU'D NEVER GUESS THIS SMILING MAN WAS A SERIAL KILLER.
MA'AM, DO YOU MIND IF WE TAKE A LOOK AROUND YOUR SON'S ROOM?
HIS ROOM?
OH... UM, OF COURSE.
RIGHT THIS WAY.

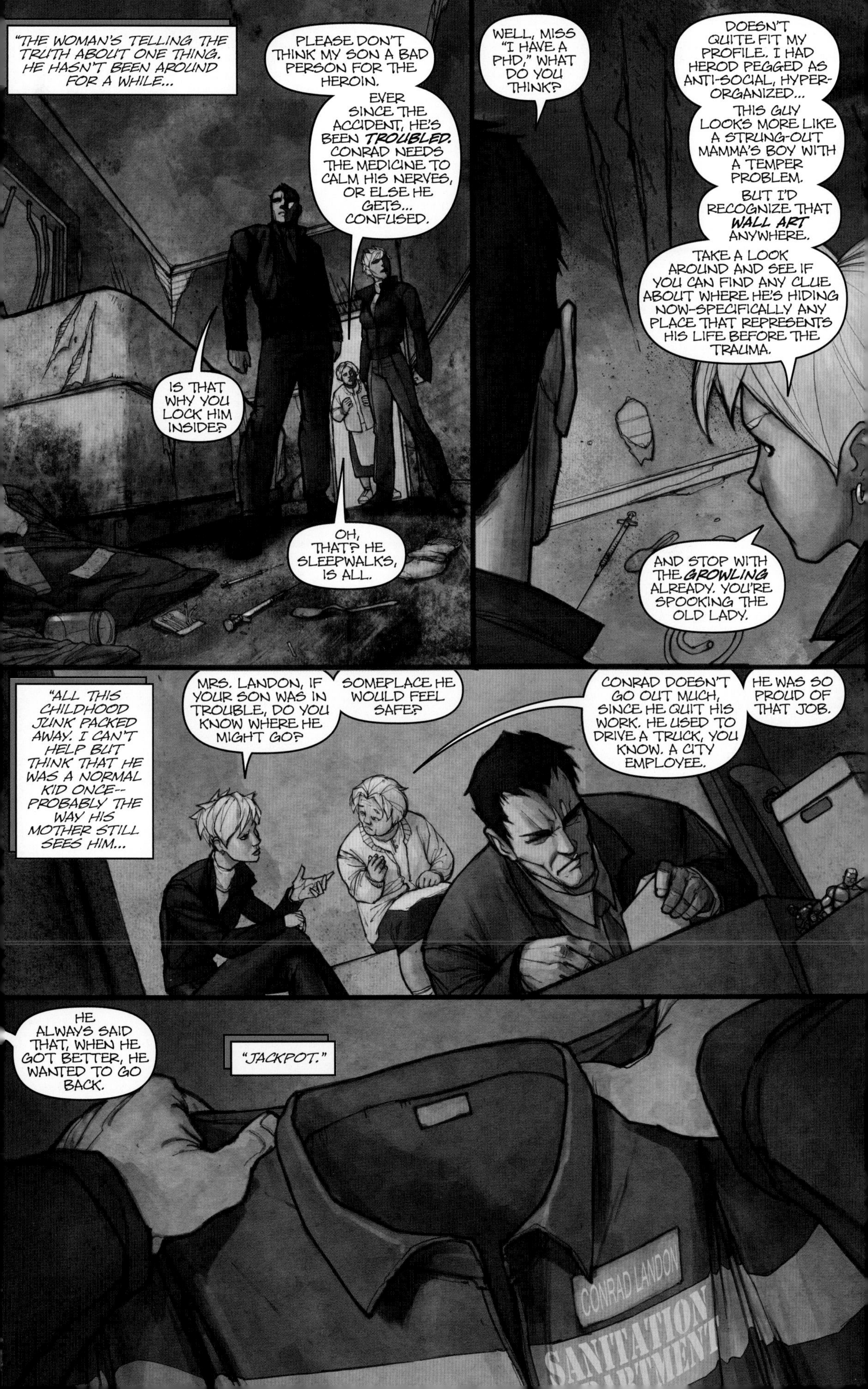
"THE WOMAN'S TELLING THE TRUTH ABOUT ONE THING. HE HASN'T BEEN AROUND FOR A WHILE...
PLEASE DON'T THINK MY SON A BAD PERSON FOR THE HEROIN.
EVER SINCE THE ACCIDENT, HE'S BEEN TROUBLED. CONRAD NEEDS THE MEDICINE TO CALM HIS NERVES, OR ELSE HE GETS... CONFUSED.
IS THAT WHY YOU LOCK HIM INSIDE?
OH, THAT? HE SLEEPWALKS, IS ALL.
WELL, MISS "I HAVE A PHD," WHAT DO YOU THINK?
DOESN'T QUITE FIT MY PROFILE. I HAD HEROD PEGGED AS ANTI-SOCIAL, HYPER-ORGANIZED...
THIS GUY LOOKS MORE LIKE A STRUNG-OUT MAMMA'S BOY WITH A TEMPER PROBLEM.
BUT I'D RECOGNIZE THAT WALL ART ANYWHERE.
TAKE A LOOK AROUND AND SEE IF YOU CAN FIND ANY CLUE ABOUT WHERE HE'S HIDING NOW--SPECIFICALLY ANY PLACE THAT REPRESENTS HIS LIFE BEFORE THE TRAUMA.
AND STOP WITH THE GROWLING ALREADY. YOU'RE SPOOKING THE OLD LADY.
"ALL THIS CHILDHOOD JUNK PACKED AWAY. I CAN'T HELP BUT THINK THAT HE WAS A NORMAL KID ONCE-- PROBABLY THE WAY HIS MOTHER STILL SEES HIM...
MRS. LANDON, IF YOUR SON WAS IN TROUBLE, DO YOU KNOW WHERE HE MIGHT GO?
SOMEPLACE HE WOULD FEEL SAFE?
CONRAD DOESN'T GO OUT MUCH, SINCE HE QUIT HIS WORK. HE USED TO DRIVE A TRUCK, YOU KNOW. A CITY EMPLOYEE.
HE WAS SO PROUD OF THAT JOB.
HE ALWAYS SAID THAT, WHEN HE GOT BETTER, HE WANTED TO GO BACK.
"JACKPOT."
CONRAD LANDON
SANITATION

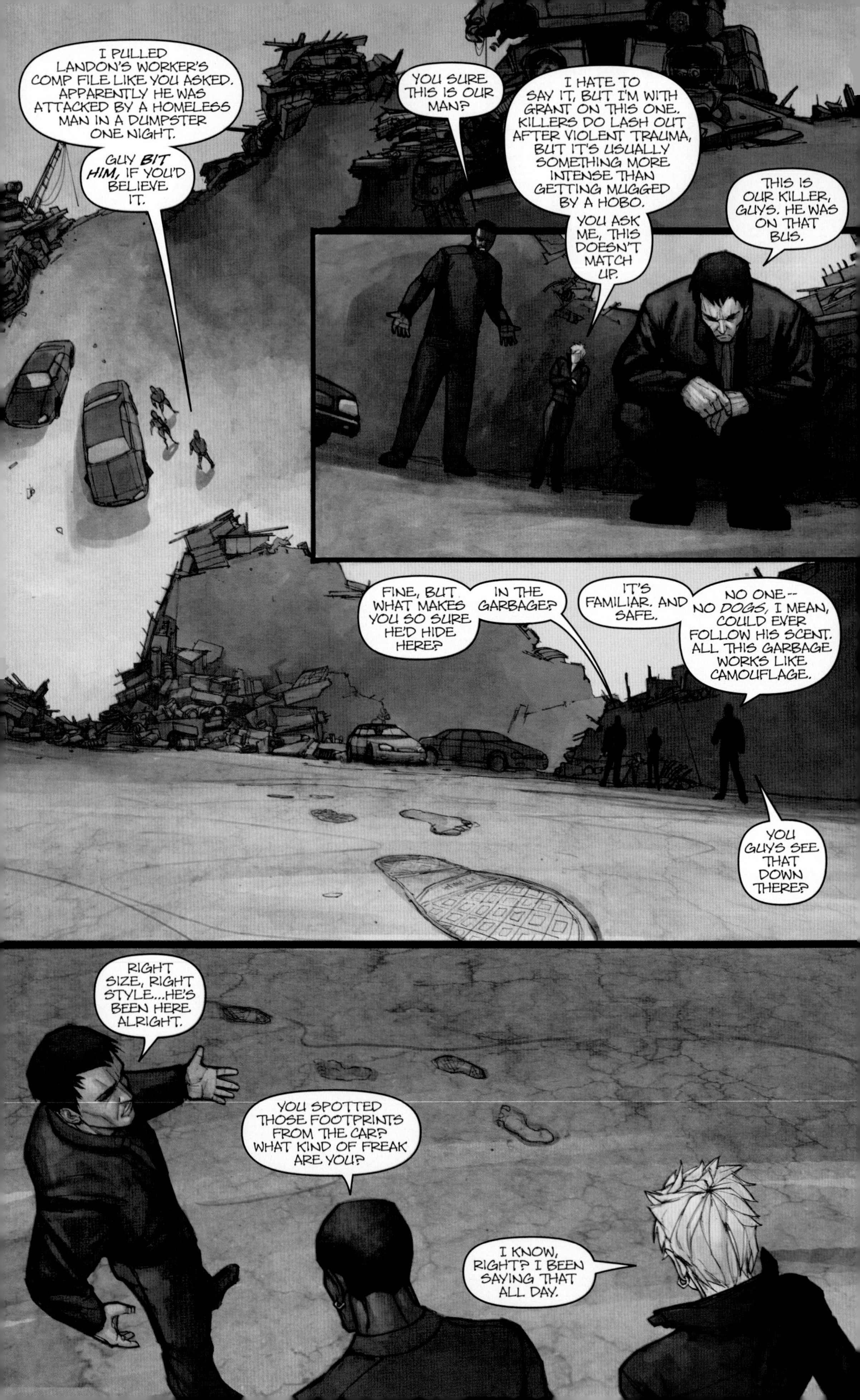
I PULLED LANDON'S WORKER'S COMP FILE LIKE YOU ASKED. APPARENTLY HE WAS ATTACKED BY A HOMELESS MAN IN A DUMPSTER ONE NIGHT.
GUY **BIT HIM,** IF YOU'D BELIEVE IT.
YOU SURE THIS IS OUR MAN?
I HATE TO SAY IT, BUT I'M WITH GRANT ON THIS ONE. KILLERS DO LASH OUT AFTER VIOLENT TRAUMA, BUT IT'S USUALLY SOMETHING MORE INTENSE THAN GETTING MUGGED BY A HOBO.
YOU ASK ME, THIS DOESN'T MATCH UP.
THIS IS OUR KILLER, GUYS. HE WAS ON THAT BUS.
FINE, BUT WHAT MAKES YOU SO SURE HE'D HIDE HERE?
IN THE GARBAGE?
IT'S FAMILIAR. AND SAFE.
NO ONE-- NO *DOGS,* I MEAN, COULD EVER FOLLOW HIS SCENT. ALL THIS GARBAGE WORKS LIKE CAMOUFLAGE.
YOU GUYS SEE THAT DOWN THERE?
RIGHT SIZE, RIGHT STYLE...HE'S BEEN HERE ALRIGHT.
YOU SPOTTED THOSE FOOTPRINTS FROM THE CAR? WHAT KIND OF FREAK ARE YOU?
I KNOW, RIGHT? I BEEN SAYING THAT ALL DAY.

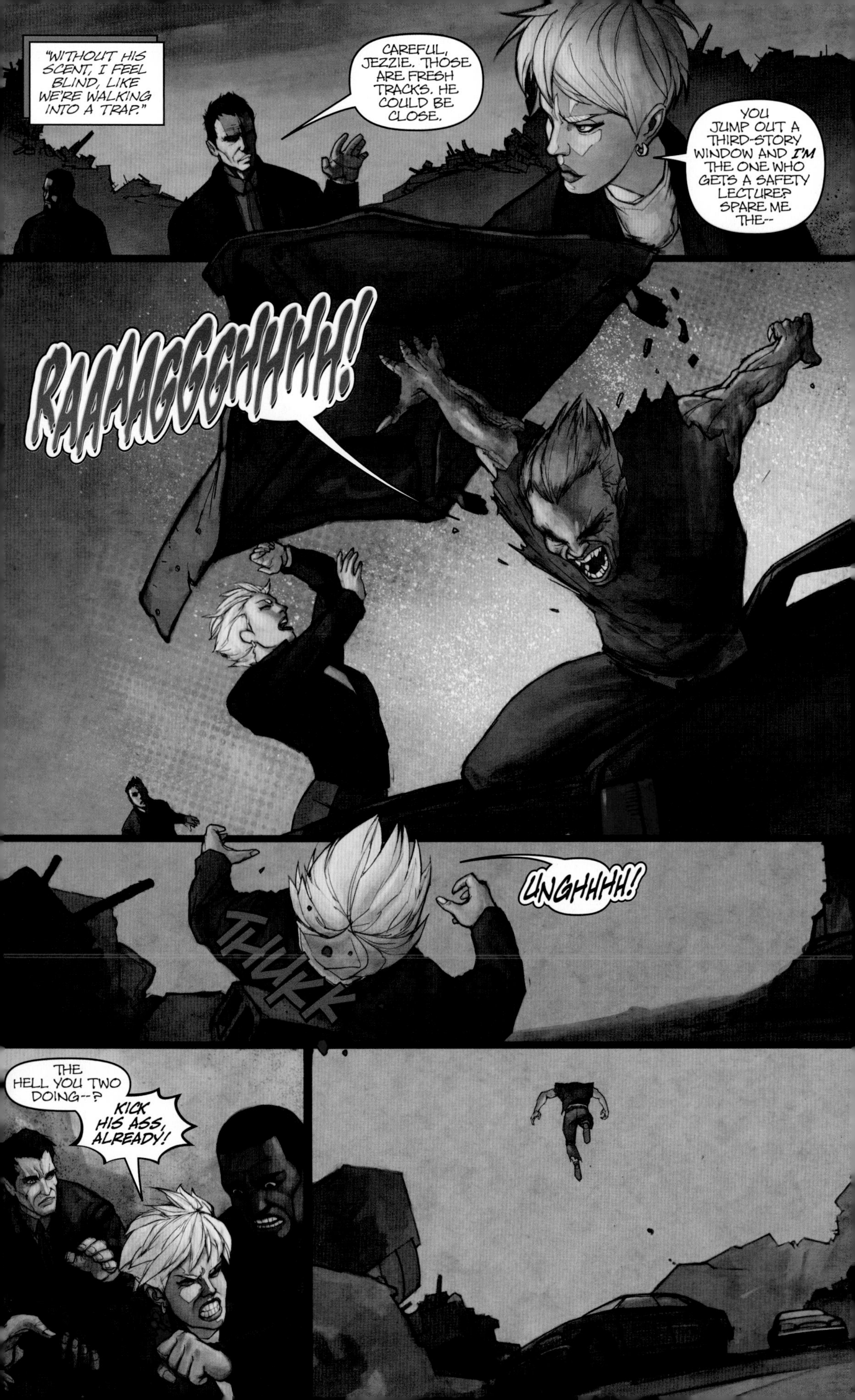
"WITHOUT HIS SCENT, I FEEL BLIND, LIKE WE'RE WALKING INTO A TRAP."
CAREFUL, JEZZIE. THOSE ARE FRESH TRACKS. HE COULD BE CLOSE.
YOU JUMP OUT A THIRD-STORY WINDOW AND I'M THE ONE WHO GETS A SAFETY LECTURE? SPARE ME THE--
RAAAAGGGHHHH!
UNGHHHH!
THUKK
THE HELL YOU TWO DOING--?
KICK HIS ASS, ALREADY!

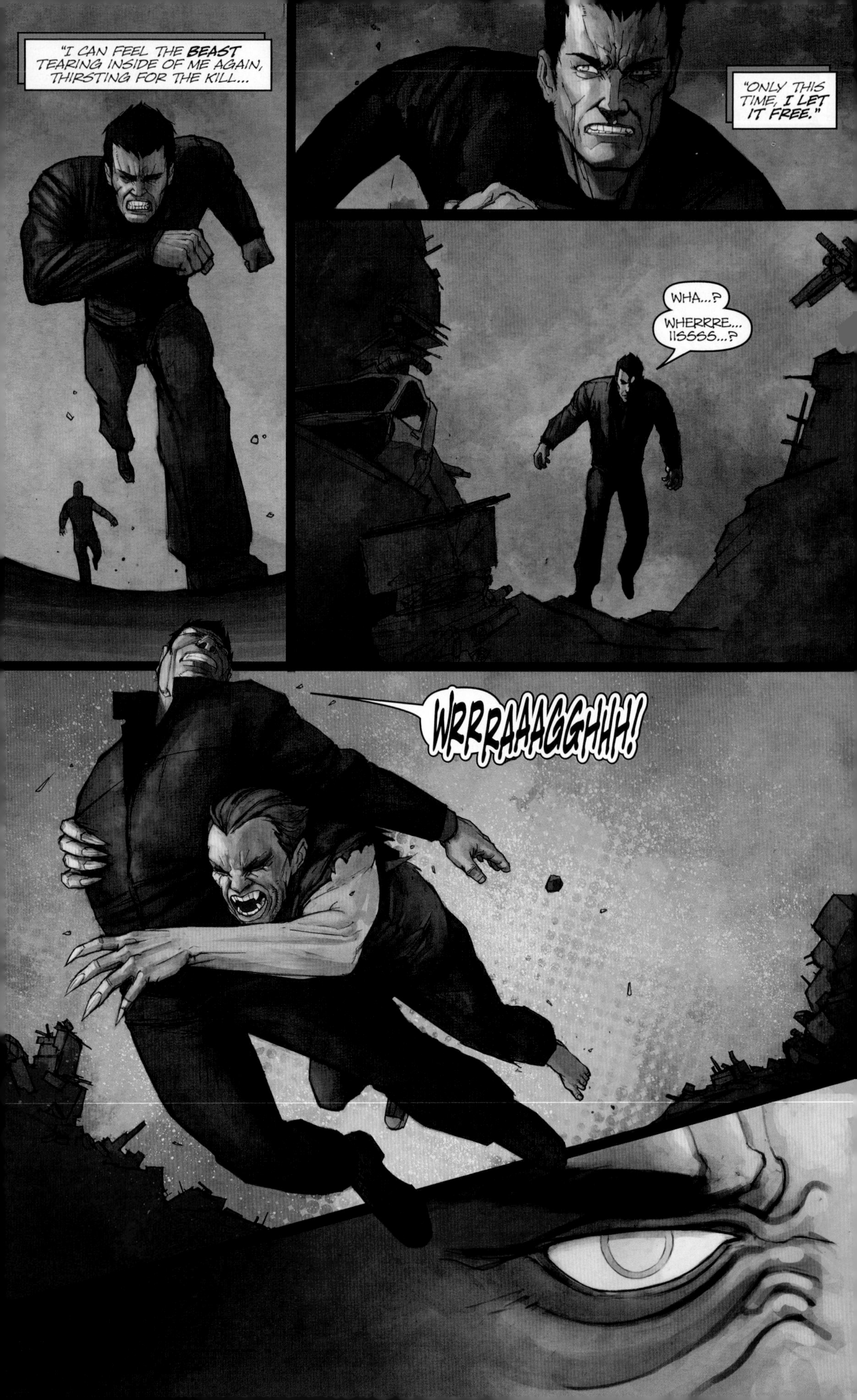
"I CAN FEEL THE BEAST TEARING INSIDE OF ME AGAIN, THIRSTING FOR THE KILL...
"ONLY THIS TIME, I LET IT FREE."
WHA...?
WHERRRE... IISSSS...?
WRRRAAAGGHHH!

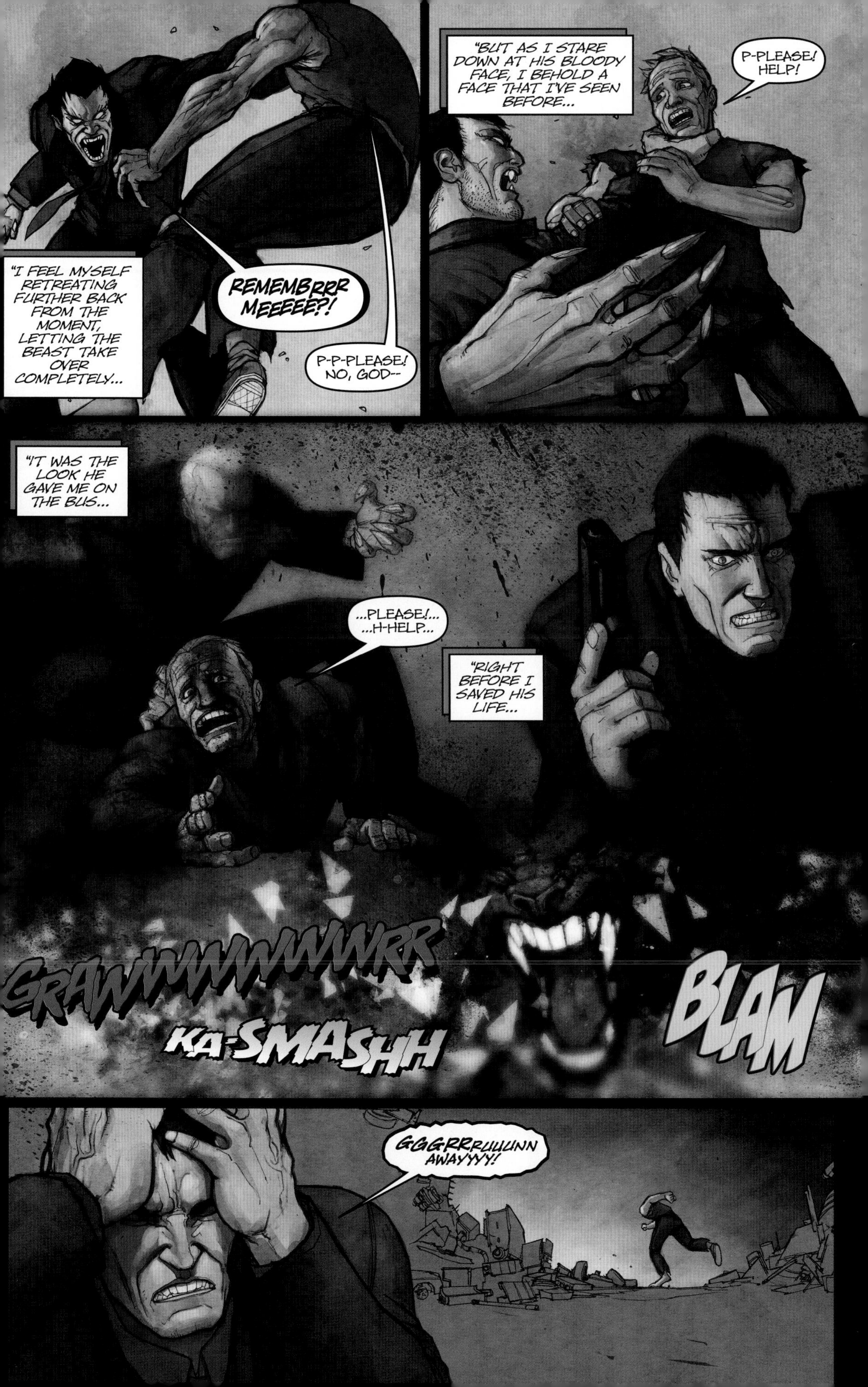
"I FEEL MYSELF RETREATING FURTHER BACK FROM THE MOMENT, LETTING THE BEAST TAKE OVER COMPLETELY...
REMEMBRRR MEEEEE?!
P-P-PLEASE! NO, GOD--
"BUT AS I STARE DOWN AT HIS BLOODY FACE, I BEHOLD A FACE THAT I'VE SEEN BEFORE...
P-PLEASE! HELP!
"IT WAS THE LOOK HE GAVE ME ON THE BUS...
...PLEASE!... ...H-HELP...
"RIGHT BEFORE I SAVED HIS LIFE...
GRAWWWWWWRR
KA-SMASHH
BLAM
GGGRRuuuNN AWAYYYY!

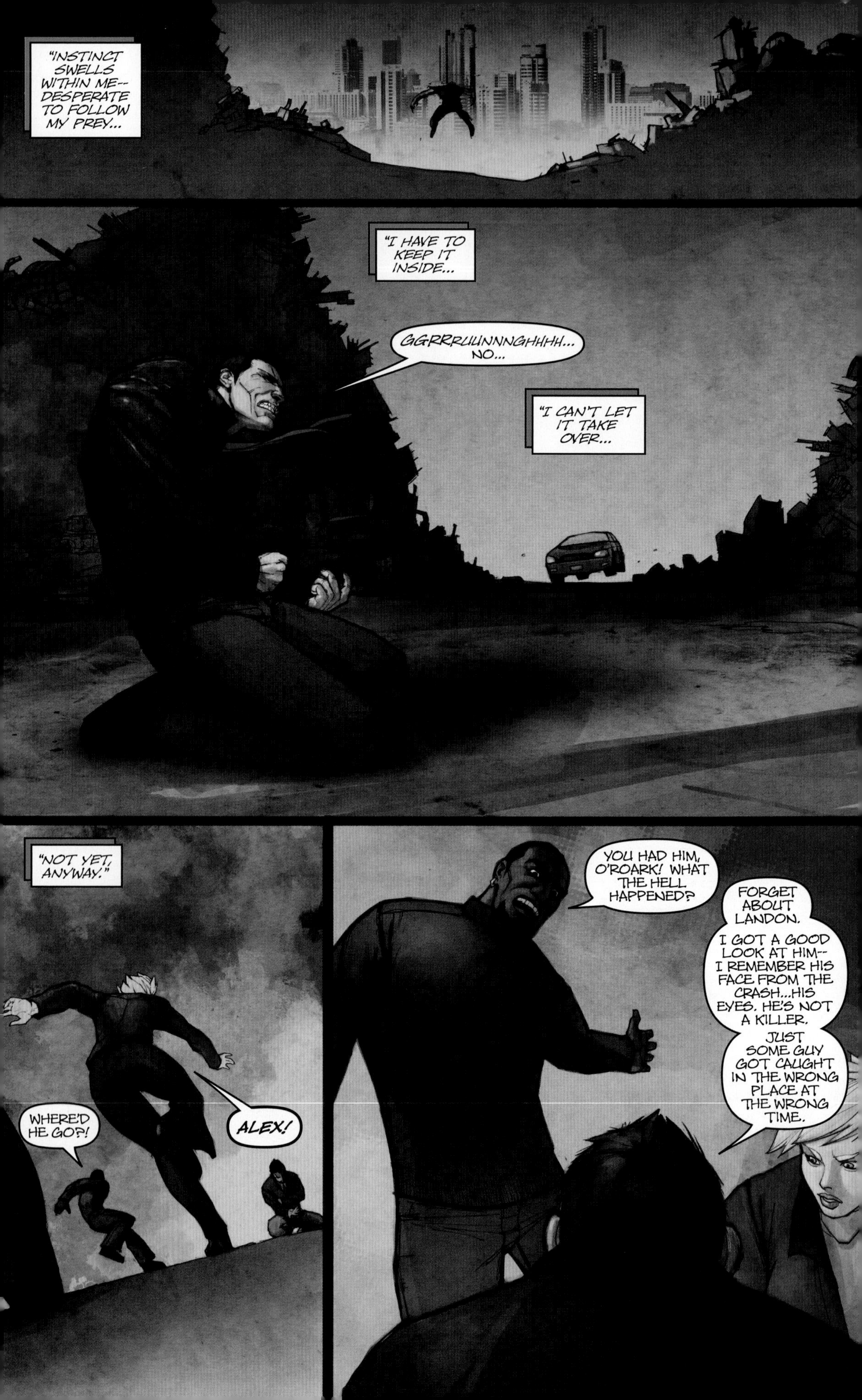
"INSTINCT SWELLS WITHIN ME-- DESPERATE TO FOLLOW MY PREY...
"I HAVE TO KEEP IT INSIDE...
GGRRRUUNNNGHHHH... NO...
"I CAN'T LET IT TAKE OVER...
"NOT YET, ANYWAY."
WHERE'D HE GO?!
ALEX!
YOU HAD HIM, O'ROARK! WHAT THE HELL HAPPENED?
FORGET ABOUT LANDON.
I GOT A GOOD LOOK AT HIM-- I REMEMBER HIS FACE FROM THE CRASH...HIS EYES. HE'S NOT A KILLER.
JUST SOME GUY GOT CAUGHT IN THE WRONG PLACE AT THE WRONG TIME.

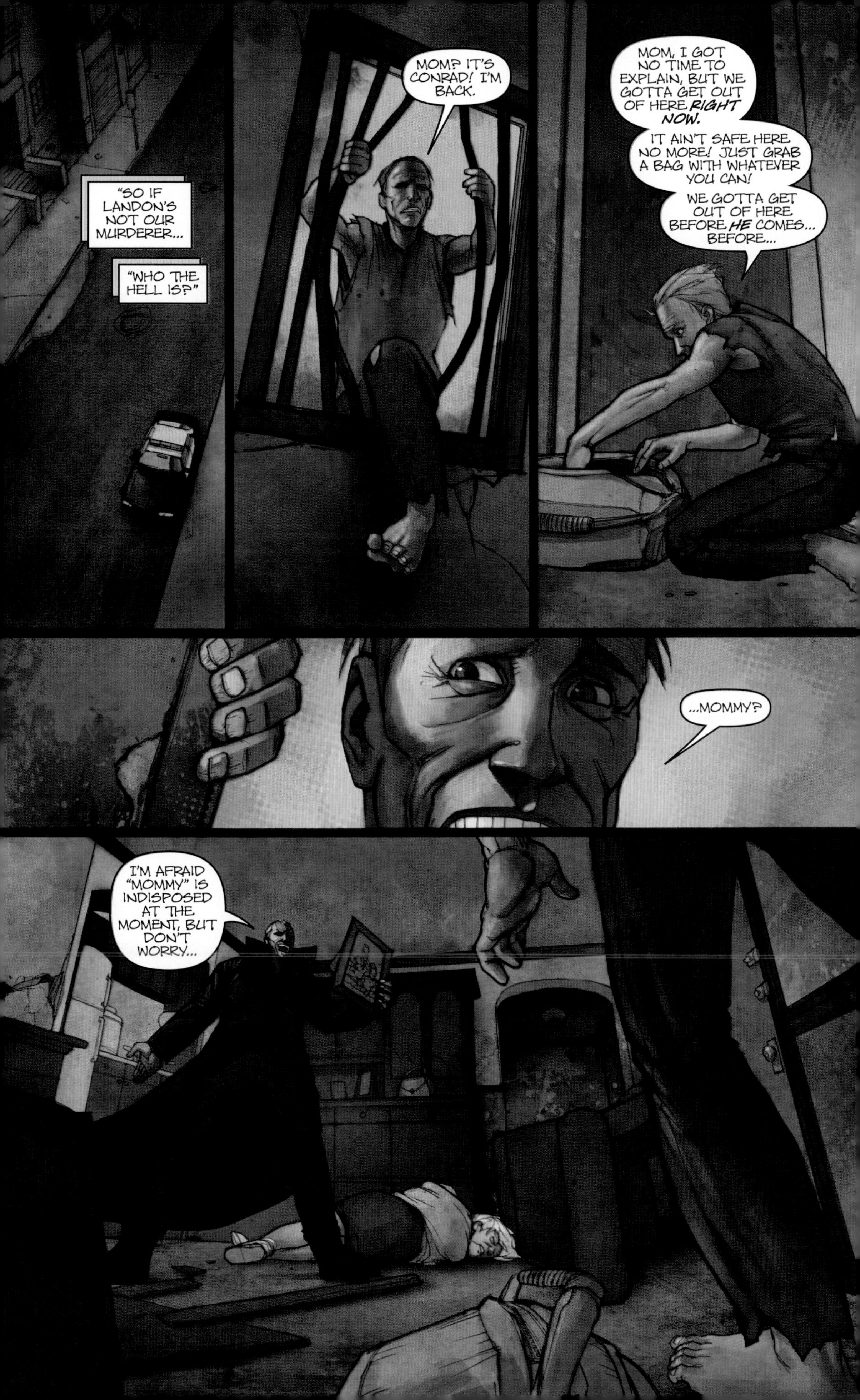
"SO IF LANDON'S NOT OUR MURDERER...
"WHO THE HELL IS?"
MOM? IT'S CONRAD! I'M BACK.
MOM, I GOT NO TIME TO EXPLAIN, BUT WE GOTTA GET OUT OF HERE RIGHT NOW.
IT AIN'T SAFE HERE NO MORE! JUST GRAB A BAG WITH WHATEVER YOU CAN!
WE GOTTA GET OUT OF HERE BEFORE HE COMES... BEFORE...
...MOMMY?
I'M AFRAID "MOMMY" IS INDISPOSED AT THE MOMENT, BUT DON'T WORRY...

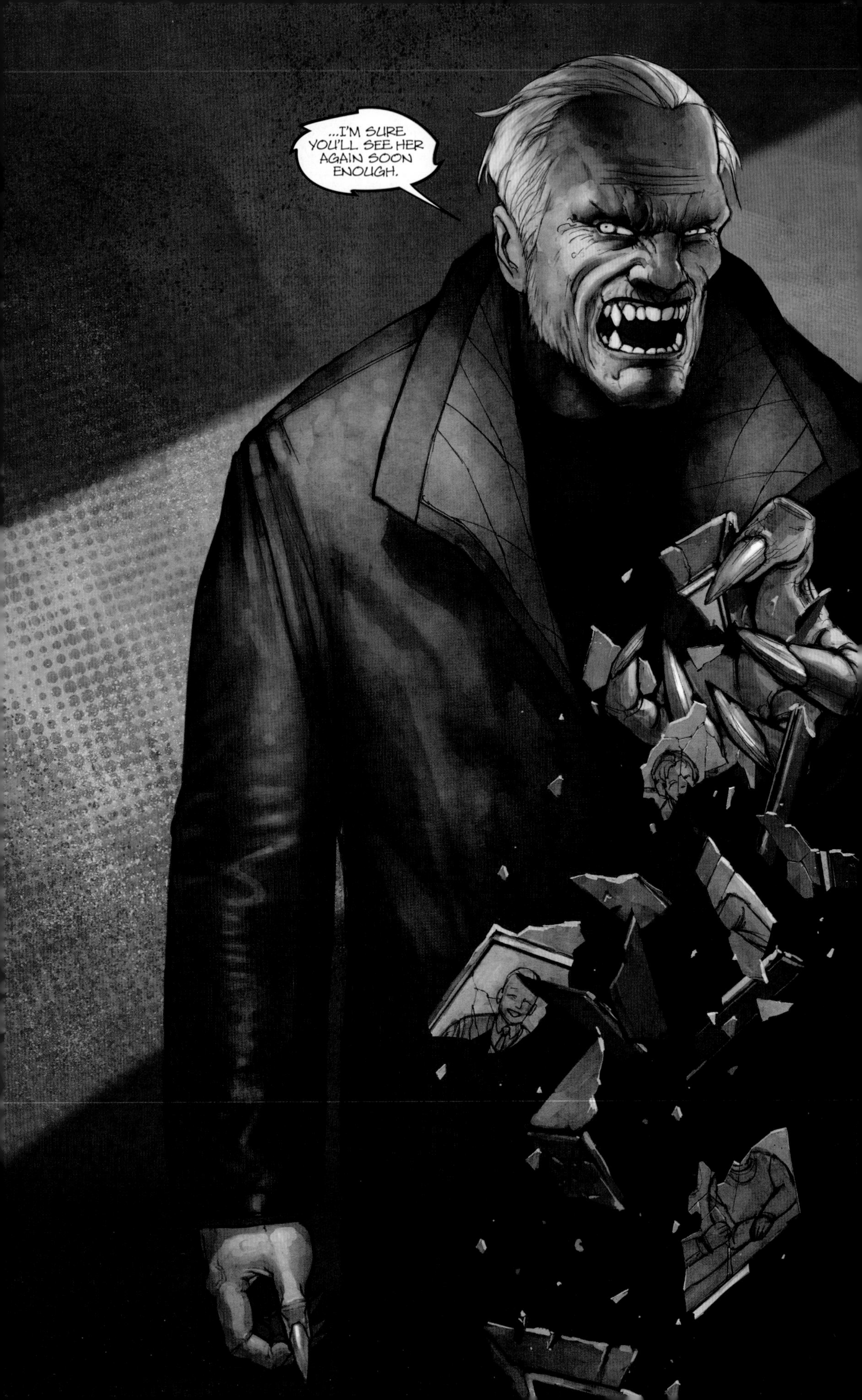
...I'M SURE YOU'LL SEE HER AGAIN SOON ENOUGH.

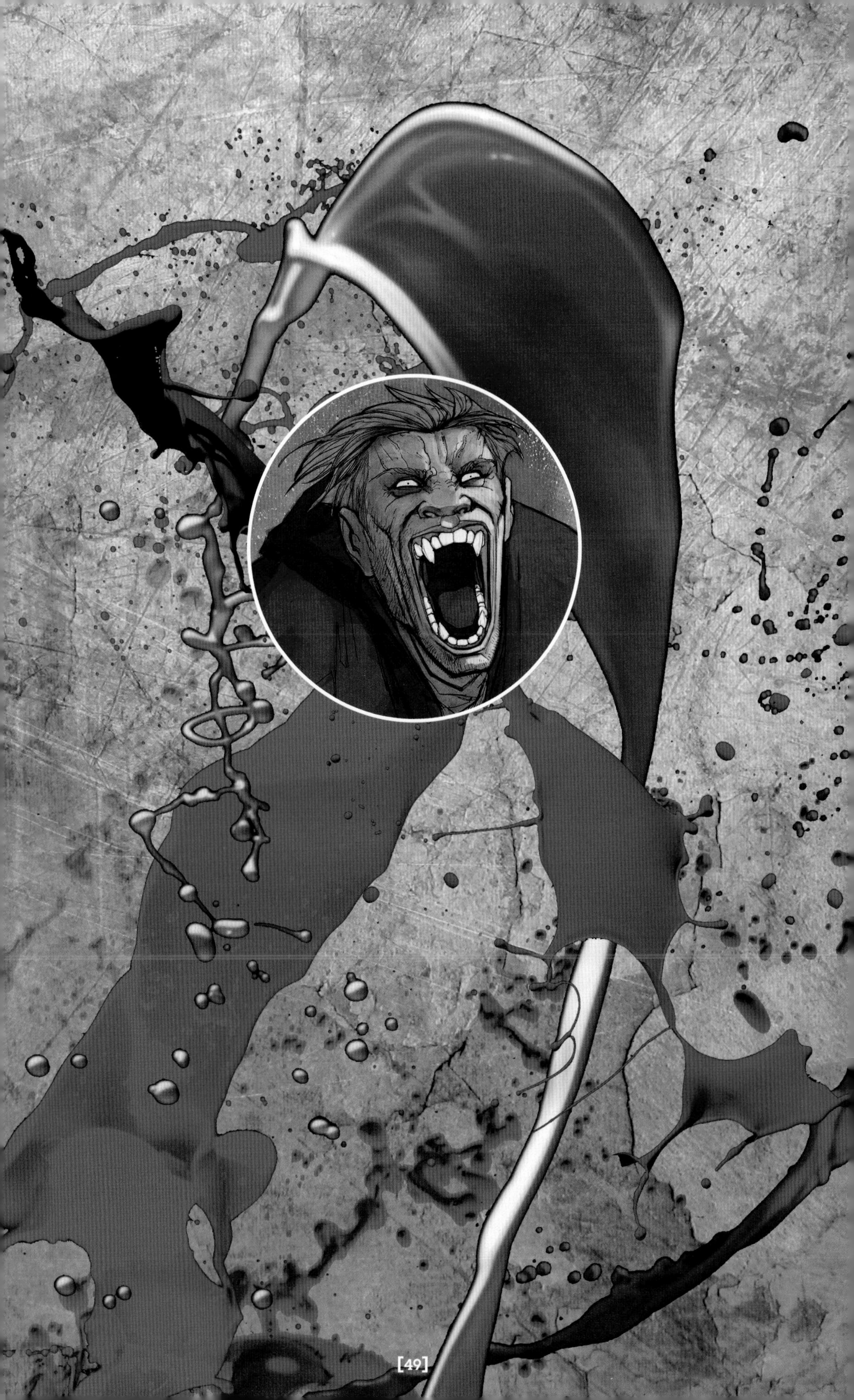

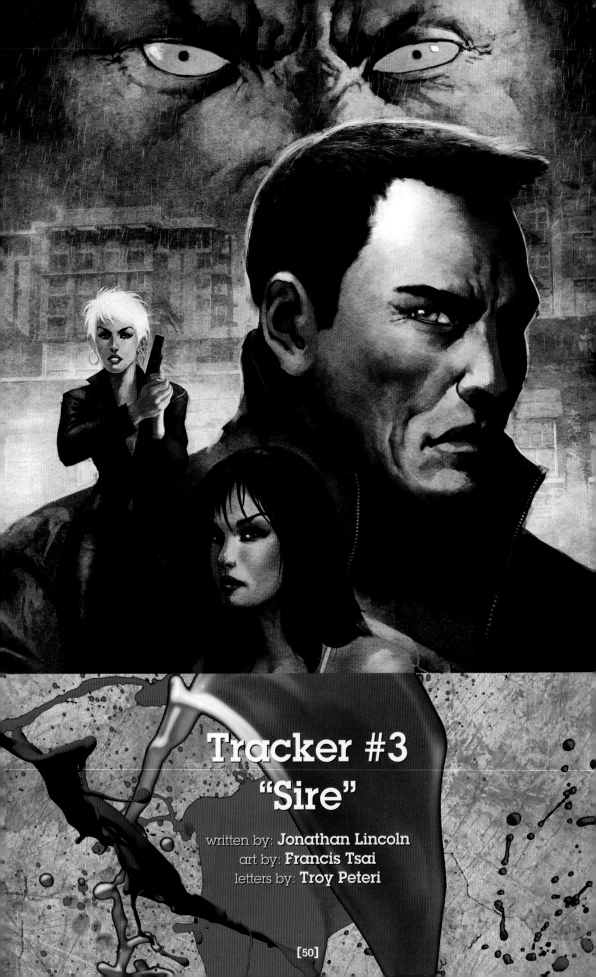

Tracker #3
"Sire"

written by: **Jonathan Lincoln**
art by: **Francis Tsai**
letters by: **Troy Peteri**

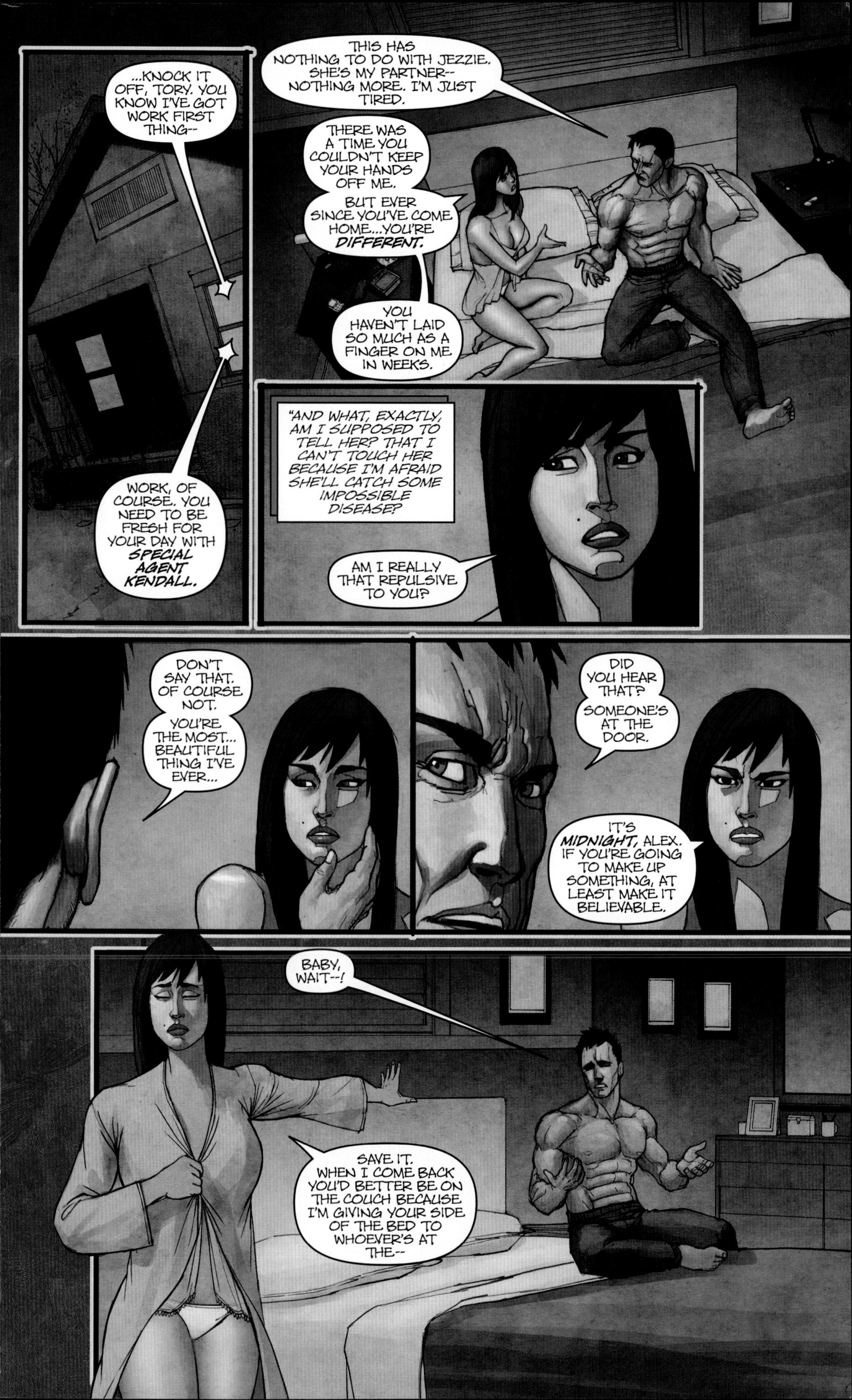
...KNOCK IT OFF, TORY. YOU KNOW I'VE GOT WORK FIRST THING--
THIS HAS NOTHING TO DO WITH JEZZIE. SHE'S MY PARTNER-- NOTHING MORE. I'M JUST TIRED.
THERE WAS A TIME YOU COULDN'T KEEP YOUR HANDS OFF ME.
BUT EVER SINCE YOU'VE COME HOME...YOU'RE DIFFERENT.
YOU HAVEN'T LAID SO MUCH AS A FINGER ON ME IN WEEKS.
WORK, OF COURSE. YOU NEED TO BE FRESH FOR YOUR DAY WITH SPECIAL AGENT KENDALL.
"AND WHAT, EXACTLY, AM I SUPPOSED TO TELL HER? THAT I CAN'T TOUCH HER BECAUSE I'M AFRAID SHE'LL CATCH SOME IMPOSSIBLE DISEASE?
AM I REALLY THAT REPULSIVE TO YOU?
DON'T SAY THAT. OF COURSE NOT.
YOU'RE THE MOST... BEAUTIFUL THING I'VE EVER...
DID YOU HEAR THAT?
SOMEONE'S AT THE DOOR.
IT'S MIDNIGHT, ALEX. IF YOU'RE GOING TO MAKE UP SOMETHING, AT LEAST MAKE IT BELIEVABLE.
BABY, WAIT--!
SAVE IT. WHEN I COME BACK YOU'D BETTER BE ON THE COUCH BECAUSE I'M GIVING YOUR SIDE OF THE BED TO WHOEVER'S AT THE--

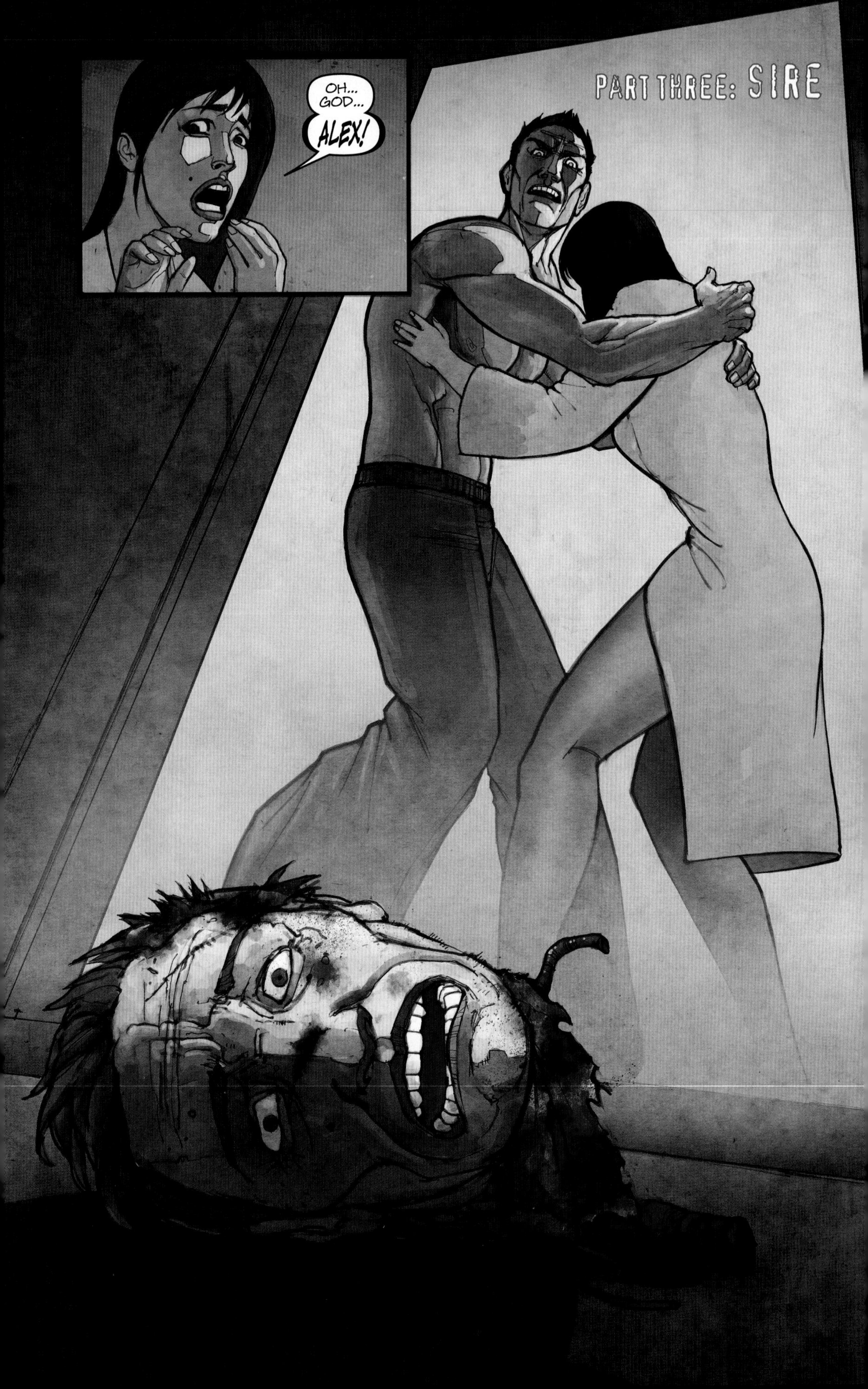
OH... GOD... ALEX!
PART THREE: SIRE

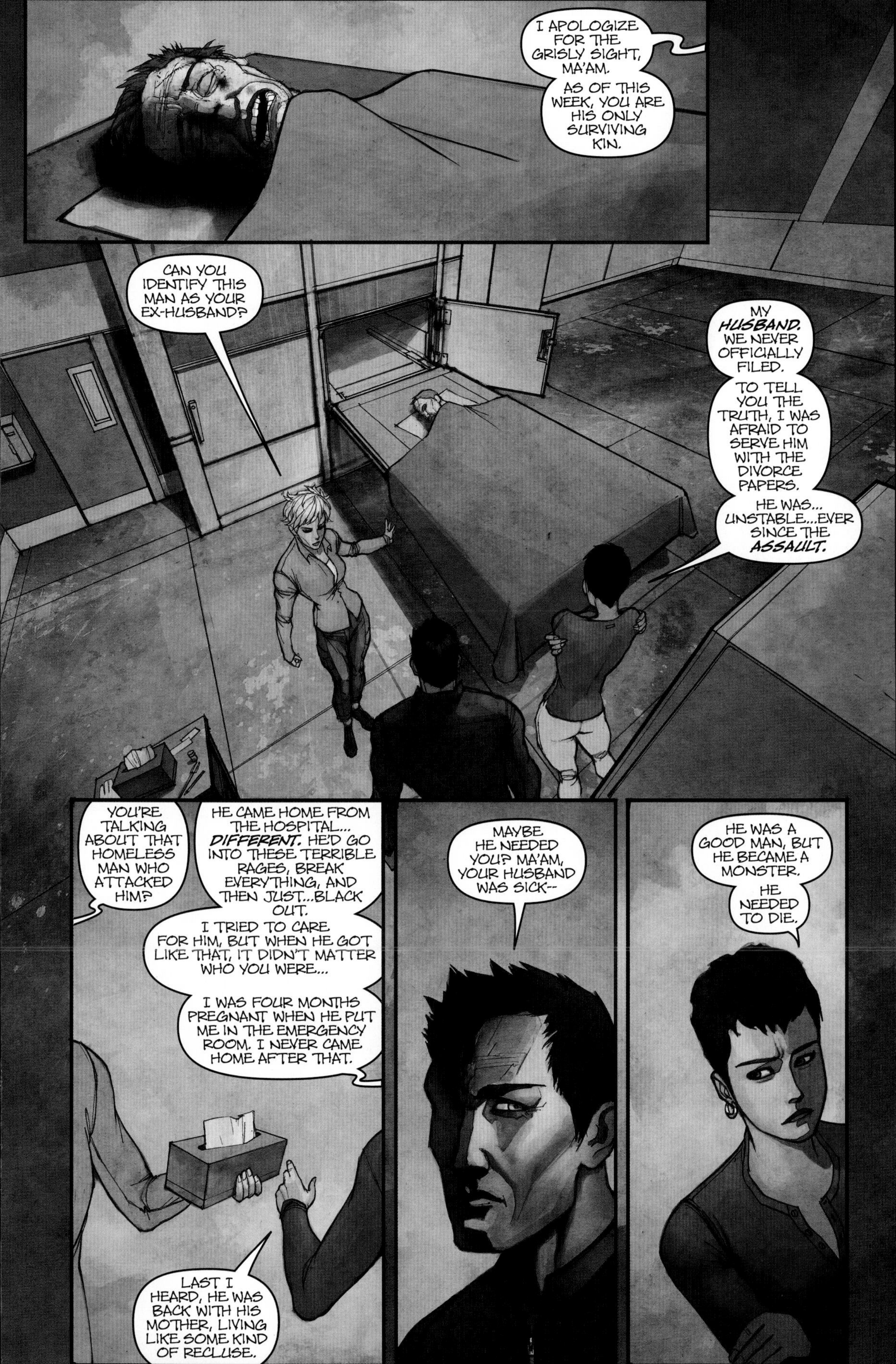
I APOLOGIZE FOR THE GRISLY SIGHT, MA'AM.
AS OF THIS WEEK, YOU ARE HIS ONLY SURVIVING KIN.
CAN YOU IDENTIFY THIS MAN AS YOUR EX-HUSBAND?
MY HUSBAND. WE NEVER OFFICIALLY FILED.
TO TELL YOU THE TRUTH, I WAS AFRAID TO SERVE HIM WITH THE DIVORCE PAPERS.
HE WAS... UNSTABLE...EVER SINCE THE ASSAULT.
YOU'RE TALKING ABOUT THAT HOMELESS MAN WHO ATTACKED HIM?
HE CAME HOME FROM THE HOSPITAL... DIFFERENT. HE'D GO INTO THESE TERRIBLE RAGES, BREAK EVERYTHING, AND THEN JUST...BLACK OUT.
I TRIED TO CARE FOR HIM, BUT WHEN HE GOT LIKE THAT, IT DIDN'T MATTER WHO YOU WERE...
I WAS FOUR MONTHS PREGNANT WHEN HE PUT ME IN THE EMERGENCY ROOM. I NEVER CAME HOME AFTER THAT.
LAST I HEARD, HE WAS BACK WITH HIS MOTHER, LIVING LIKE SOME KIND OF RECLUSE.
MAYBE HE NEEDED YOU? MA'AM, YOUR HUSBAND WAS SICK--
HE WAS A GOOD MAN, BUT HE BECAME A MONSTER.
HE NEEDED TO DIE.

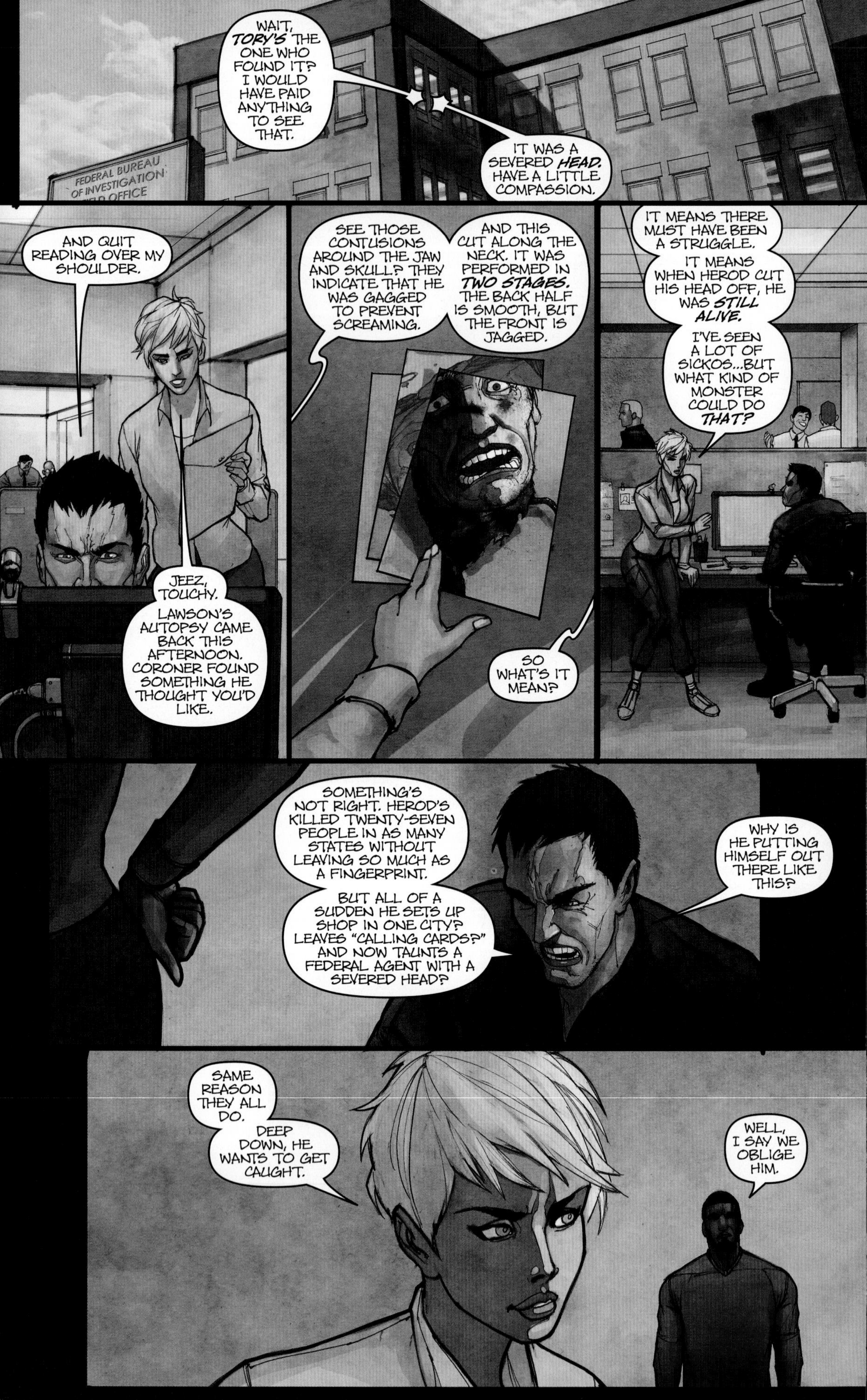
FEDERAL BUREAU OF INVESTIGATION FIELD OFFICE
WAIT, TORY'S THE ONE WHO FOUND IT? I WOULD HAVE PAID ANYTHING TO SEE THAT.
IT WAS A SEVERED HEAD. HAVE A LITTLE COMPASSION.
AND QUIT READING OVER MY SHOULDER.
JEEZ, TOUCHY.
LAWSON'S AUTOPSY CAME BACK THIS AFTERNOON. CORONER FOUND SOMETHING HE THOUGHT YOU'D LIKE.
SEE THOSE CONTUSIONS AROUND THE JAW AND SKULL? THEY INDICATE THAT HE WAS GAGGED TO PREVENT SCREAMING.
AND THIS CUT ALONG THE NECK. IT WAS PERFORMED IN TWO STAGES. THE BACK HALF IS SMOOTH, BUT THE FRONT IS JAGGED.
SO WHAT'S IT MEAN?
IT MEANS THERE MUST HAVE BEEN A STRUGGLE.
IT MEANS WHEN HEROD CUT HIS HEAD OFF, HE WAS STILL ALIVE.
I'VE SEEN A LOT OF SICKOS...BUT WHAT KIND OF MONSTER COULD DO THAT?
SOMETHING'S NOT RIGHT. HEROD'S KILLED TWENTY-SEVEN PEOPLE IN AS MANY STATES WITHOUT LEAVING SO MUCH AS A FINGERPRINT.
BUT ALL OF A SUDDEN HE SETS UP SHOP IN ONE CITY? LEAVES "CALLING CARDS?" AND NOW TAUNTS A FEDERAL AGENT WITH A SEVERED HEAD?
WHY IS HE PUTTING HIMSELF OUT THERE LIKE THIS?
SAME REASON THEY ALL DO.
DEEP DOWN, HE WANTS TO GET CAUGHT.
WELL, I SAY WE OBLIGE HIM.

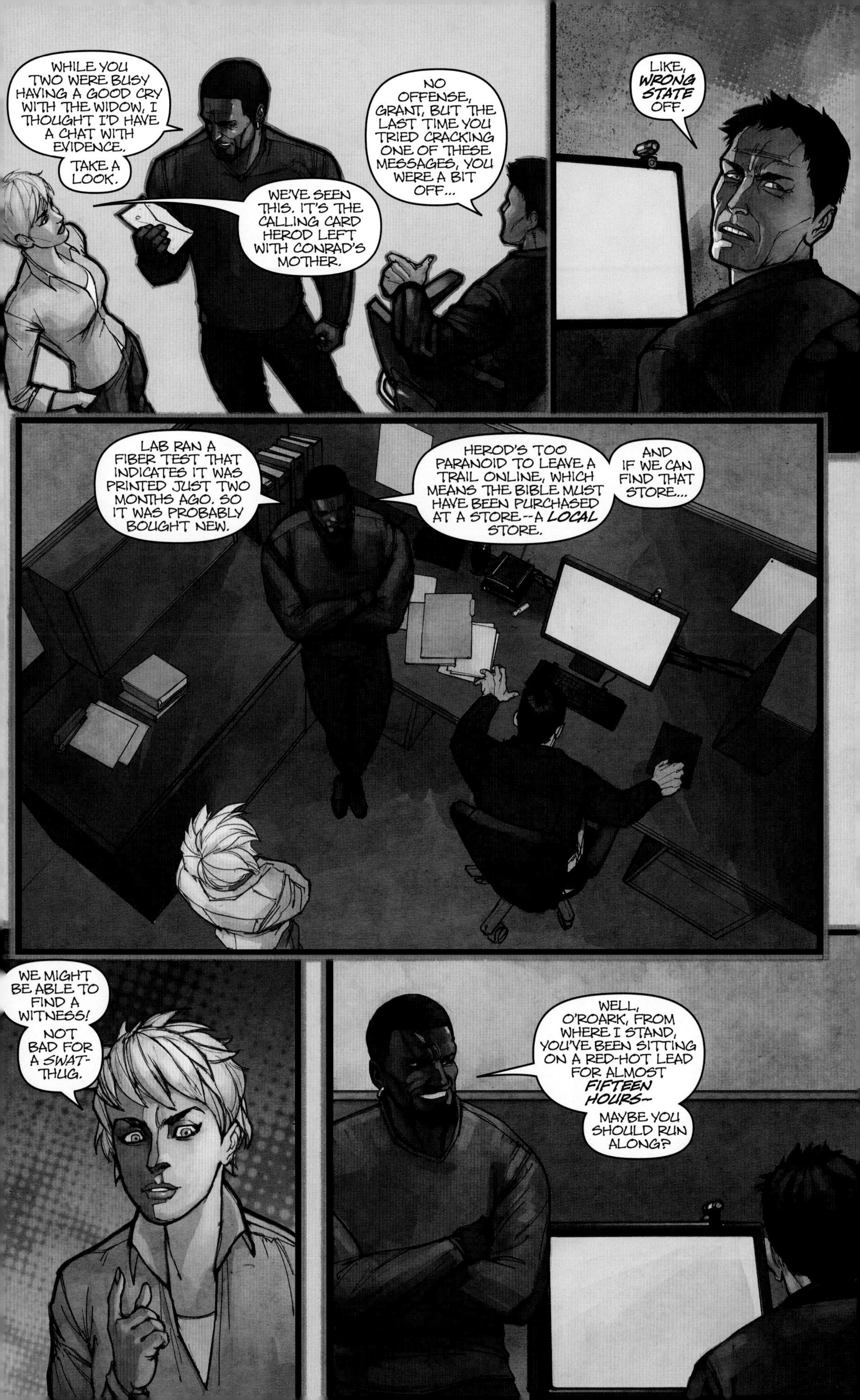
WHILE YOU TWO WERE BUSY HAVING A GOOD CRY WITH THE WIDOW, I THOUGHT I'D HAVE A CHAT WITH EVIDENCE.
TAKE A LOOK.
WE'VE SEEN THIS. IT'S THE CALLING CARD HEROD LEFT WITH CONRAD'S MOTHER.
NO OFFENSE, GRANT, BUT THE LAST TIME YOU TRIED CRACKING ONE OF THESE MESSAGES, YOU WERE A BIT OFF...
LIKE, *WRONG STATE* OFF.
LAB RAN A FIBER TEST THAT INDICATES IT WAS PRINTED JUST TWO MONTHS AGO. SO IT WAS PROBABLY BOUGHT NEW.
HEROD'S TOO PARANOID TO LEAVE A TRAIL ONLINE, WHICH MEANS THE BIBLE MUST HAVE BEEN PURCHASED AT A STORE--A *LOCAL* STORE.
AND IF WE CAN FIND THAT STORE...
WE MIGHT BE ABLE TO FIND A WITNESS!
NOT BAD FOR A *SWAT-THUG.*
WELL, O'ROARK, FROM WHERE I STAND, YOU'VE BEEN SITTING ON A RED-HOT LEAD FOR ALMOST *FIFTEEN HOURS--*
MAYBE YOU SHOULD RUN ALONG?

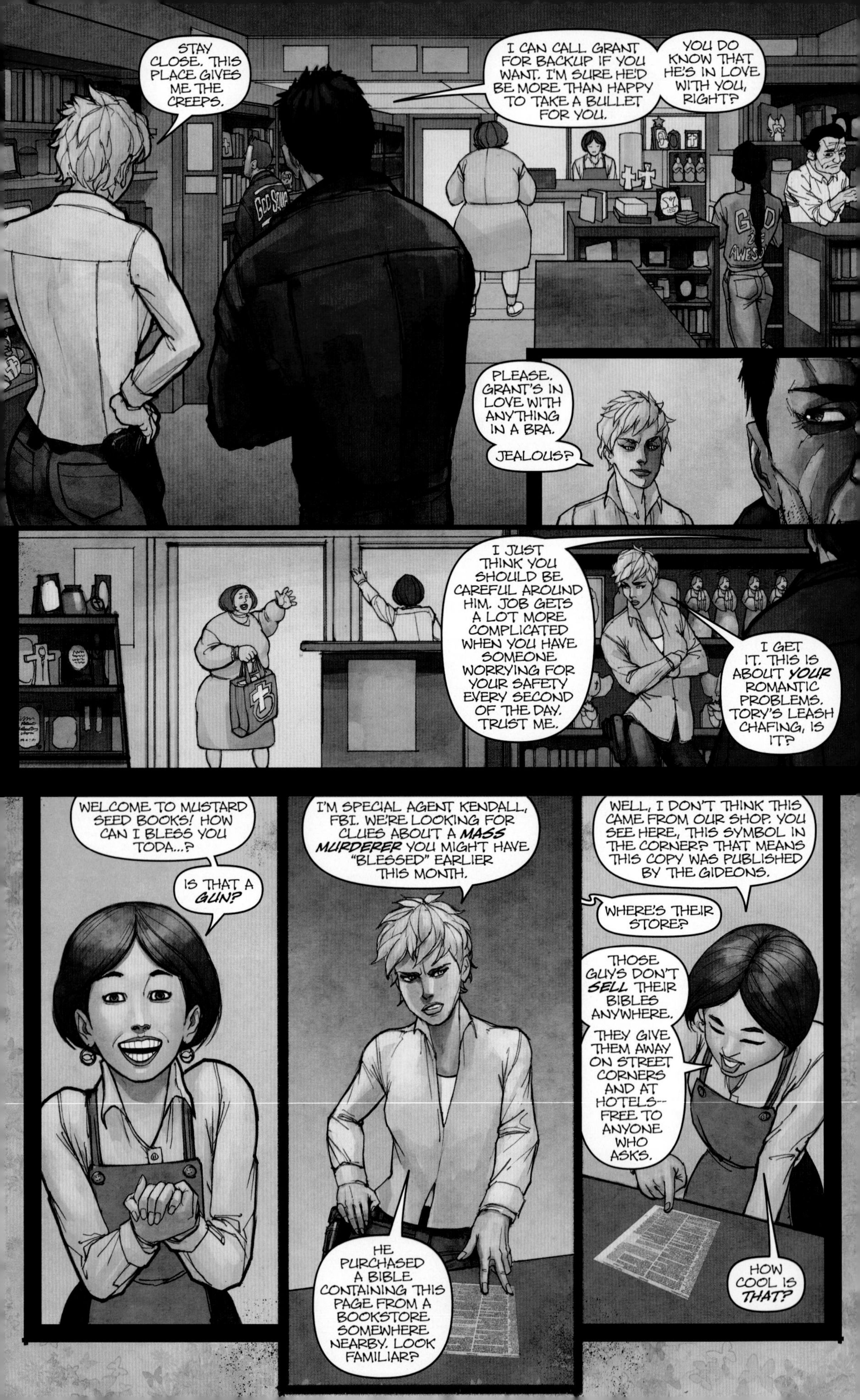
STAY CLOSE. THIS PLACE GIVES ME THE CREEPS.
I CAN CALL GRANT FOR BACKUP IF YOU WANT. I'M SURE HE'D BE MORE THAN HAPPY TO TAKE A BULLET FOR YOU.
YOU DO KNOW THAT HE'S IN LOVE WITH YOU, RIGHT?
PLEASE. GRANT'S IN LOVE WITH ANYTHING IN A BRA.
JEALOUS?
I JUST THINK YOU SHOULD BE CAREFUL AROUND HIM. JOB GETS A LOT MORE COMPLICATED WHEN YOU HAVE SOMEONE WORRYING FOR YOUR SAFETY EVERY SECOND OF THE DAY. TRUST ME.
I GET IT. THIS IS ABOUT YOUR ROMANTIC PROBLEMS. TORY'S LEASH CHAFING, IS IT?
WELCOME TO MUSTARD SEED BOOKS! HOW CAN I BLESS YOU TODA...?
IS THAT A GUN?
I'M SPECIAL AGENT KENDALL, FBI. WE'RE LOOKING FOR CLUES ABOUT A MASS MURDERER YOU MIGHT HAVE "BLESSED" EARLIER THIS MONTH.
HE PURCHASED A BIBLE CONTAINING THIS PAGE FROM A BOOKSTORE SOMEWHERE NEARBY. LOOK FAMILIAR?
WELL, I DON'T THINK THIS CAME FROM OUR SHOP. YOU SEE HERE, THIS SYMBOL IN THE CORNER? THAT MEANS THIS COPY WAS PUBLISHED BY THE GIDEONS.
WHERE'S THEIR STORE?
THOSE GUYS DON'T SELL THEIR BIBLES ANYWHERE.
THEY GIVE THEM AWAY ON STREET CORNERS AND AT HOTELS-- FREE TO ANYONE WHO ASKS.
HOW COOL IS THAT?

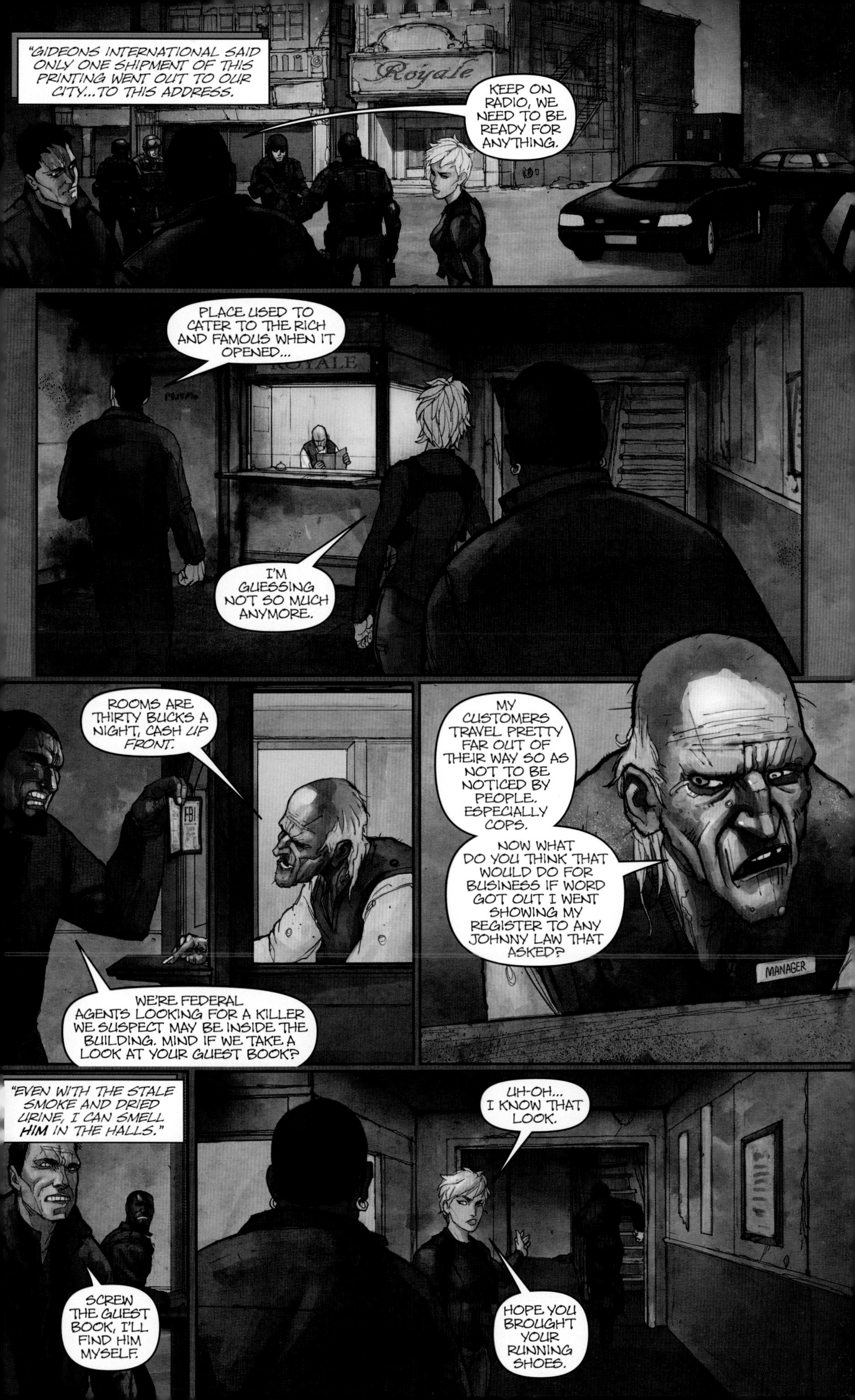
"GIDEONS INTERNATIONAL SAID ONLY ONE SHIPMENT OF THIS PRINTING WENT OUT TO OUR CITY...TO THIS ADDRESS.
Royale
KEEP ON RADIO, WE NEED TO BE READY FOR ANYTHING.
PLACE USED TO CATER TO THE RICH AND FAMOUS WHEN IT OPENED...
ROYALE
I'M GUESSING NOT SO MUCH ANYMORE.
ROOMS ARE THIRTY BUCKS A NIGHT, CASH UP FRONT.
FBI
WE'RE FEDERAL AGENTS LOOKING FOR A KILLER WE SUSPECT MAY BE INSIDE THE BUILDING. MIND IF WE TAKE A LOOK AT YOUR GUEST BOOK?
MY CUSTOMERS TRAVEL PRETTY FAR OUT OF THEIR WAY SO AS NOT TO BE NOTICED BY PEOPLE. ESPECIALLY COPS.
NOW WHAT DO YOU THINK THAT WOULD DO FOR BUSINESS IF WORD GOT OUT I WENT SHOWING MY REGISTER TO ANY JOHNNY LAW THAT ASKED?
MANAGER
"EVEN WITH THE STALE SMOKE AND DRIED URINE, I CAN SMELL **HIM** IN THE HALLS."
SCREW THE GUEST BOOK, I'LL FIND HIM MYSELF.
UH-OH... I KNOW THAT LOOK.
HOPE YOU BROUGHT YOUR RUNNING SHOES.

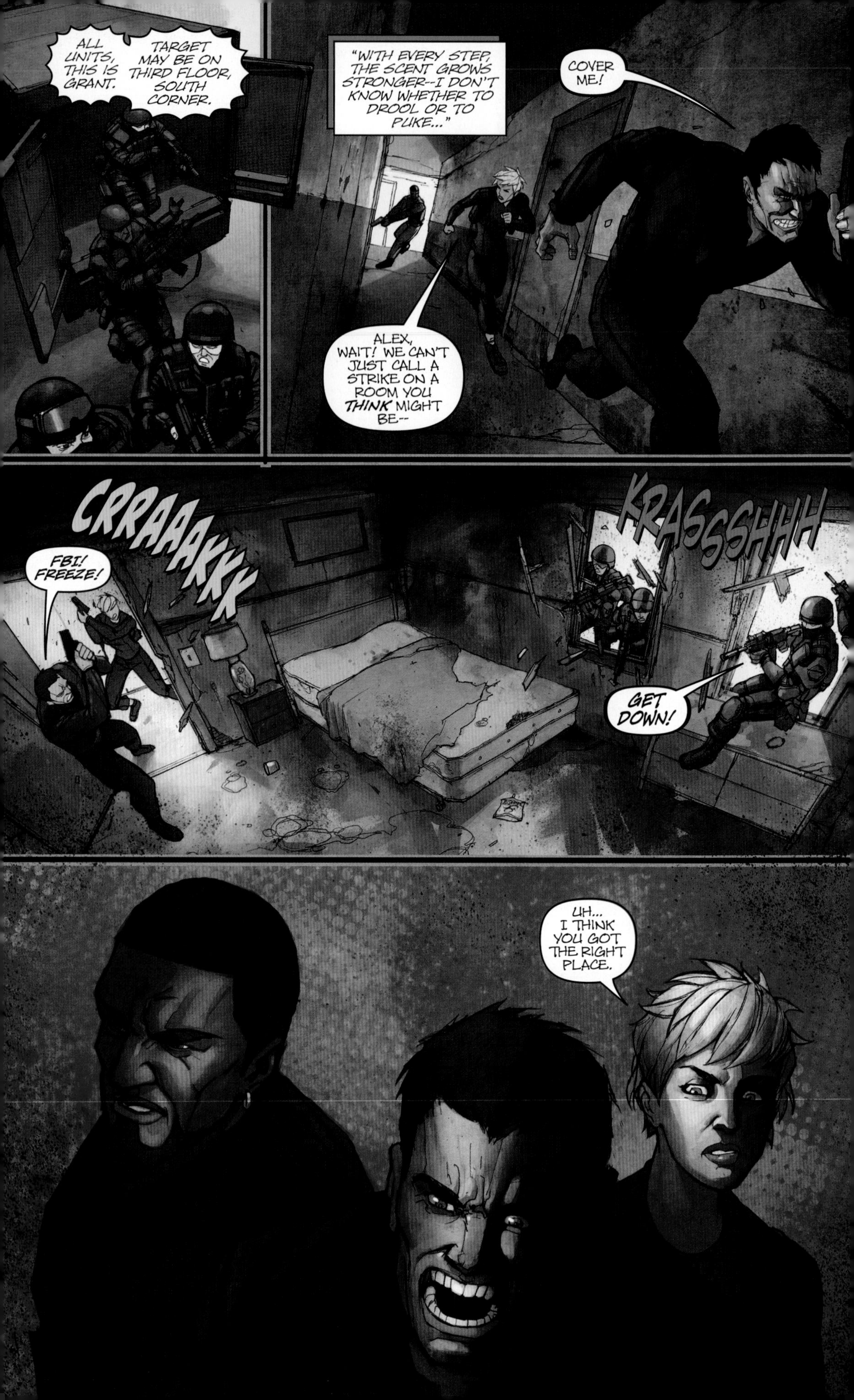
ALL UNITS, THIS IS GRANT.
TARGET MAY BE ON THIRD FLOOR, SOUTH CORNER.
"WITH EVERY STEP, THE SCENT GROWS STRONGER--I DON'T KNOW WHETHER TO DROOL OR TO PUKE..."
COVER ME!
ALEX, WAIT! WE CAN'T JUST CALL A STRIKE ON A ROOM YOU THINK MIGHT BE--
CRRAAAKKK
FBI! FREEZE!
KRASSSHHH
GET DOWN!
UH... I THINK YOU GOT THE RIGHT PLACE.

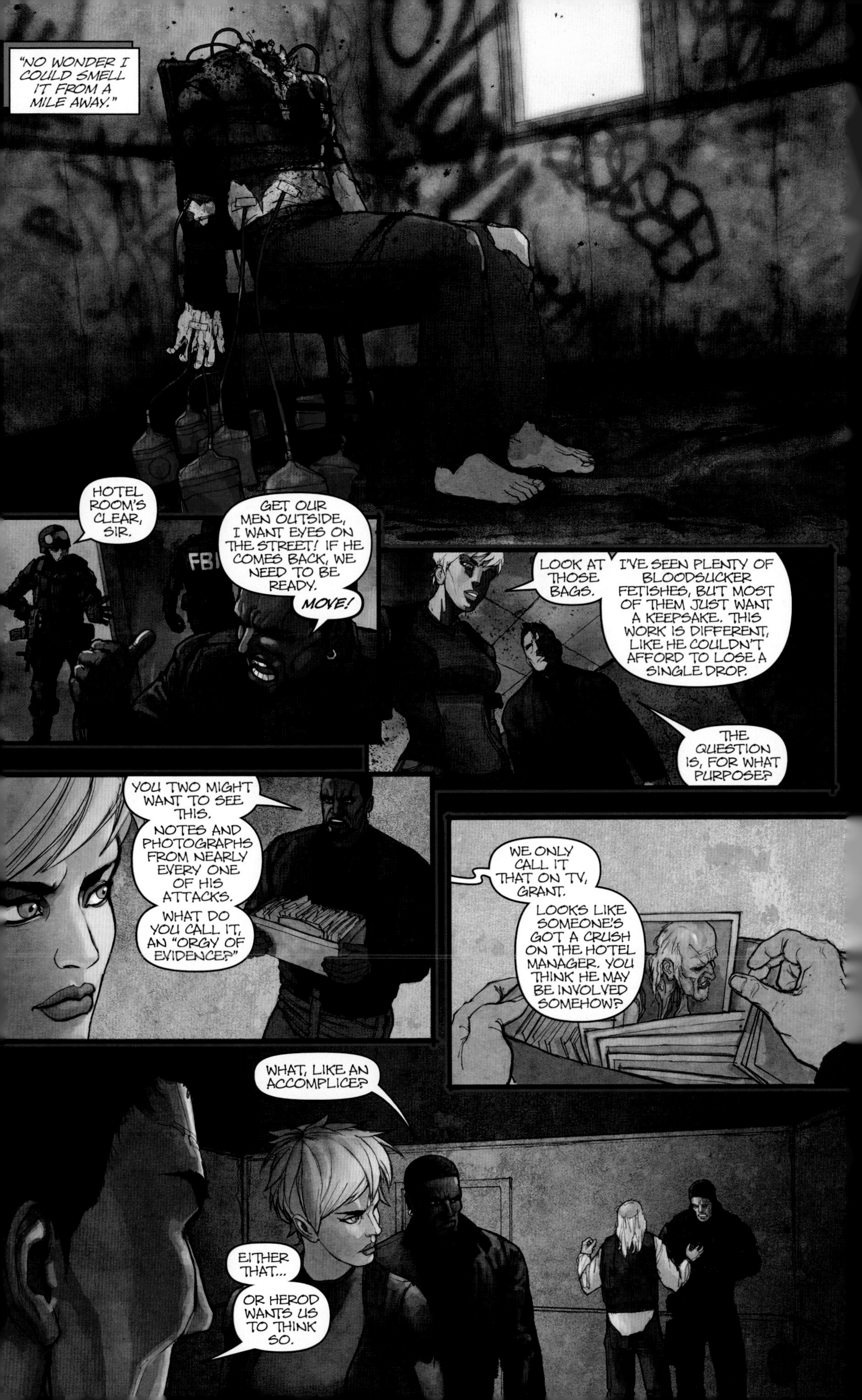
"NO WONDER I COULD SMELL IT FROM A MILE AWAY."
HOTEL ROOM'S CLEAR, SIR.
GET OUR MEN OUTSIDE, I WANT EYES ON THE STREET! IF HE COMES BACK, WE NEED TO BE READY.
MOVE!
FBI
LOOK AT THOSE BAGS.
I'VE SEEN PLENTY OF BLOODSUCKER FETISHES, BUT MOST OF THEM JUST WANT A KEEPSAKE. THIS WORK IS DIFFERENT, LIKE HE COULDN'T AFFORD TO LOSE A SINGLE DROP.
THE QUESTION IS, FOR WHAT PURPOSE?
YOU TWO MIGHT WANT TO SEE THIS.
NOTES AND PHOTOGRAPHS FROM NEARLY EVERY ONE OF HIS ATTACKS.
WHAT DO YOU CALL IT, AN "ORGY OF EVIDENCE?"
WE ONLY CALL IT THAT ON TV, GRANT.
LOOKS LIKE SOMEONE'S GOT A CRUSH ON THE HOTEL MANAGER. YOU THINK HE MAY BE INVOLVED SOMEHOW?
WHAT, LIKE AN ACCOMPLICE?
EITHER THAT...
OR HEROD WANTS US TO THINK SO.

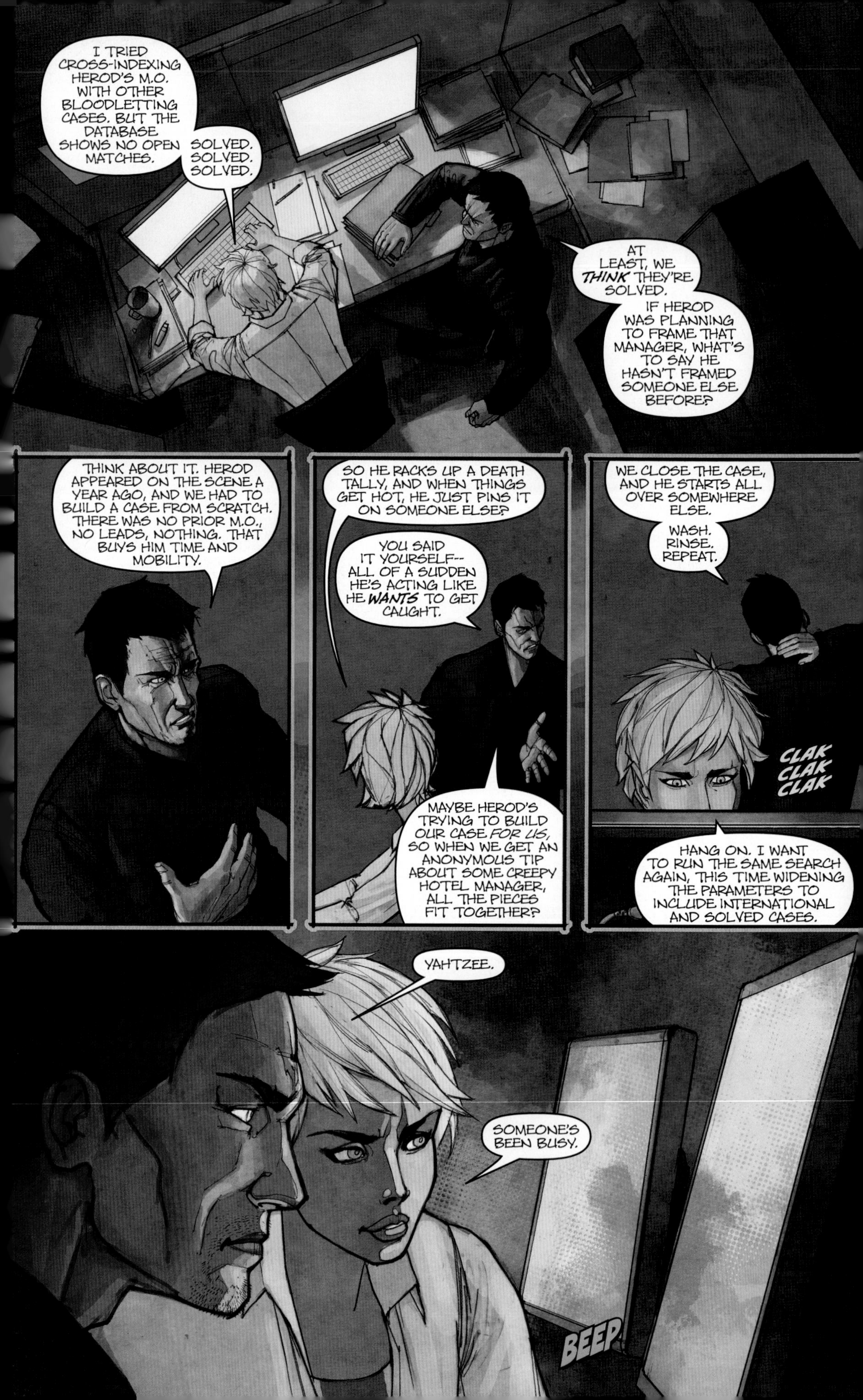
I TRIED CROSS-INDEXING HEROD'S M.O. WITH OTHER BLOODLETTING CASES. BUT THE DATABASE SHOWS NO OPEN MATCHES.
SOLVED. SOLVED. SOLVED.
AT LEAST, WE THINK THEY'RE SOLVED.
IF HEROD WAS PLANNING TO FRAME THAT MANAGER, WHAT'S TO SAY HE HASN'T FRAMED SOMEONE ELSE BEFORE?
THINK ABOUT IT. HEROD APPEARED ON THE SCENE A YEAR AGO, AND WE HAD TO BUILD A CASE FROM SCRATCH. THERE WAS NO PRIOR M.O., NO LEADS, NOTHING. THAT BUYS HIM TIME AND MOBILITY.
SO HE RACKS UP A DEATH TALLY, AND WHEN THINGS GET HOT, HE JUST PINS IT ON SOMEONE ELSE?
YOU SAID IT YOURSELF-- ALL OF A SUDDEN HE'S ACTING LIKE HE WANTS TO GET CAUGHT.
MAYBE HEROD'S TRYING TO BUILD OUR CASE FOR US, SO WHEN WE GET AN ANONYMOUS TIP ABOUT SOME CREEPY HOTEL MANAGER, ALL THE PIECES FIT TOGETHER?
WE CLOSE THE CASE, AND HE STARTS ALL OVER SOMEWHERE ELSE.
WASH. RINSE. REPEAT.
CLAK CLAK CLAK
HANG ON. I WANT TO RUN THE SAME SEARCH AGAIN, THIS TIME WIDENING THE PARAMETERS TO INCLUDE INTERNATIONAL AND SOLVED CASES.
YAHTZEE.
SOMEONE'S BEEN BUSY.
BEEP

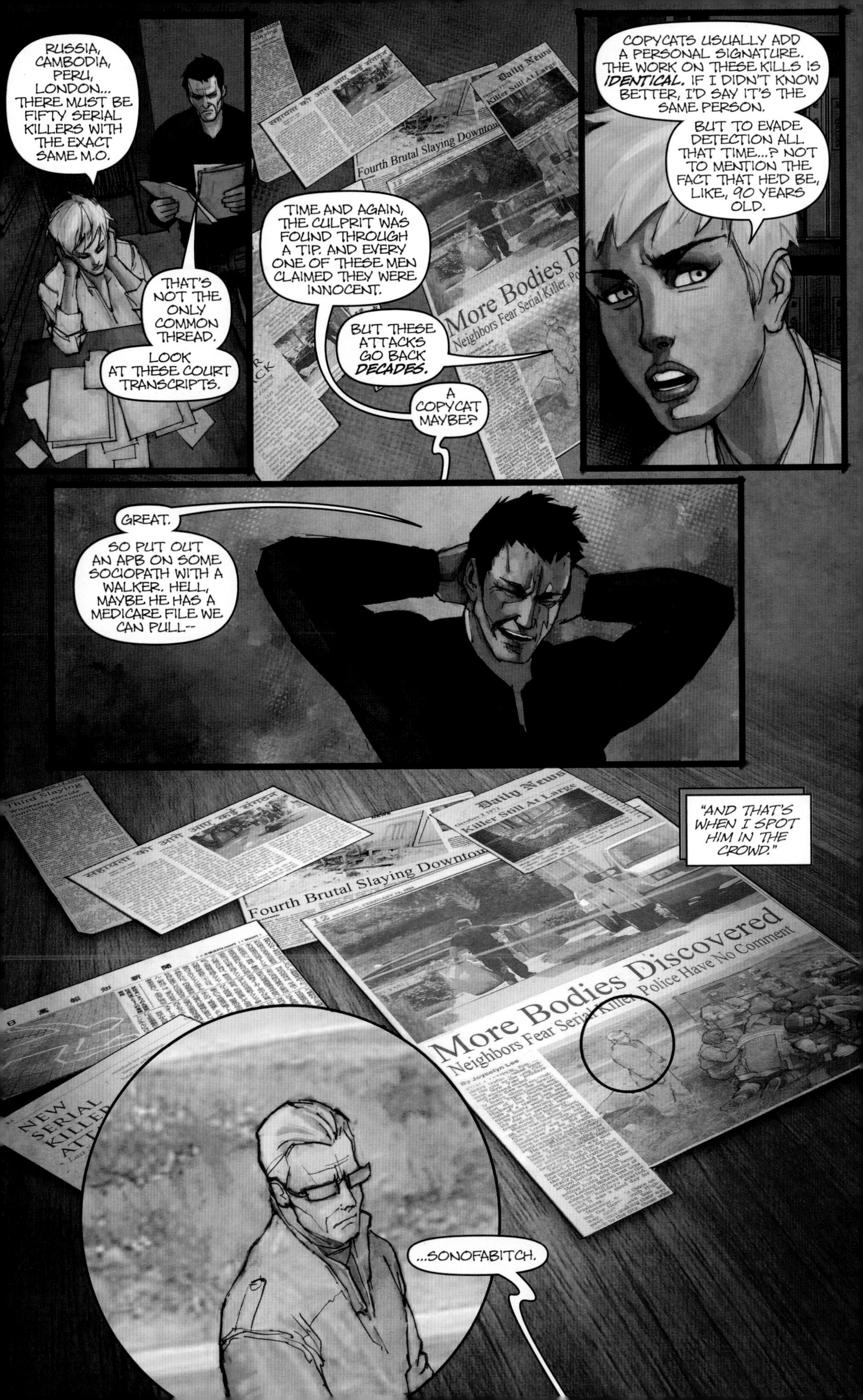
RUSSIA, CAMBODIA, PERU, LONDON... THERE MUST BE FIFTY SERIAL KILLERS WITH THE EXACT SAME M.O.
THAT'S NOT THE ONLY COMMON THREAD.
LOOK AT THESE COURT TRANSCRIPTS.
TIME AND AGAIN, THE CULPRIT WAS FOUND THROUGH A TIP. AND EVERY ONE OF THESE MEN CLAIMED THEY WERE INNOCENT.
BUT THESE ATTACKS GO BACK *DECADES.*
A COPYCAT MAYBE?
COPYCATS USUALLY ADD A PERSONAL SIGNATURE. THE WORK ON THESE KILLS IS *IDENTICAL.* IF I DIDN'T KNOW BETTER, I'D SAY IT'S THE SAME PERSON.
BUT TO EVADE DETECTION ALL THAT TIME...? NOT TO MENTION THE FACT THAT HE'D BE, LIKE, 90 YEARS OLD.
GREAT.
SO PUT OUT AN APB ON SOME SOCIOPATH WITH A WALKER. HELL, MAYBE HE HAS A MEDICARE FILE WE CAN PULL--
"AND THAT'S WHEN I SPOT HIM IN THE CROWD."
Third Slaying
Daily News
Killer Still At Large
Fourth Brutal Slaying Downtow
More Bodies Discovered
Neighbors Fear Serial Killer, Police Have No Comment
By Joycelyn Lee
NEW SERIAL KILLER
...SONOFABITCH.

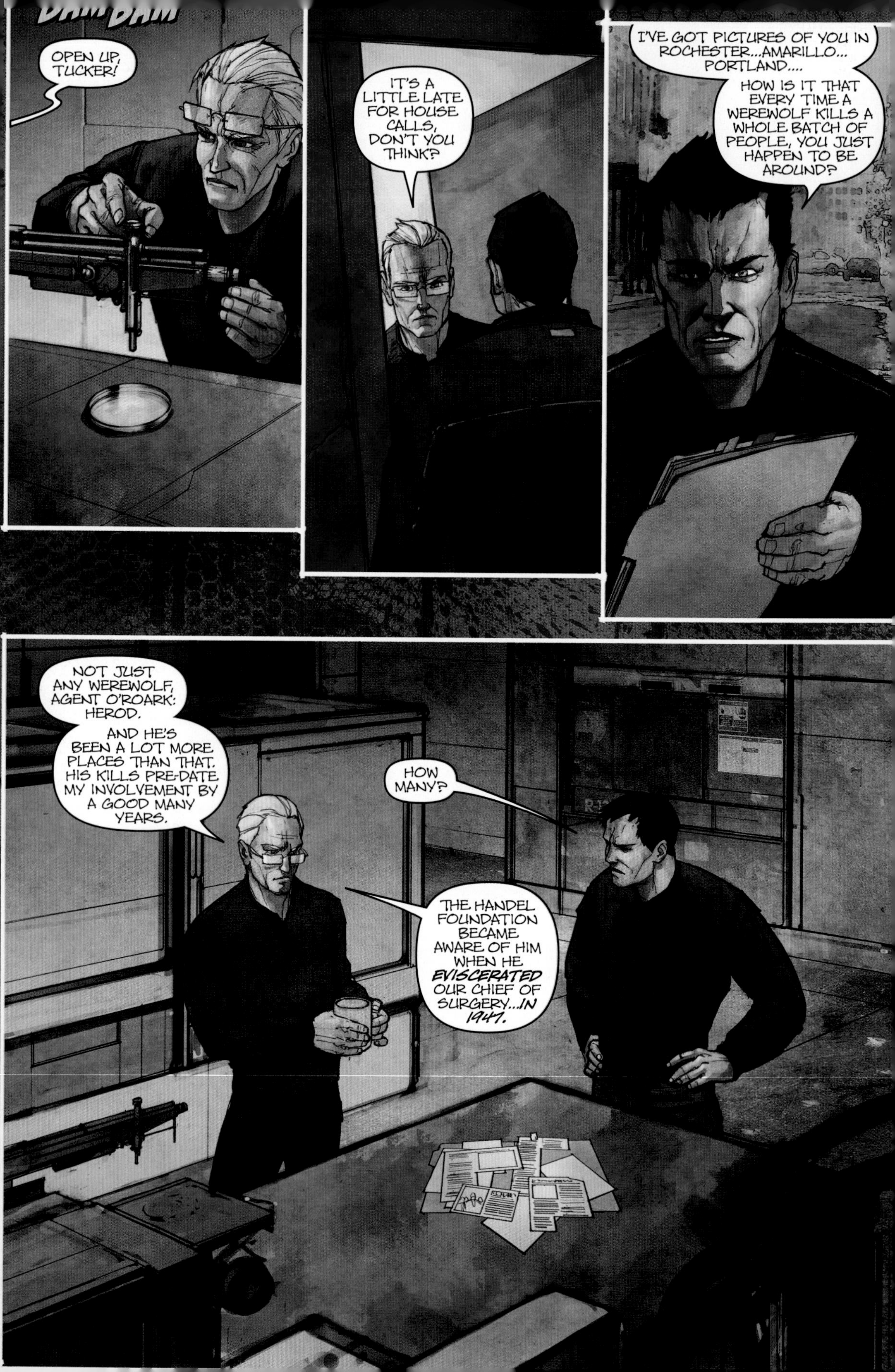
BAM BAM
OPEN UP, TUCKER!
IT'S A LITTLE LATE FOR HOUSE CALLS, DON'T YOU THINK?
I'VE GOT PICTURES OF YOU IN ROCHESTER...AMARILLO... PORTLAND....
HOW IS IT THAT EVERY TIME A WEREWOLF KILLS A WHOLE BATCH OF PEOPLE, YOU JUST HAPPEN TO BE AROUND?
NOT JUST ANY WEREWOLF, AGENT O'ROARK: HEROD.
AND HE'S BEEN A LOT MORE PLACES THAN THAT. HIS KILLS PRE-DATE MY INVOLVEMENT BY A GOOD MANY YEARS.
HOW MANY?
THE HANDEL FOUNDATION BECAME AWARE OF HIM WHEN HE EVISCERATED OUR CHIEF OF SURGERY...IN 1947.

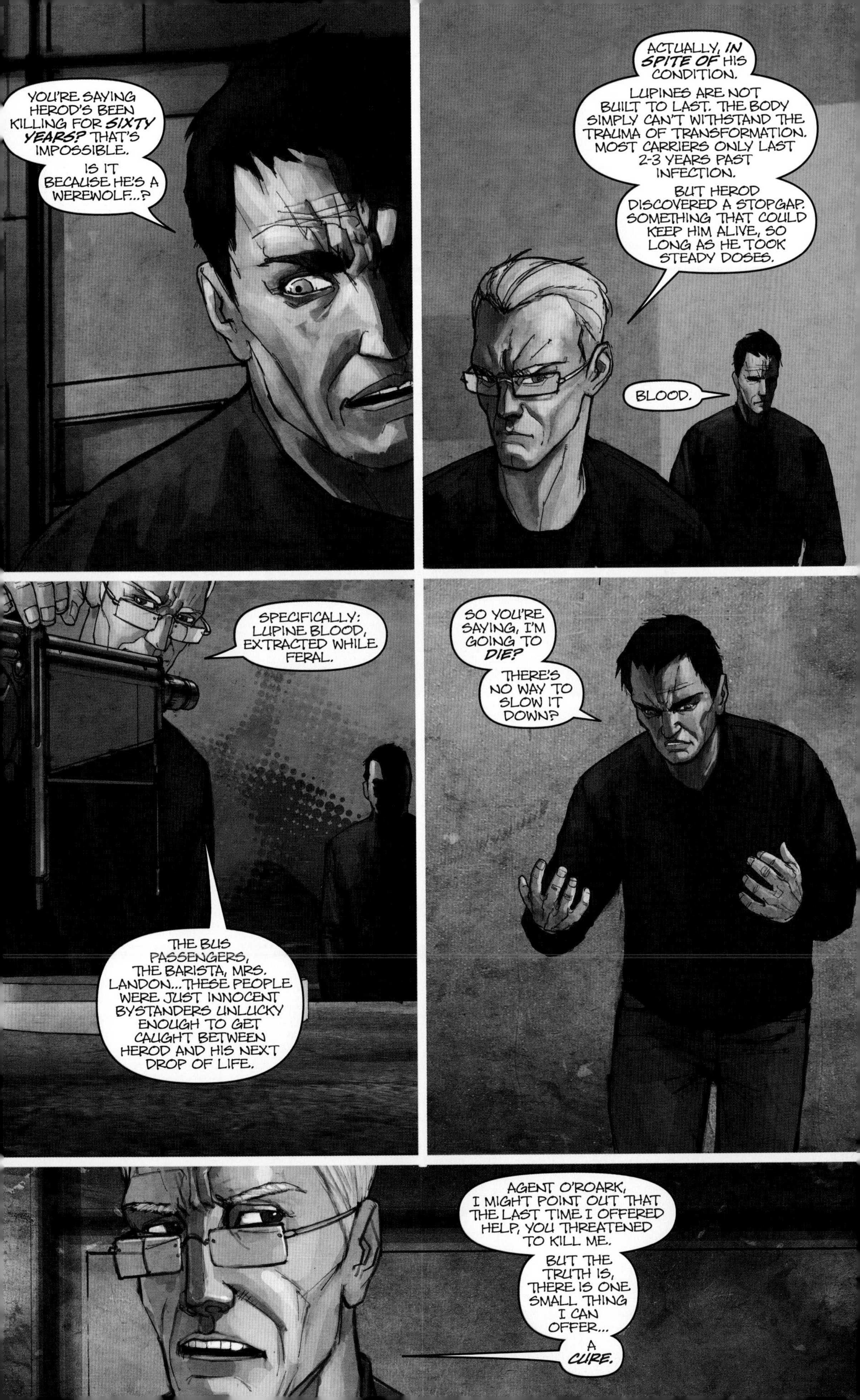
YOU'RE SAYING HEROD'S BEEN KILLING FOR *SIXTY YEARS?* THAT'S IMPOSSIBLE.
IS IT BECAUSE HE'S A WEREWOLF...?
ACTUALLY, *IN SPITE OF* HIS CONDITION.
LUPINES ARE NOT BUILT TO LAST. THE BODY SIMPLY CAN'T WITHSTAND THE TRAUMA OF TRANSFORMATION. MOST CARRIERS ONLY LAST 2-3 YEARS PAST INFECTION.
BUT HEROD DISCOVERED A STOPGAP. SOMETHING THAT COULD KEEP HIM ALIVE, SO LONG AS HE TOOK STEADY DOSES.
BLOOD.
SPECIFICALLY: LUPINE BLOOD, EXTRACTED WHILE FERAL.
THE BUS PASSENGERS, THE BARISTA, MRS. LANDON... THESE PEOPLE WERE JUST INNOCENT BYSTANDERS UNLUCKY ENOUGH TO GET CAUGHT BETWEEN HEROD AND HIS NEXT DROP OF LIFE.
SO YOU'RE SAYING, I'M GOING TO *DIE?*
THERE'S NO WAY TO SLOW IT DOWN?
AGENT O'ROARK, I MIGHT POINT OUT THAT THE LAST TIME I OFFERED HELP, YOU THREATENED TO KILL ME.
BUT THE TRUTH IS, THERE IS ONE SMALL THING I CAN OFFER...
A *CURE.*

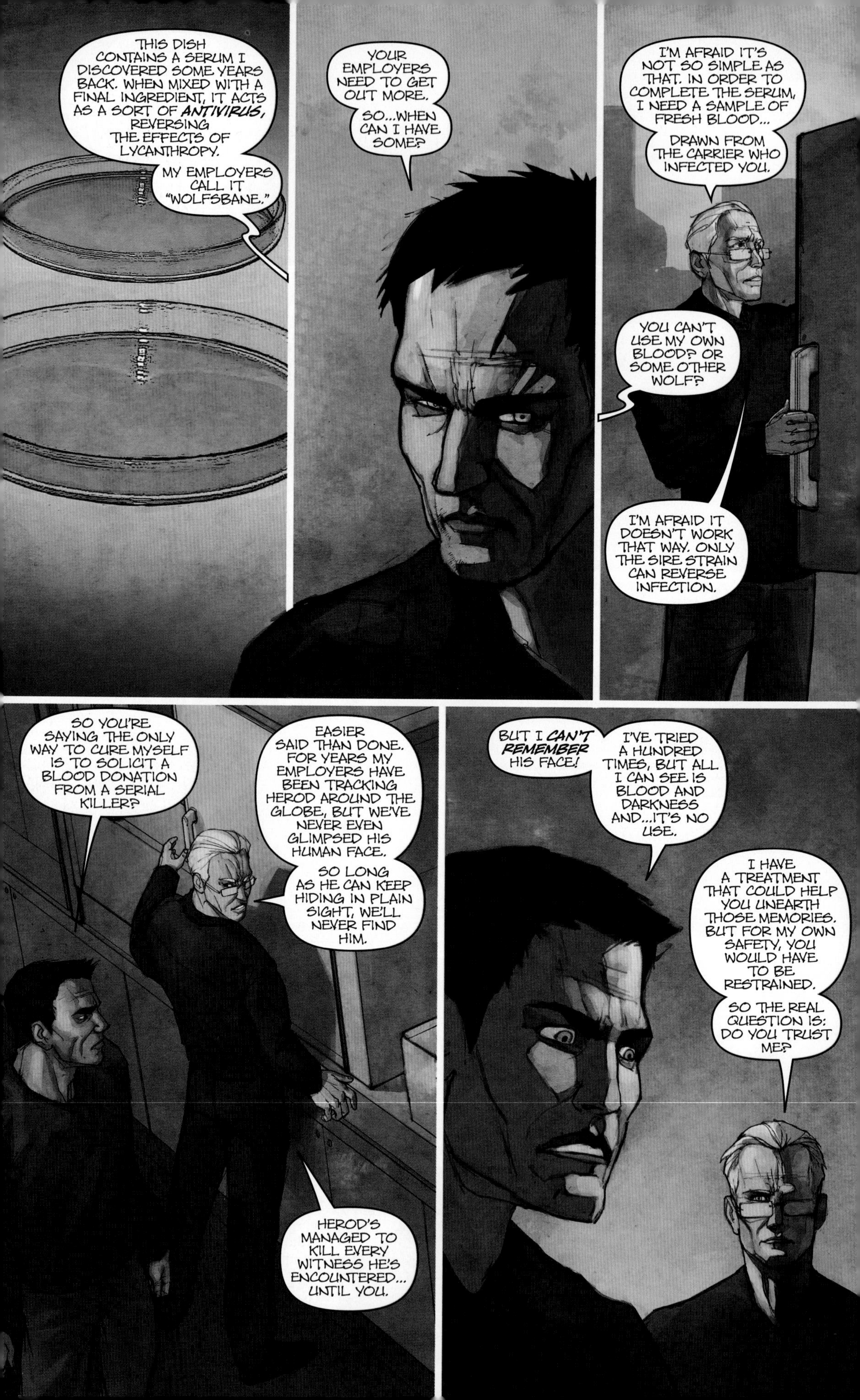
THIS DISH CONTAINS A SERUM I DISCOVERED SOME YEARS BACK. WHEN MIXED WITH A FINAL INGREDIENT, IT ACTS AS A SORT OF *ANTIVIRUS,* REVERSING THE EFFECTS OF LYCANTHROPY.
MY EMPLOYERS CALL IT "WOLFSBANE."
YOUR EMPLOYERS NEED TO GET OUT MORE.
SO...WHEN CAN I HAVE SOME?
I'M AFRAID IT'S NOT SO SIMPLE AS THAT. IN ORDER TO COMPLETE THE SERUM, I NEED A SAMPLE OF FRESH BLOOD...
DRAWN FROM THE CARRIER WHO INFECTED YOU.
YOU CAN'T USE MY OWN BLOOD? OR SOME OTHER WOLF?
I'M AFRAID IT DOESN'T WORK THAT WAY. ONLY THE SIRE STRAIN CAN REVERSE INFECTION.
SO YOU'RE SAYING THE ONLY WAY TO CURE MYSELF IS TO SOLICIT A BLOOD DONATION FROM A SERIAL KILLER?
EASIER SAID THAN DONE. FOR YEARS MY EMPLOYERS HAVE BEEN TRACKING HEROD AROUND THE GLOBE, BUT WE'VE NEVER EVEN GLIMPSED HIS HUMAN FACE.
SO LONG AS HE CAN KEEP HIDING IN PLAIN SIGHT, WE'LL NEVER FIND HIM.
HEROD'S MANAGED TO KILL EVERY WITNESS HE'S ENCOUNTERED... UNTIL YOU.
BUT I *CAN'T REMEMBER* HIS FACE!
I'VE TRIED A HUNDRED TIMES, BUT ALL I CAN SEE IS BLOOD AND DARKNESS AND...IT'S NO USE.
I HAVE A TREATMENT THAT COULD HELP YOU UNEARTH THOSE MEMORIES. BUT FOR MY OWN SAFETY, YOU WOULD HAVE TO BE RESTRAINED.
SO THE REAL QUESTION IS: DO YOU TRUST ME?

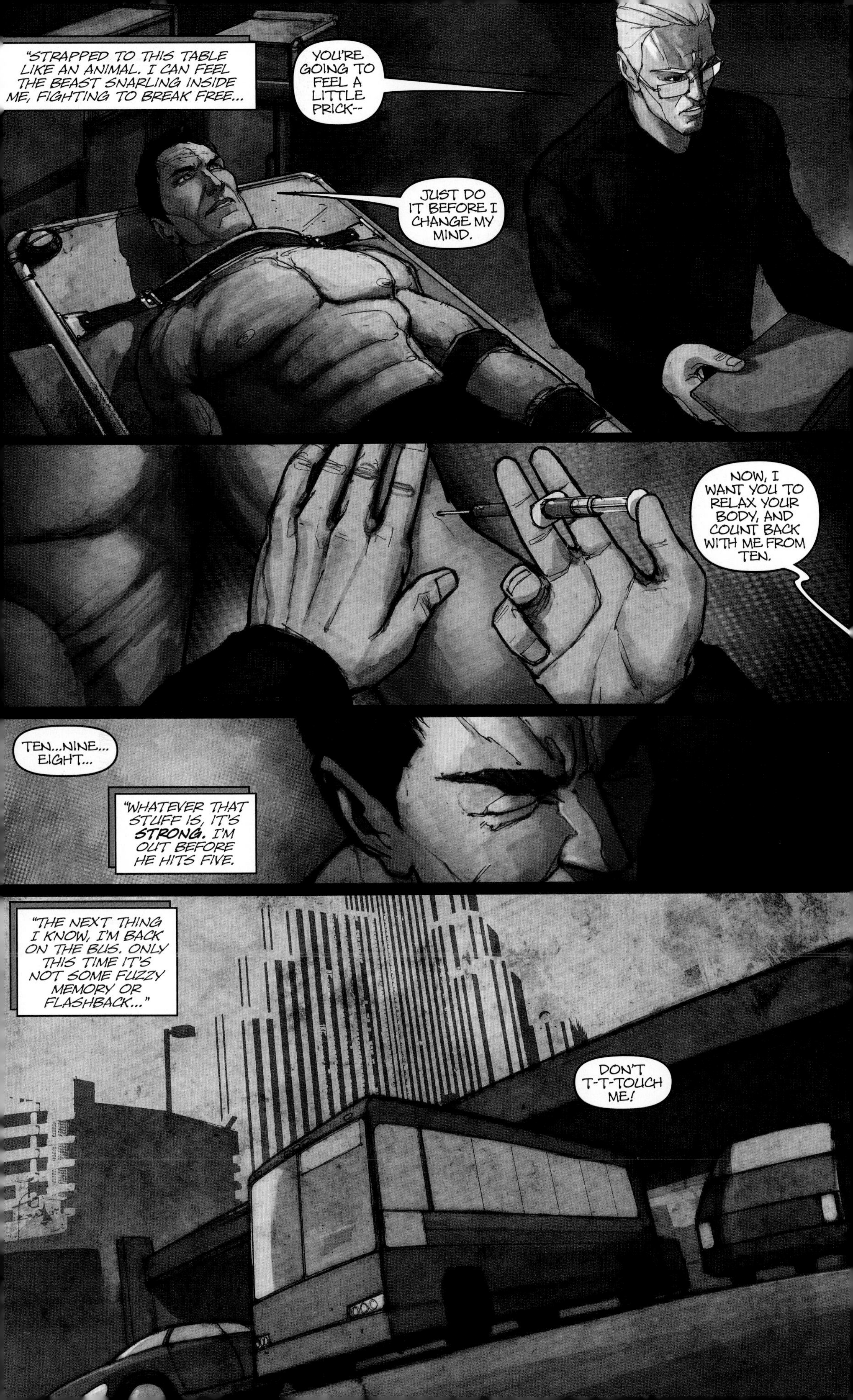
"STRAPPED TO THIS TABLE LIKE AN ANIMAL. I CAN FEEL THE BEAST SNARLING INSIDE ME, FIGHTING TO BREAK FREE...
YOU'RE GOING TO FEEL A LITTLE PRICK--
JUST DO IT BEFORE I CHANGE MY MIND.
NOW, I WANT YOU TO RELAX YOUR BODY, AND COUNT BACK WITH ME FROM TEN.
TEN...NINE... EIGHT...
"WHATEVER THAT STUFF IS, IT'S STRONG. I'M OUT BEFORE HE HITS FIVE.
"THE NEXT THING I KNOW, I'M BACK ON THE BUS. ONLY THIS TIME IT'S NOT SOME FUZZY MEMORY OR FLASHBACK..."
DON'T T-T-TOUCH ME!

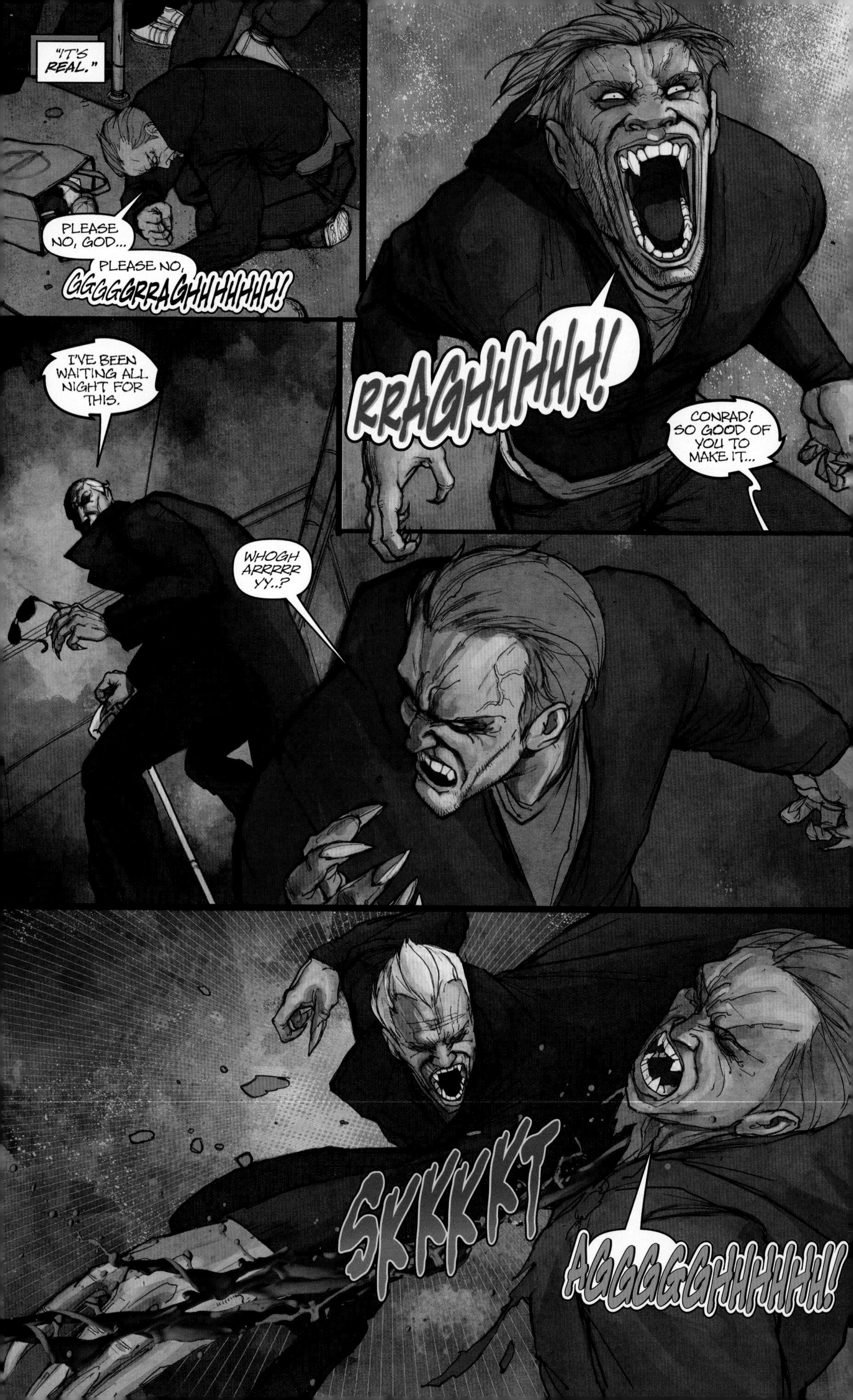
"IT'S REAL."
PLEASE NO, GOD...
PLEASE NO, GGGGGRRAGHHHHHH!
RRAGHHHHH!
I'VE BEEN WAITING ALL NIGHT FOR THIS.
CONRAD! SO GOOD OF YOU TO MAKE IT...
WHOGH ARRRRR YY..?
SKKKKT
AGGGGGHHHHH!

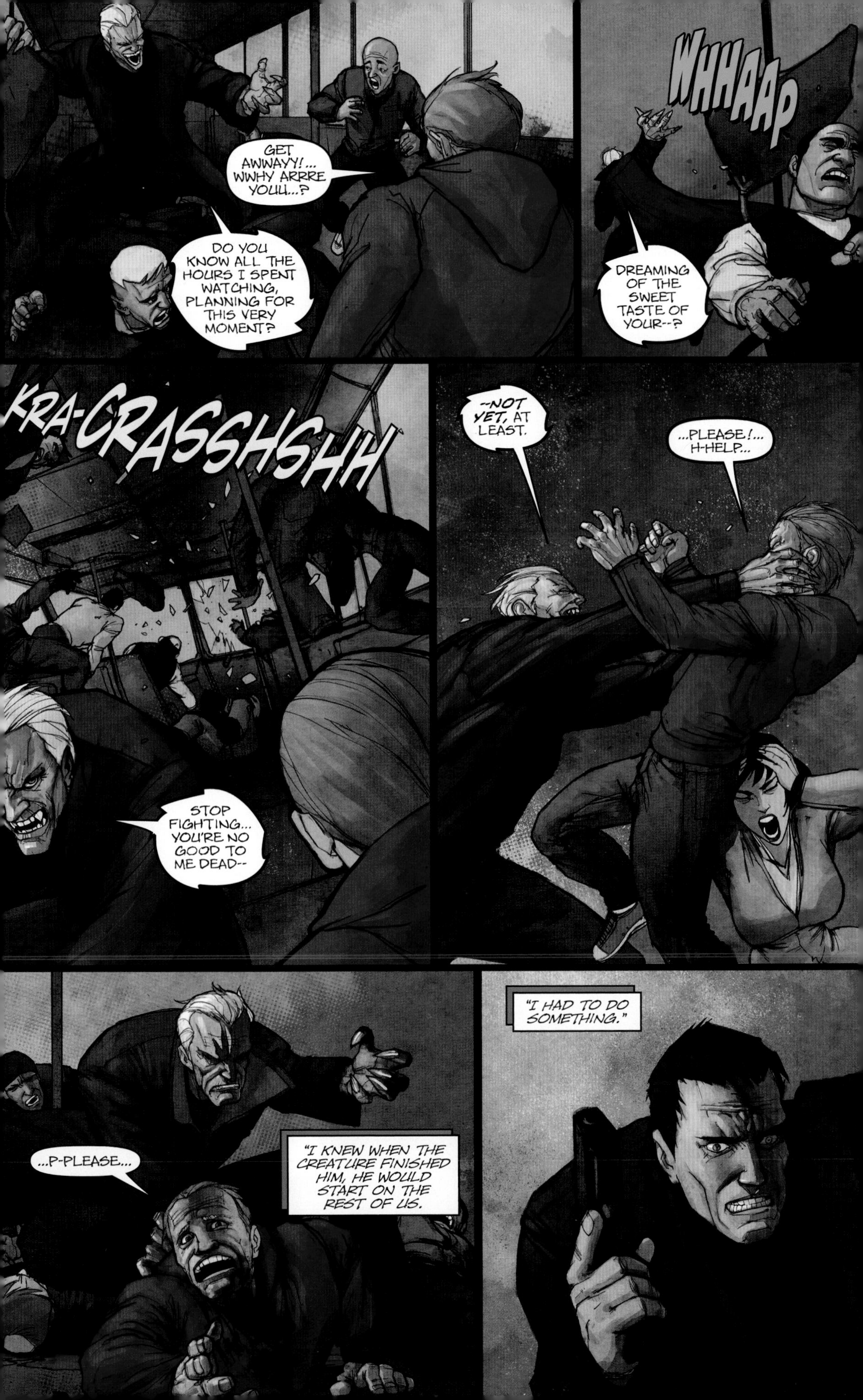
GET AWWAYY!... WWHY ARRRE YOUU...?
DO YOU KNOW ALL THE HOURS I SPENT WATCHING, PLANNING FOR THIS VERY MOMENT?
WHHAAP
DREAMING OF THE SWEET TASTE OF YOUR--?
KRA-CRASSHSHH
STOP FIGHTING... YOU'RE NO GOOD TO ME DEAD--
--NOT YET, AT LEAST.
...PLEASE!... H-HELP...
...P-PLEASE...
"I KNEW WHEN THE CREATURE FINISHED HIM, HE WOULD START ON THE REST OF US.
"I HAD TO DO SOMETHING."

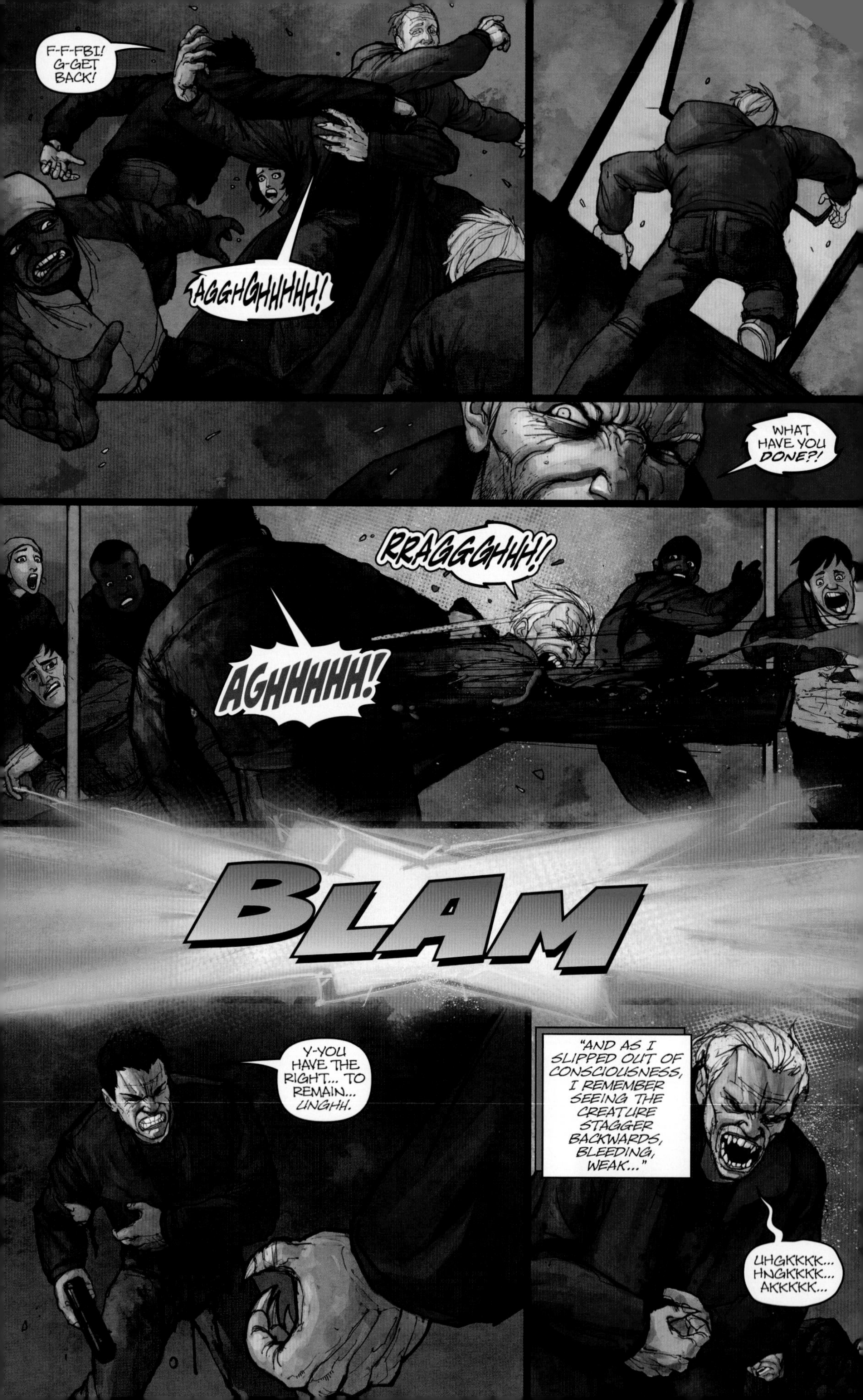
F-F-FBI! G-GET BACK!
AGGHGHHHHH!
WHAT HAVE YOU DONE?!
RRAGGGHHH!
AGHHHHH!
BLAM
Y-YOU HAVE THE RIGHT... TO REMAIN... UNGHH.
"AND AS I SLIPPED OUT OF CONSCIOUSNESS, I REMEMBER SEEING THE CREATURE STAGGER BACKWARDS, BLEEDING, WEAK..."
UHGKKKK... HNGKKKK... AKKKKK...

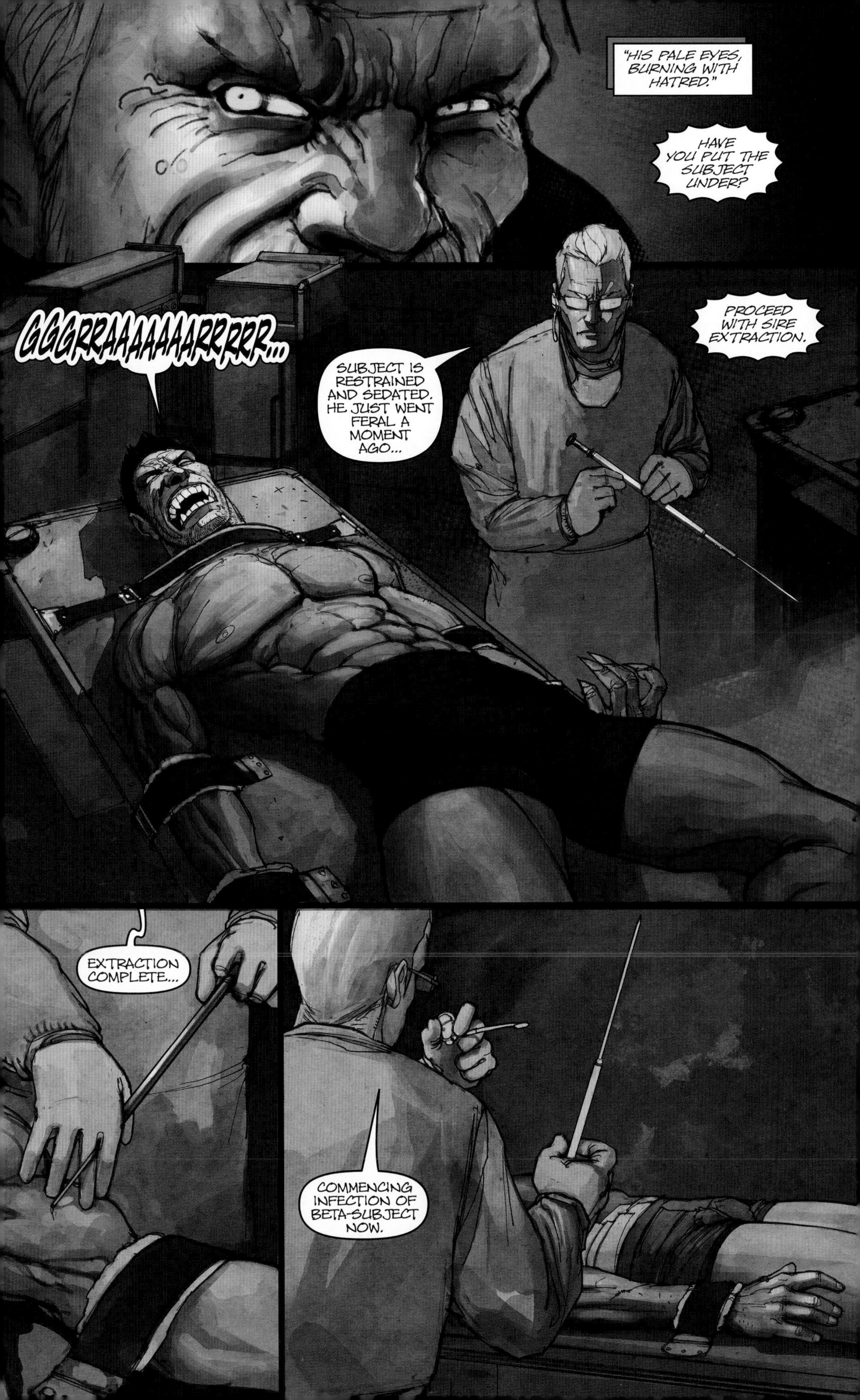
"HIS PALE EYES, BURNING WITH HATRED."
HAVE YOU PUT THE SUBJECT UNDER?
GGGRRAAAAAAARRRRR...
SUBJECT IS RESTRAINED AND SEDATED. HE JUST WENT FERAL A MOMENT AGO...
PROCEED WITH SIRE EXTRACTION.
EXTRACTION COMPLETE...
COMMENCING INFECTION OF BETA-SUBJECT NOW.

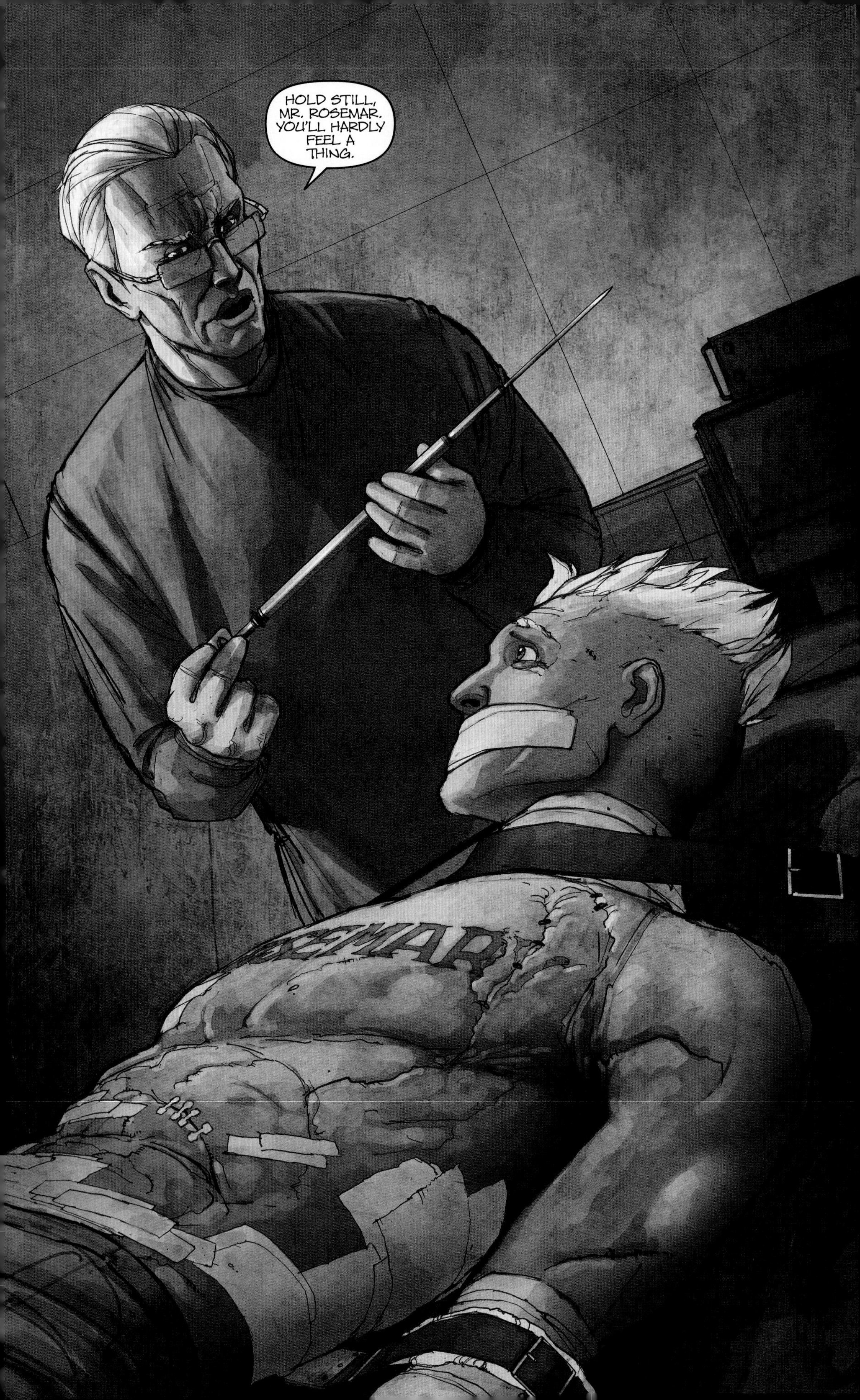
HOLD STILL, MR. ROSEMAR. YOU'LL HARDLY FEEL A THING.

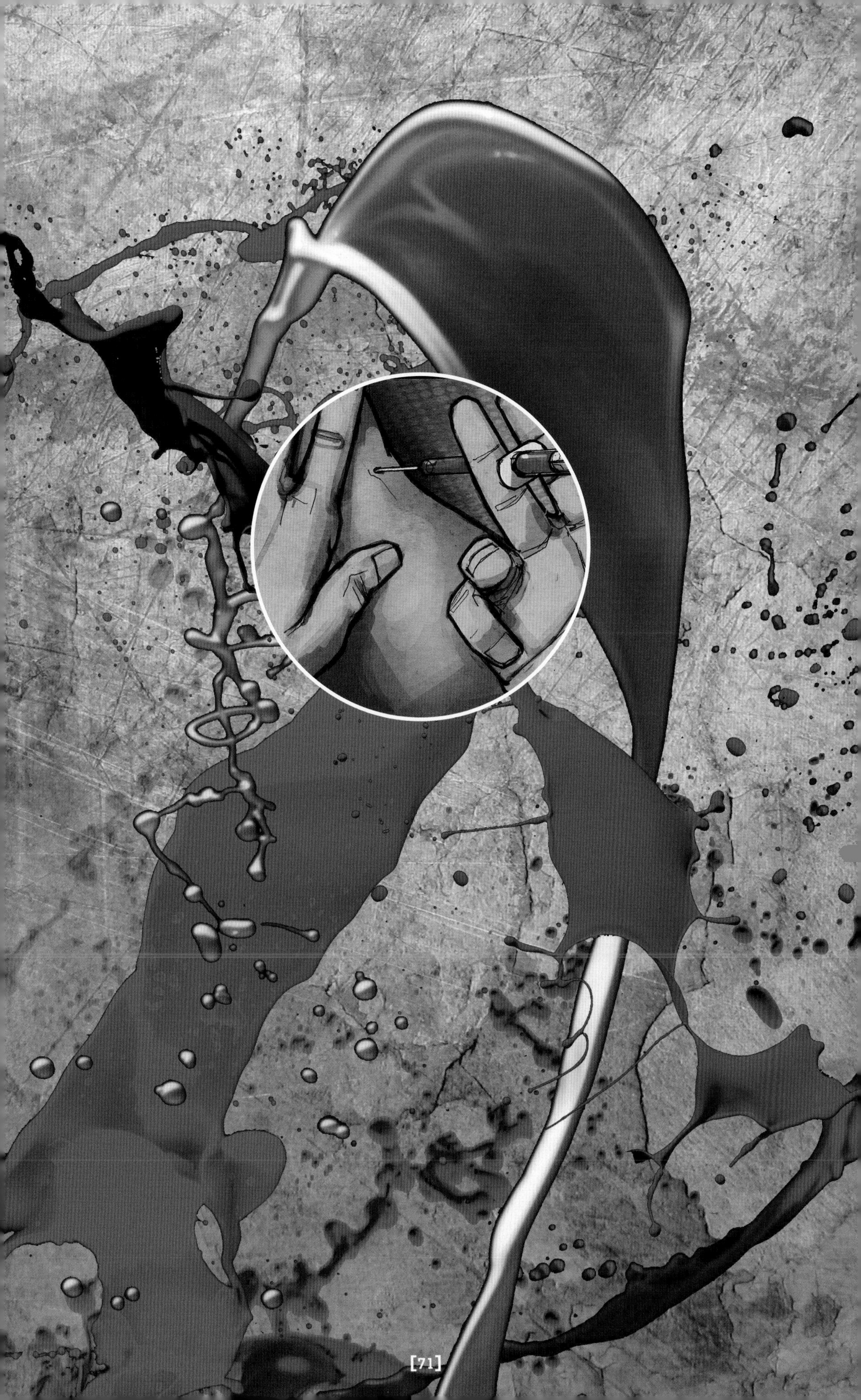

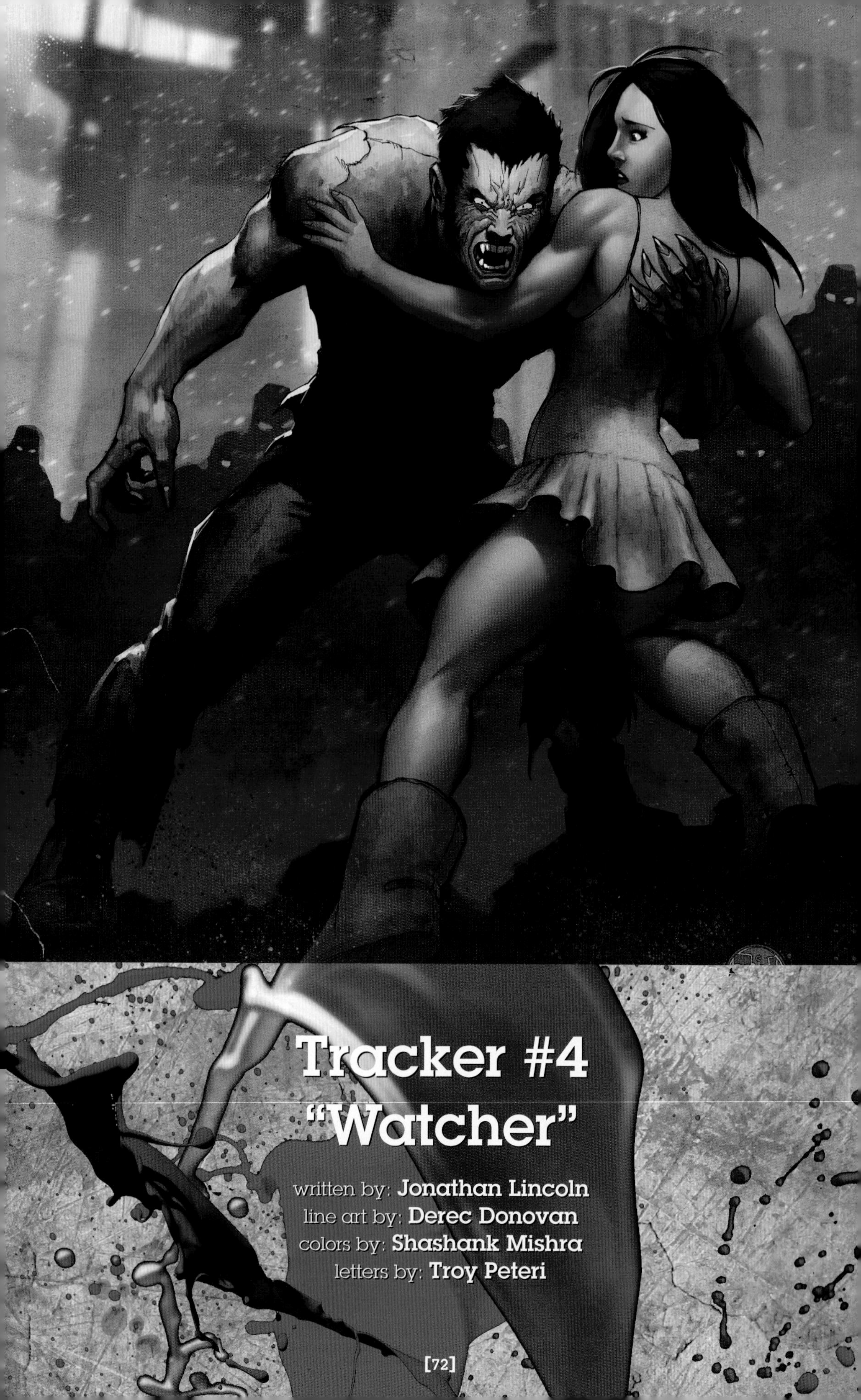

Tracker #4
"Watcher"

written by: **Jonathan Lincoln**
line art by: **Derec Donovan**
colors by: **Shashank Mishra**
letters by: **Troy Peteri**

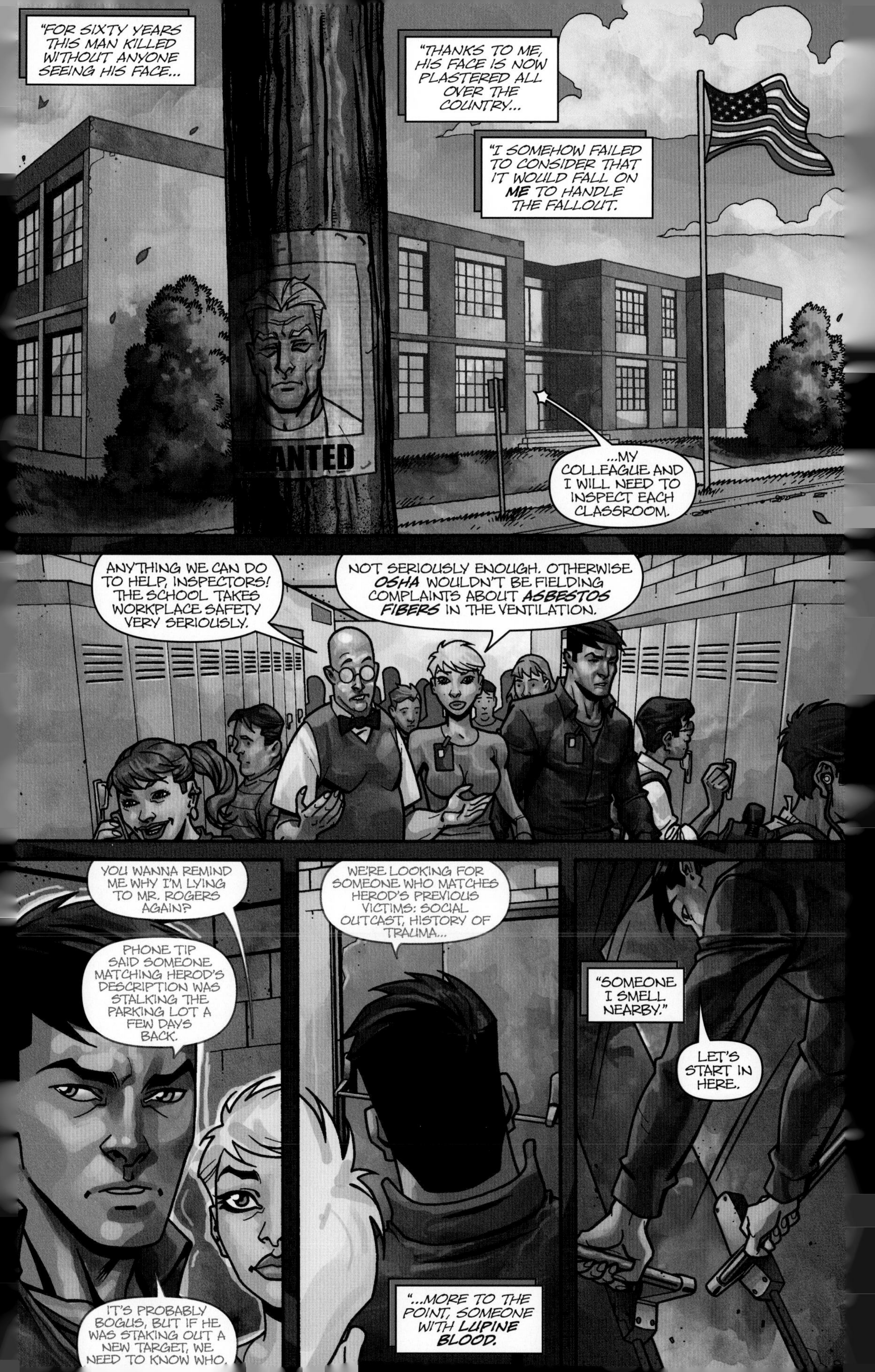
"FOR SIXTY YEARS THIS MAN KILLED WITHOUT ANYONE SEEING HIS FACE...
"THANKS TO ME, HIS FACE IS NOW PLASTERED ALL OVER THE COUNTRY...
"I SOMEHOW FAILED TO CONSIDER THAT IT WOULD FALL ON ME TO HANDLE THE FALLOUT.
ANTED
...MY COLLEAGUE AND I WILL NEED TO INSPECT EACH CLASSROOM.
ANYTHING WE CAN DO TO HELP, INSPECTORS! THE SCHOOL TAKES WORKPLACE SAFETY VERY SERIOUSLY.
NOT SERIOUSLY ENOUGH. OTHERWISE OSHA WOULDN'T BE FIELDING COMPLAINTS ABOUT ASBESTOS FIBERS IN THE VENTILATION.
YOU WANNA REMIND ME WHY I'M LYING TO MR. ROGERS AGAIN?
PHONE TIP SAID SOMEONE MATCHING HEROD'S DESCRIPTION WAS STALKING THE PARKING LOT A FEW DAYS BACK.
IT'S PROBABLY BOGUS, BUT IF HE WAS STAKING OUT A NEW TARGET, WE NEED TO KNOW WHO.
WE'RE LOOKING FOR SOMEONE WHO MATCHES HEROD'S PREVIOUS VICTIMS: SOCIAL OUTCAST, HISTORY OF TRAUMA...
"...MORE TO THE POINT, SOMEONE WITH LUPINE BLOOD.
"SOMEONE I SMELL NEARBY."
LET'S START IN HERE.

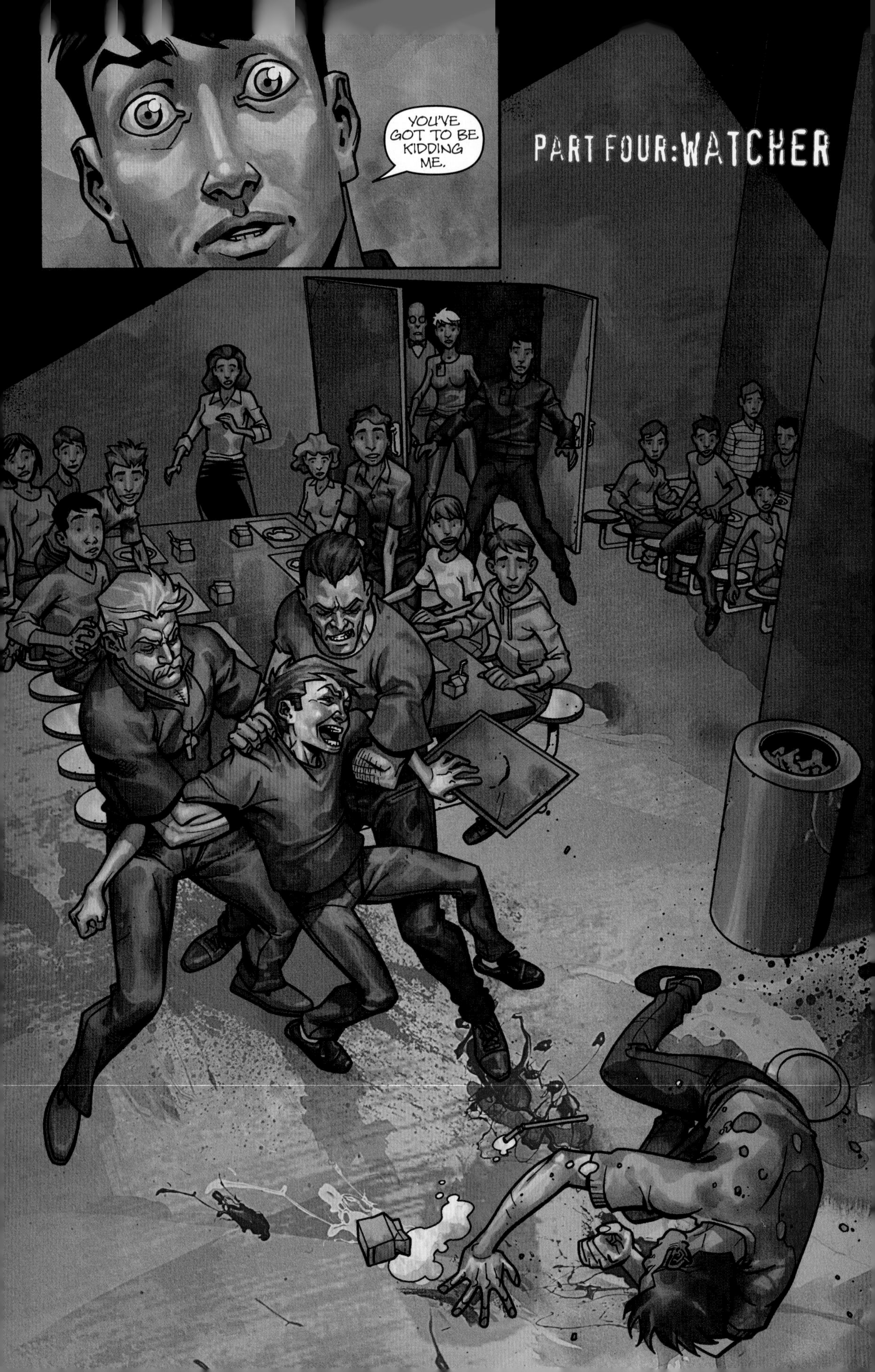
YOU'VE GOT TO BE KIDDING ME.
PART FOUR: WATCHER

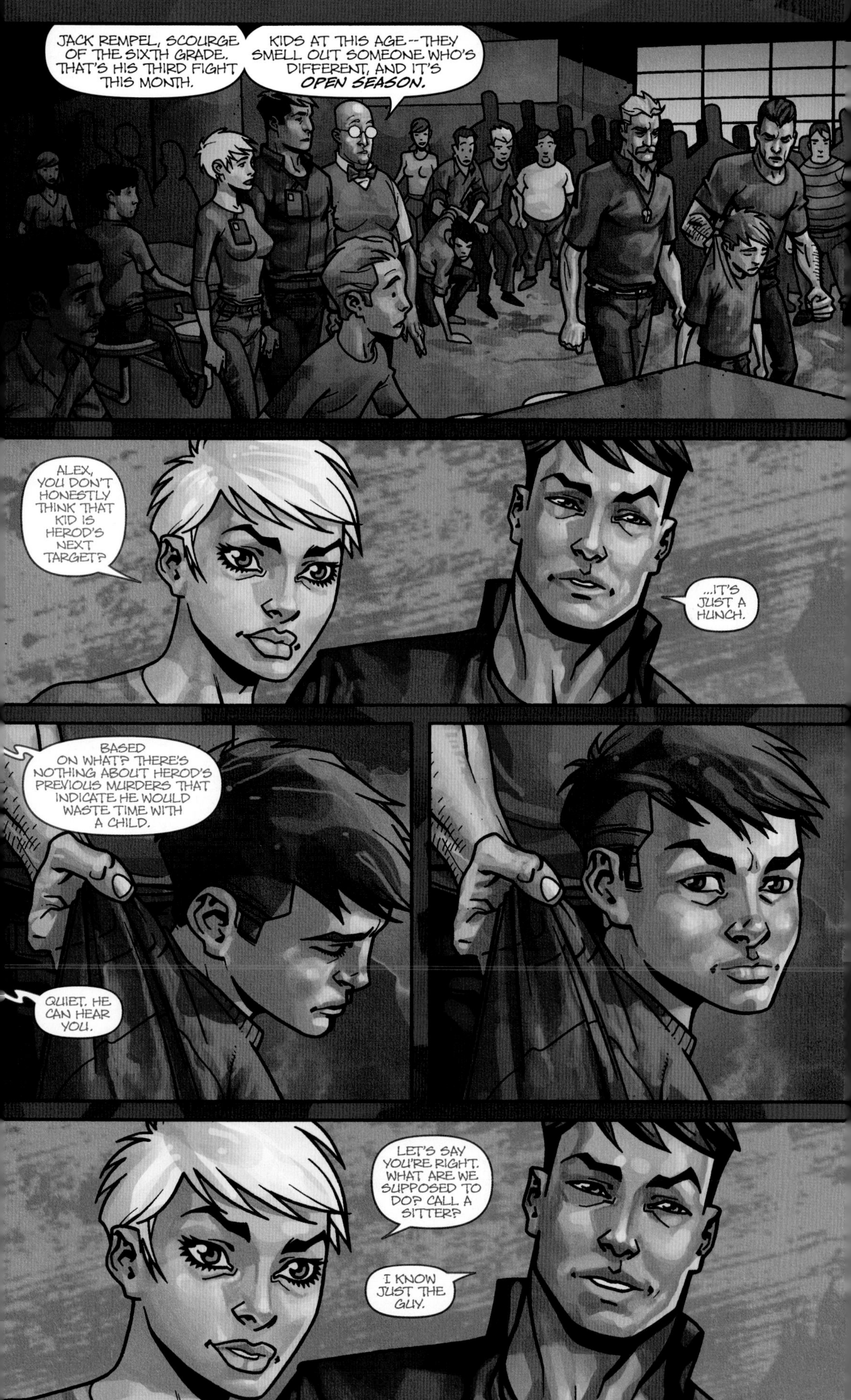
JACK REMPEL, SCOURGE OF THE SIXTH GRADE. THAT'S HIS THIRD FIGHT THIS MONTH.
KIDS AT THIS AGE--THEY SMELL OUT SOMEONE WHO'S DIFFERENT, AND IT'S *OPEN SEASON.*
ALEX, YOU DON'T HONESTLY THINK THAT KID IS HEROD'S NEXT TARGET?
...IT'S JUST A HUNCH.
BASED ON WHAT? THERE'S NOTHING ABOUT HEROD'S PREVIOUS MURDERS THAT INDICATE HE WOULD WASTE TIME WITH A CHILD.
QUIET. HE CAN HEAR YOU.
LET'S SAY YOU'RE RIGHT. WHAT ARE WE SUPPOSED TO DO? CALL A SITTER?
I KNOW JUST THE GUY.

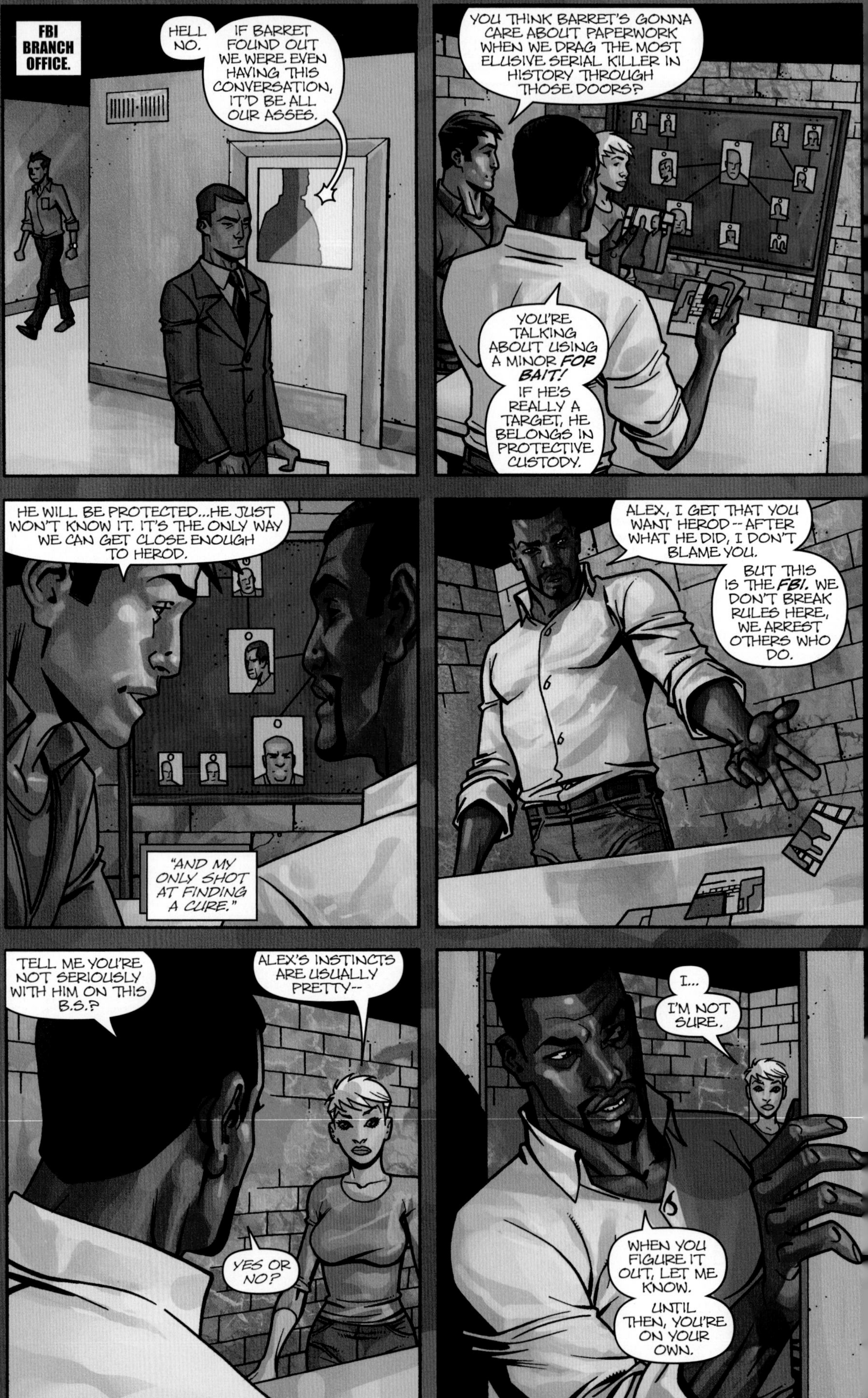
FBI BRANCH OFFICE.
HELL NO.
IF BARRET FOUND OUT WE WERE EVEN HAVING THIS CONVERSATION, IT'D BE ALL OUR ASSES.
YOU THINK BARRET'S GONNA CARE ABOUT PAPERWORK WHEN WE DRAG THE MOST ELUSIVE SERIAL KILLER IN HISTORY THROUGH THOSE DOORS?
YOU'RE TALKING ABOUT USING A MINOR FOR BAIT!
IF HE'S REALLY A TARGET, HE BELONGS IN PROTECTIVE CUSTODY.
HE WILL BE PROTECTED...HE JUST WON'T KNOW IT. IT'S THE ONLY WAY WE CAN GET CLOSE ENOUGH TO HEROD.
"AND MY ONLY SHOT AT FINDING A CURE."
ALEX, I GET THAT YOU WANT HEROD -- AFTER WHAT HE DID, I DON'T BLAME YOU.
BUT THIS IS THE FBI. WE DON'T BREAK RULES HERE, WE ARREST OTHERS WHO DO.
TELL ME YOU'RE NOT SERIOUSLY WITH HIM ON THIS B.S.?
ALEX'S INSTINCTS ARE USUALLY PRETTY--
YES OR NO?
I...
I'M NOT SURE.
WHEN YOU FIGURE IT OUT, LET ME KNOW.
UNTIL THEN, YOU'RE ON YOUR OWN.

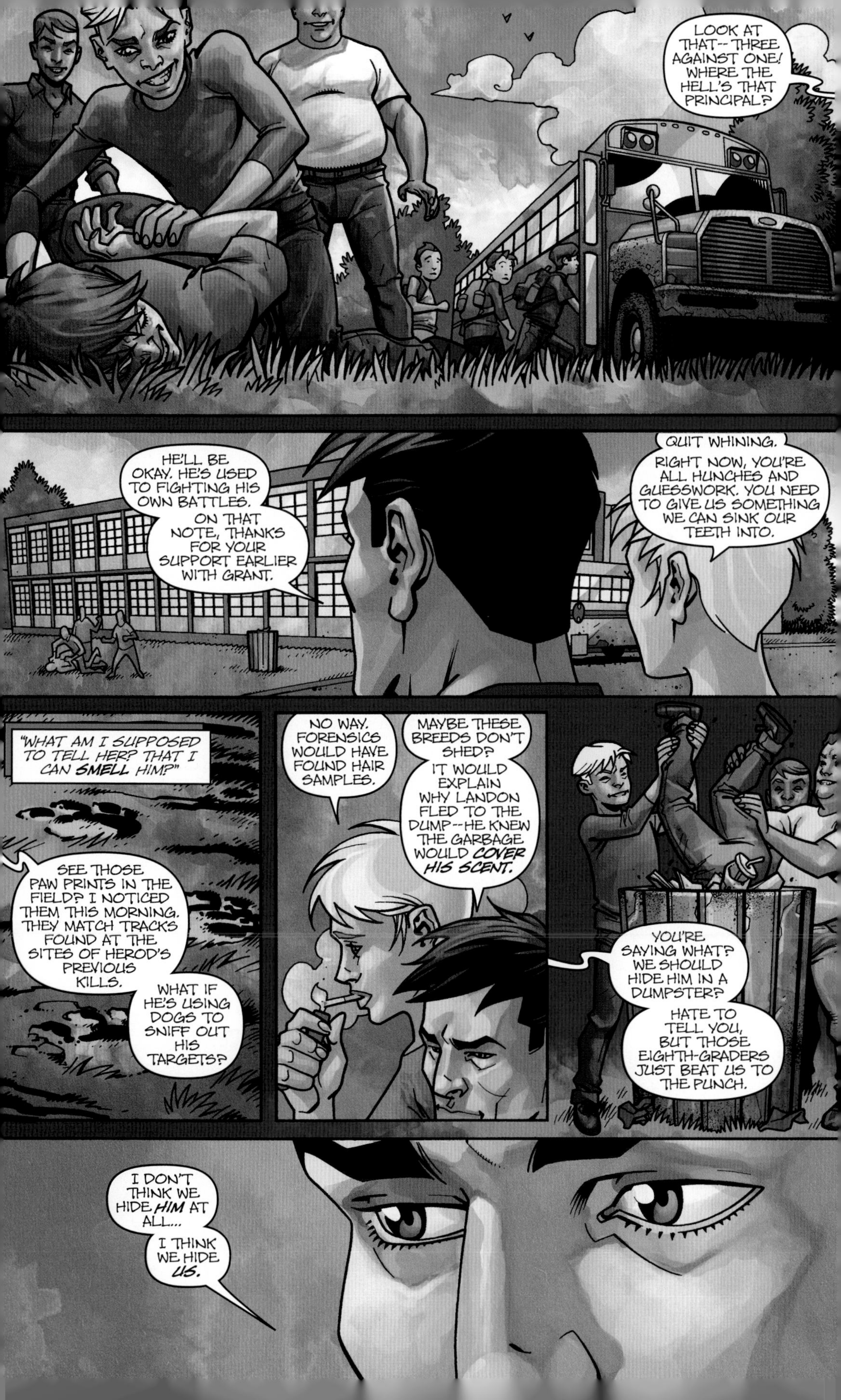
LOOK AT THAT-- THREE AGAINST ONE! WHERE THE HELL'S THAT PRINCIPAL?
HE'LL BE OKAY. HE'S USED TO FIGHTING HIS OWN BATTLES.
ON THAT NOTE, THANKS FOR YOUR SUPPORT EARLIER WITH GRANT.
QUIT WHINING.
RIGHT NOW, YOU'RE ALL HUNCHES AND GUESSWORK. YOU NEED TO GIVE US SOMETHING WE CAN SINK OUR TEETH INTO.
"WHAT AM I SUPPOSED TO TELL HER? THAT I CAN SMELL HIM?"
SEE THOSE PAW PRINTS IN THE FIELD? I NOTICED THEM THIS MORNING. THEY MATCH TRACKS FOUND AT THE SITES OF HEROD'S PREVIOUS KILLS.
WHAT IF HE'S USING DOGS TO SNIFF OUT HIS TARGETS?
NO WAY. FORENSICS WOULD HAVE FOUND HAIR SAMPLES.
MAYBE THESE BREEDS DON'T SHED?
IT WOULD EXPLAIN WHY LANDON FLED TO THE DUMP--HE KNEW THE GARBAGE WOULD COVER HIS SCENT.
YOU'RE SAYING WHAT? WE SHOULD HIDE HIM IN A DUMPSTER?
HATE TO TELL YOU, BUT THOSE EIGHTH-GRADERS JUST BEAT US TO THE PUNCH.
I DON'T THINK WE HIDE HIM AT ALL...
I THINK WE HIDE US.

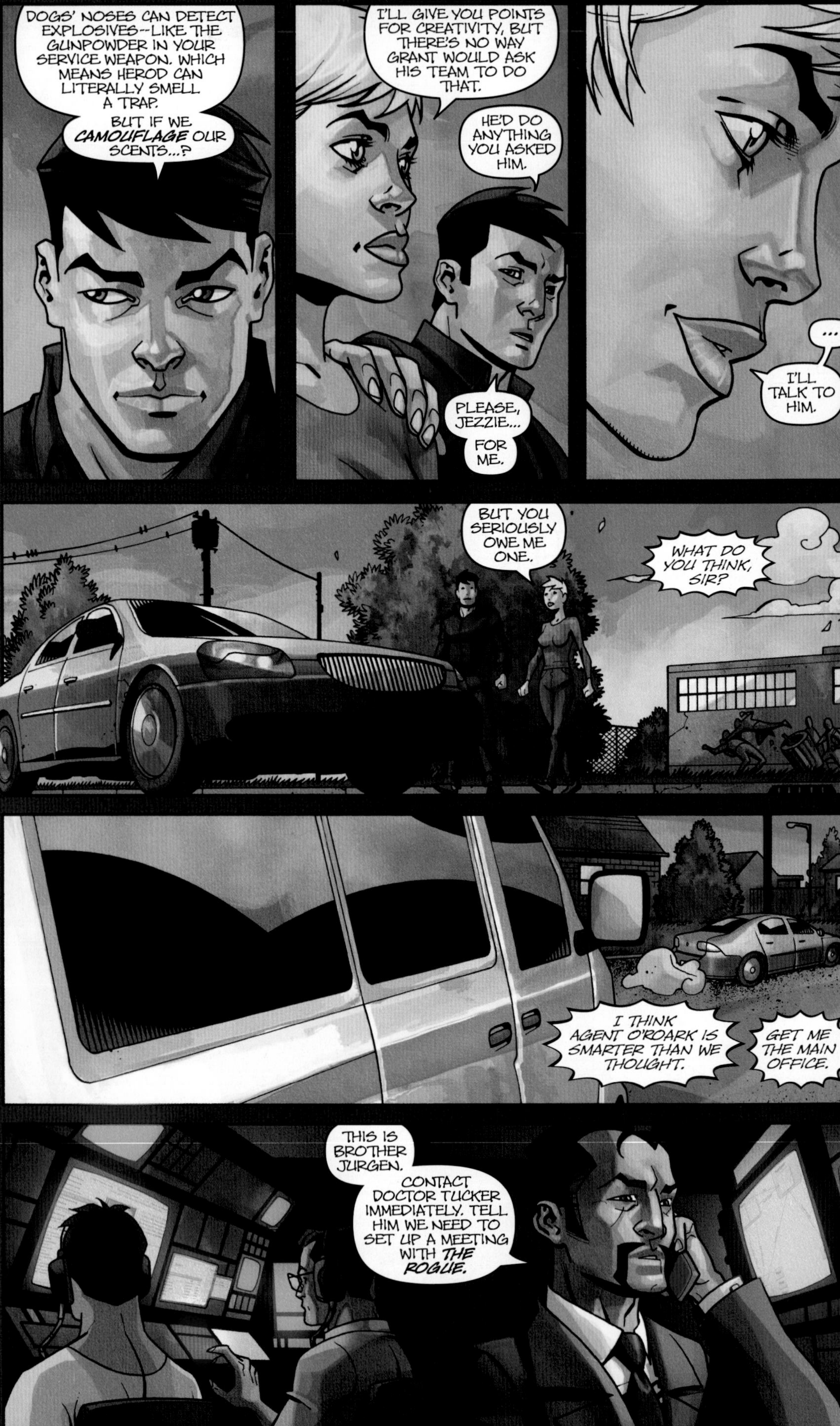
DOGS' NOSES CAN DETECT EXPLOSIVES--LIKE THE GUNPOWDER IN YOUR SERVICE WEAPON. WHICH MEANS HEROD CAN LITERALLY SMELL A TRAP.
BUT IF WE CAMOUFLAGE OUR SCENTS...?
I'LL GIVE YOU POINTS FOR CREATIVITY, BUT THERE'S NO WAY GRANT WOULD ASK HIS TEAM TO DO THAT.
HE'D DO ANYTHING YOU ASKED HIM.
PLEASE, JEZZIE...
FOR ME.
...
I'LL TALK TO HIM.
BUT YOU SERIOUSLY OWE ME ONE.
WHAT DO YOU THINK, SIR?
I THINK AGENT O'ROARK IS SMARTER THAN WE THOUGHT.
GET ME THE MAIN OFFICE.
THIS IS BROTHER JURGEN.
CONTACT DOCTOR TUCKER IMMEDIATELY. TELL HIM WE NEED TO SET UP A MEETING WITH THE ROGUE.

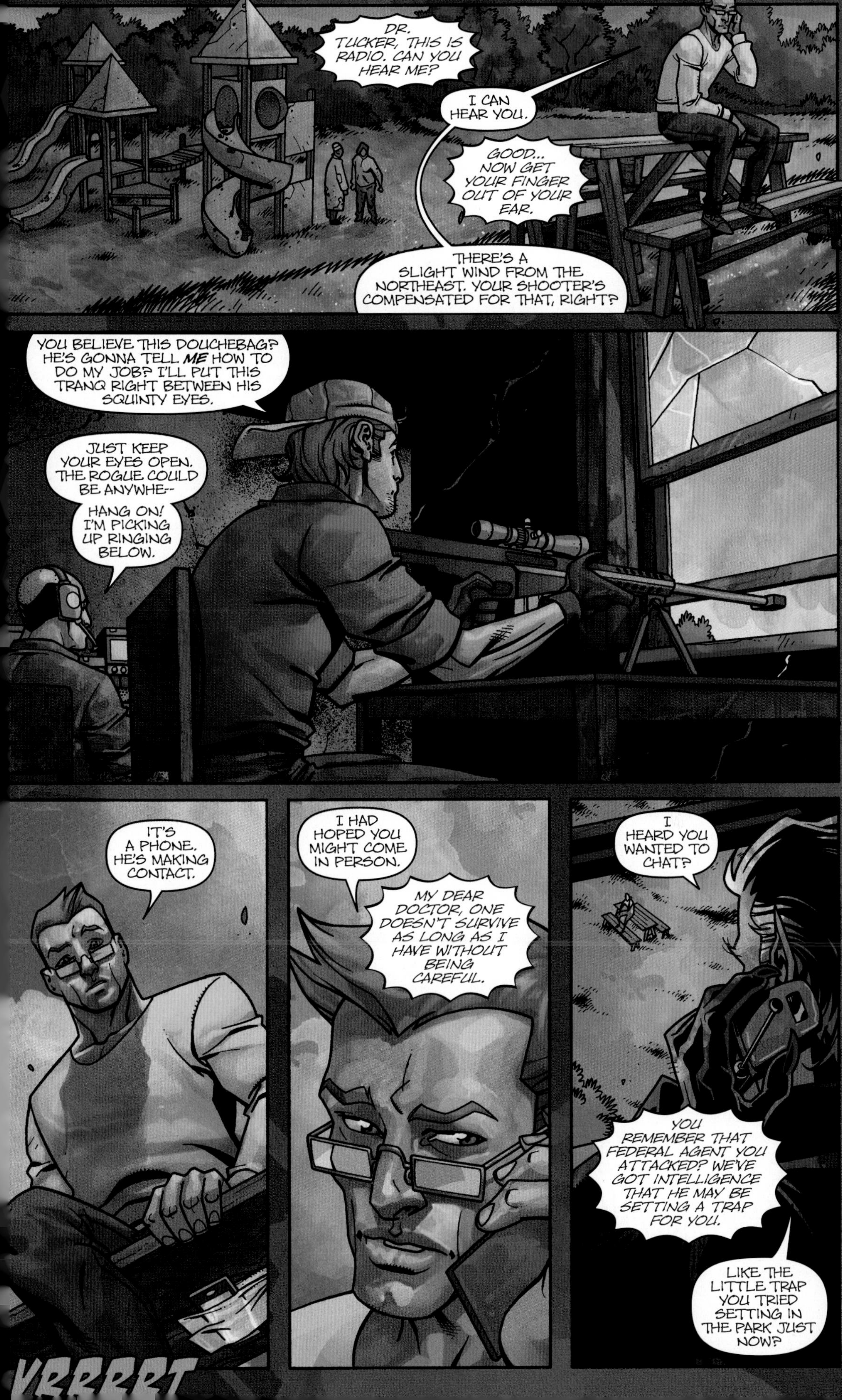
DR. TUCKER, THIS IS RADIO. CAN YOU HEAR ME?
I CAN HEAR YOU.
GOOD... NOW GET YOUR FINGER OUT OF YOUR EAR.
THERE'S A SLIGHT WIND FROM THE NORTHEAST. YOUR SHOOTER'S COMPENSATED FOR THAT, RIGHT?
YOU BELIEVE THIS DOUCHEBAG? HE'S GONNA TELL *ME* HOW TO DO MY JOB? I'LL PUT THIS TRANQ RIGHT BETWEEN HIS SQUINTY EYES.
JUST KEEP YOUR EYES OPEN. THE ROGUE COULD BE ANYWHE--
HANG ON! I'M PICKING UP RINGING BELOW.
IT'S A PHONE. HE'S MAKING CONTACT.
VRRRRT
I HAD HOPED YOU MIGHT COME IN PERSON.
MY DEAR DOCTOR, ONE DOESN'T SURVIVE AS LONG AS I HAVE WITHOUT BEING CAREFUL.
I HEARD YOU WANTED TO CHAT?
YOU REMEMBER THAT FEDERAL AGENT YOU ATTACKED? WE'VE GOT INTELLIGENCE THAT HE MAY BE SETTING A TRAP FOR YOU.
LIKE THE LITTLE TRAP YOU TRIED SETTING IN THE PARK JUST NOW?

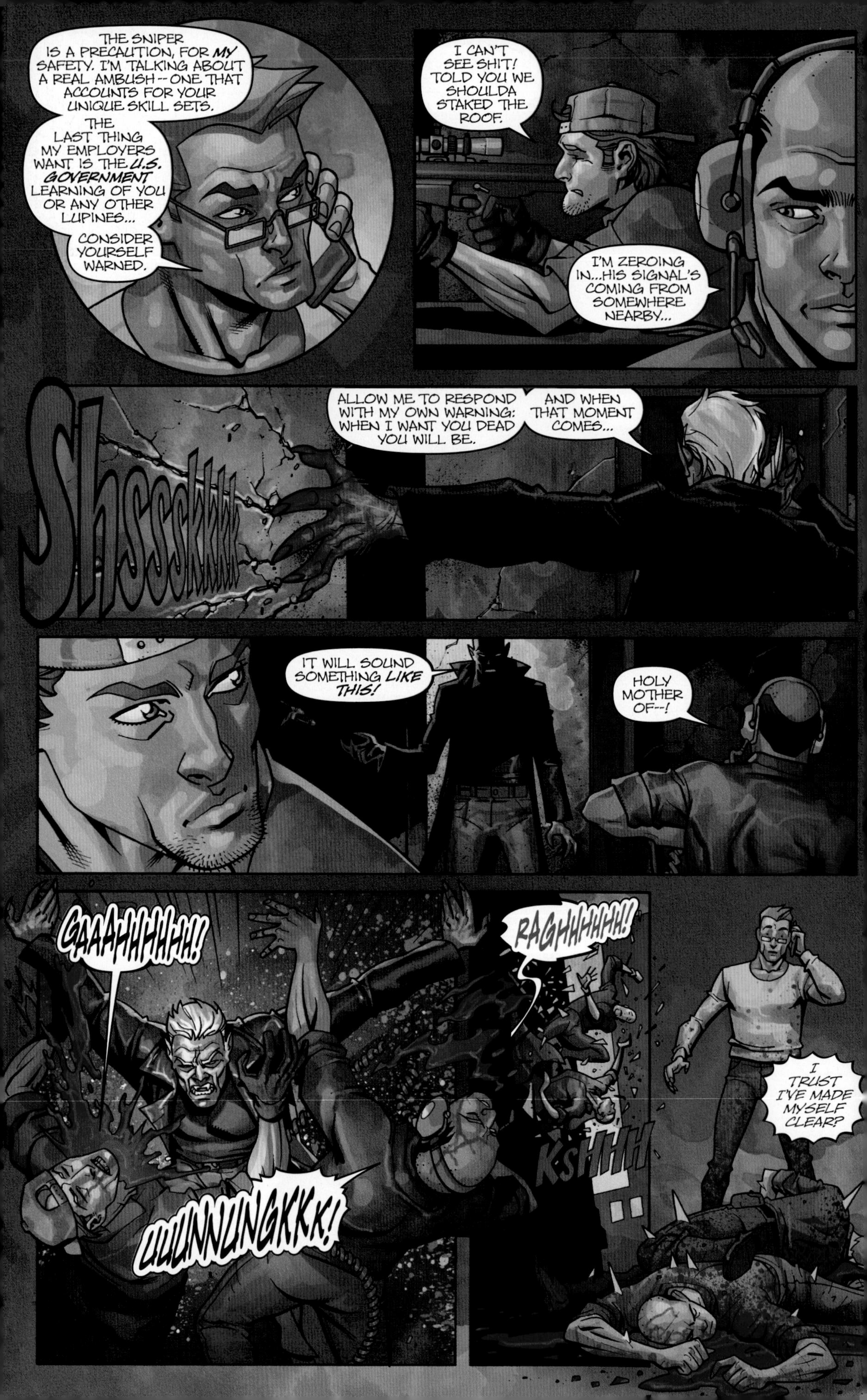
THE SNIPER IS A PRECAUTION, FOR MY SAFETY. I'M TALKING ABOUT A REAL AMBUSH -- ONE THAT ACCOUNTS FOR YOUR UNIQUE SKILL SETS.
THE LAST THING MY EMPLOYERS WANT IS THE U.S. GOVERNMENT LEARNING OF YOU OR ANY OTHER LUPINES...
CONSIDER YOURSELF WARNED.
I CAN'T SEE SHIT! TOLD YOU WE SHOULDA STAKED THE ROOF.
I'M ZEROING IN...HIS SIGNAL'S COMING FROM SOMEWHERE NEARBY...
Shssskkkk
ALLOW ME TO RESPOND WITH MY OWN WARNING: WHEN I WANT YOU DEAD YOU WILL BE.
AND WHEN THAT MOMENT COMES...
IT WILL SOUND SOMETHING LIKE THIS!
HOLY MOTHER OF--!
GAAAHHHHH!
RAGHHHHHH!
KSHHH
UUUNNUNGKKK!
I TRUST I'VE MADE MYSELF CLEAR?

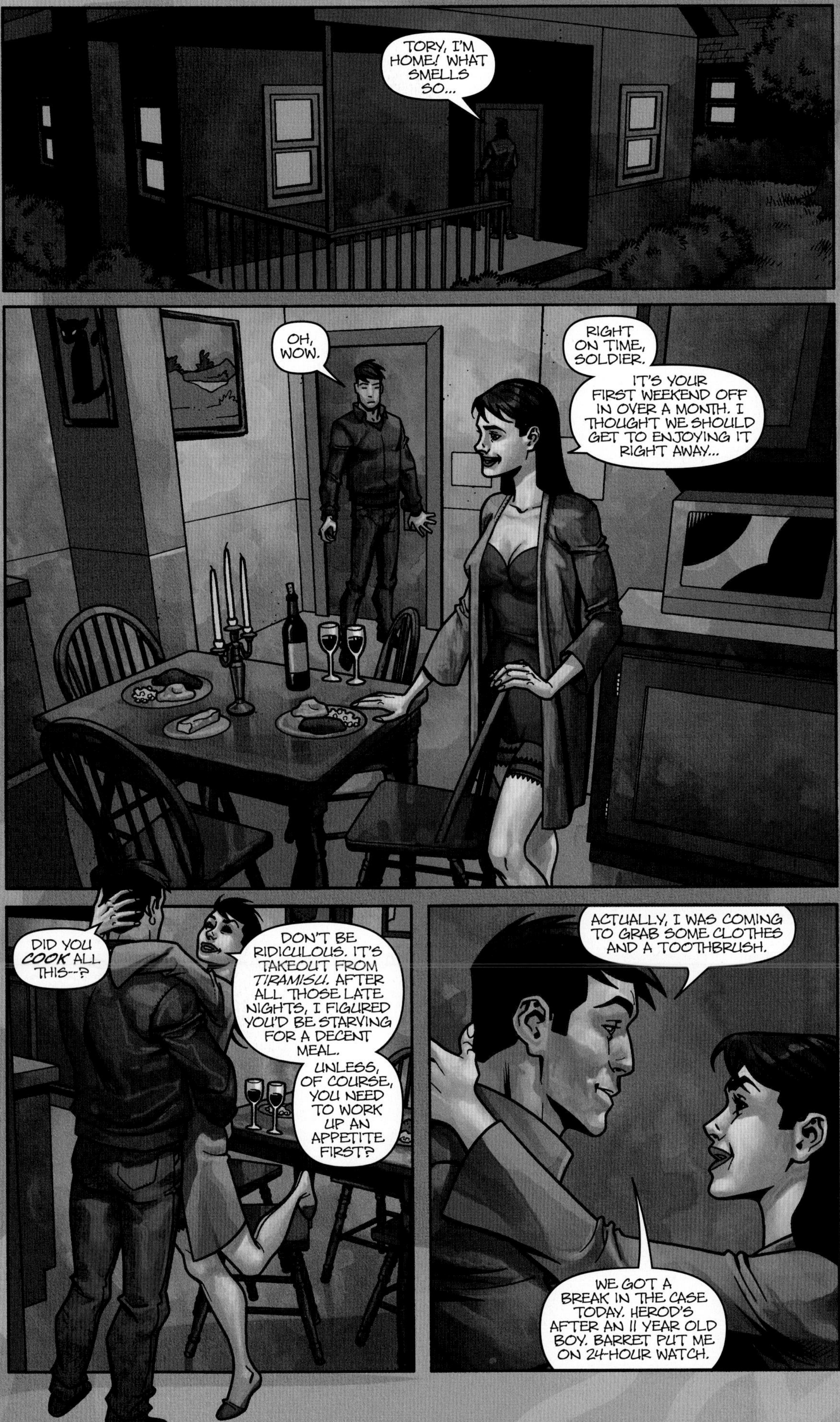
TORY, I'M HOME! WHAT SMELLS SO...
OH, WOW.
RIGHT ON TIME, SOLDIER.
IT'S YOUR FIRST WEEKEND OFF IN OVER A MONTH. I THOUGHT WE SHOULD GET TO ENJOYING IT RIGHT AWAY...
DID YOU *COOK* ALL THIS--?
DON'T BE RIDICULOUS. IT'S TAKEOUT FROM *TIRAMISU*. AFTER ALL THOSE LATE NIGHTS, I FIGURED YOU'D BE STARVING FOR A DECENT MEAL.
UNLESS, OF COURSE, YOU NEED TO WORK UP AN APPETITE FIRST?
ACTUALLY, I WAS COMING TO GRAB SOME CLOTHES AND A TOOTHBRUSH.
WE GOT A BREAK IN THE CASE TODAY. HEROD'S AFTER AN 11 YEAR OLD BOY. BARRET PUT ME ON 24-HOUR WATCH.

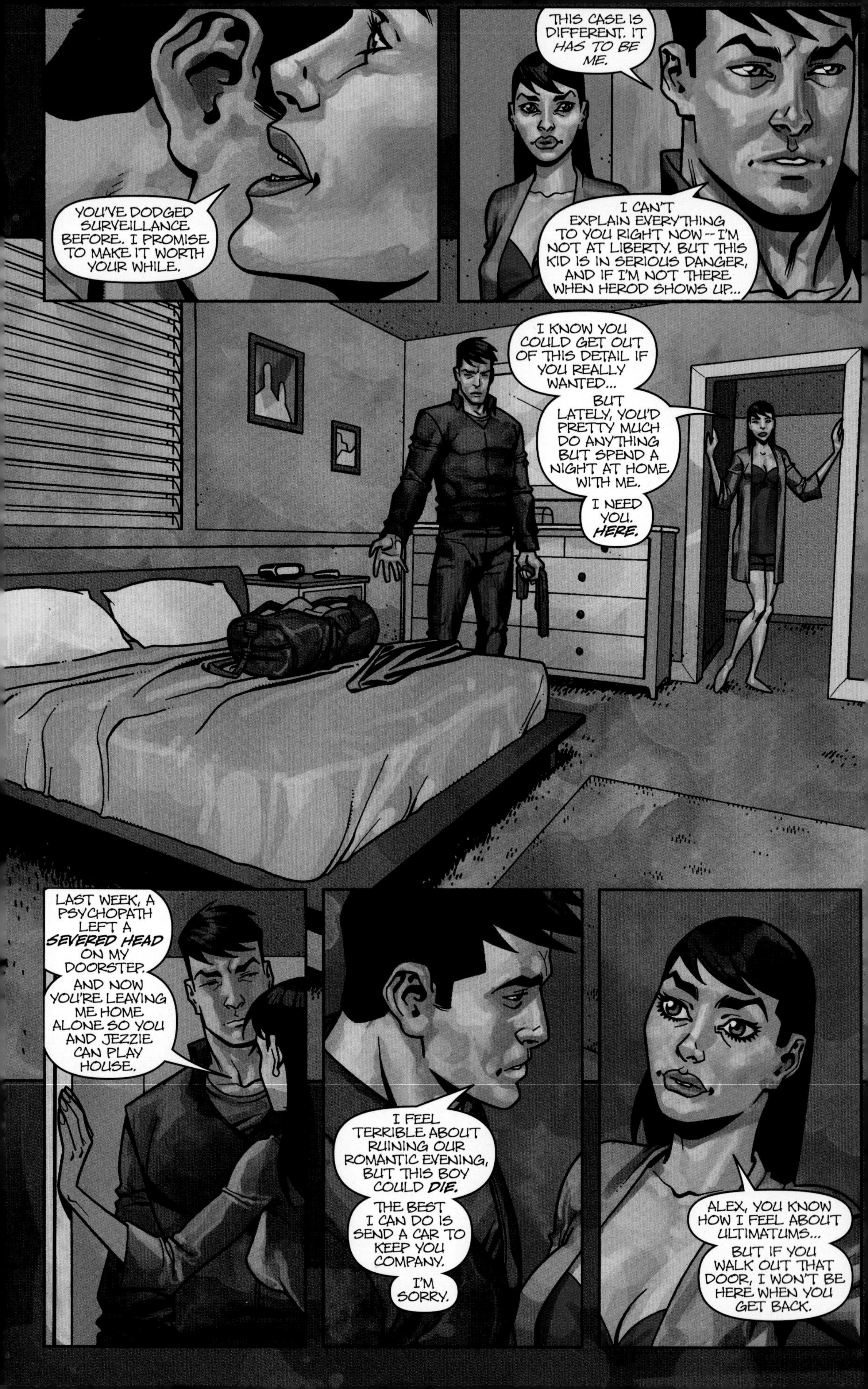
YOU'VE DODGED SURVEILLANCE BEFORE. I PROMISE TO MAKE IT WORTH YOUR WHILE.
THIS CASE IS DIFFERENT. IT HAS TO BE ME.
I CAN'T EXPLAIN EVERYTHING TO YOU RIGHT NOW -- I'M NOT AT LIBERTY. BUT THIS KID IS IN SERIOUS DANGER, AND IF I'M NOT THERE WHEN HEROD SHOWS UP...
I KNOW YOU COULD GET OUT OF THIS DETAIL IF YOU REALLY WANTED...
BUT LATELY, YOU'D PRETTY MUCH DO ANYTHING BUT SPEND A NIGHT AT HOME WITH ME.
I NEED YOU. HERE.
LAST WEEK, A PSYCHOPATH LEFT A SEVERED HEAD ON MY DOORSTEP.
AND NOW YOU'RE LEAVING ME HOME ALONE SO YOU AND JEZZIE CAN PLAY HOUSE.
I FEEL TERRIBLE ABOUT RUINING OUR ROMANTIC EVENING, BUT THIS BOY COULD DIE.
THE BEST I CAN DO IS SEND A CAR TO KEEP YOU COMPANY.
I'M SORRY.
ALEX, YOU KNOW HOW I FEEL ABOUT ULTIMATUMS...
BUT IF YOU WALK OUT THAT DOOR, I WON'T BE HERE WHEN YOU GET BACK.

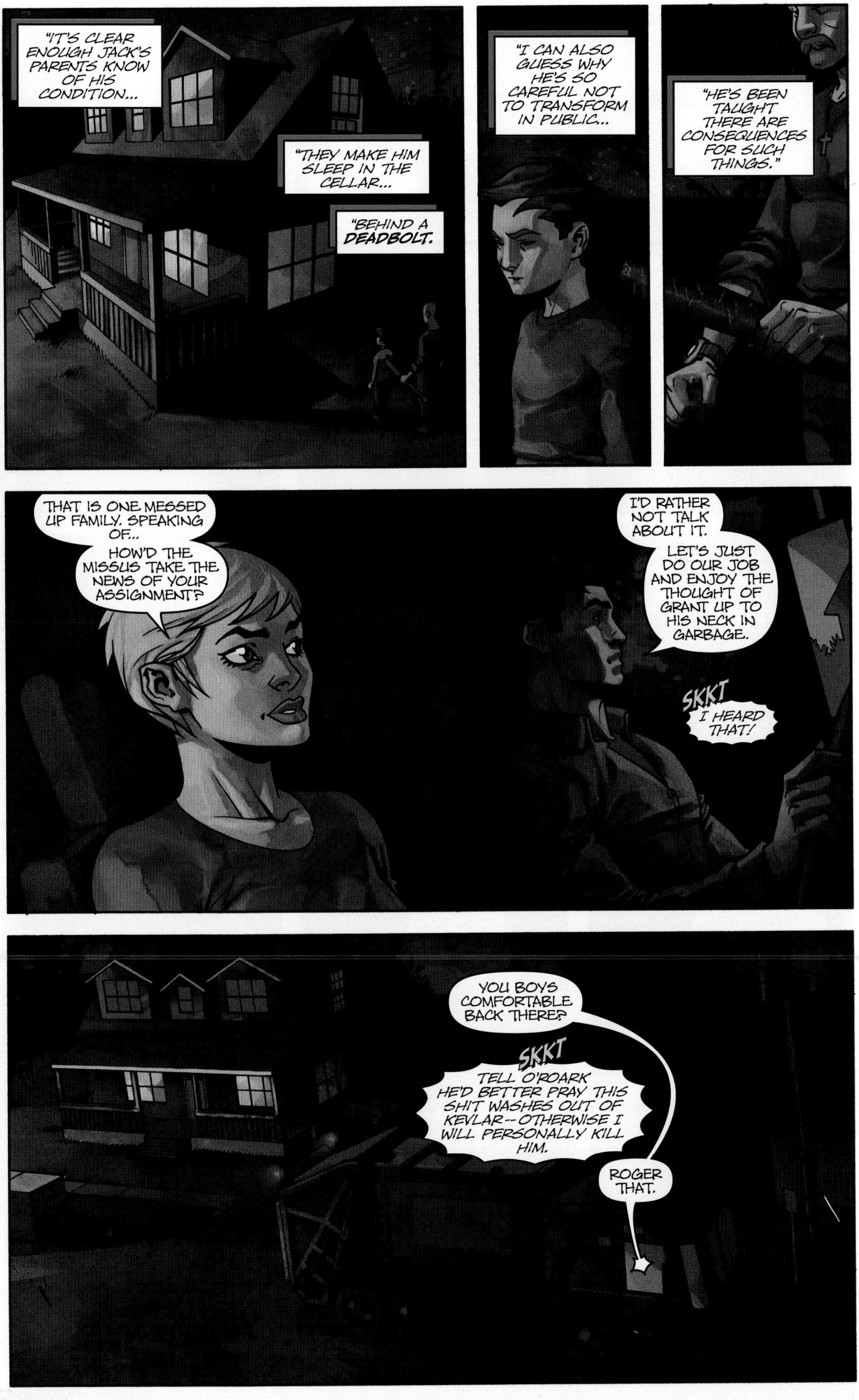
"IT'S CLEAR ENOUGH JACK'S PARENTS KNOW OF HIS CONDITION...
"THEY MAKE HIM SLEEP IN THE CELLAR...
"BEHIND A DEADBOLT.
"I CAN ALSO GUESS WHY HE'S SO CAREFUL NOT TO TRANSFORM IN PUBLIC...
"HE'S BEEN TAUGHT THERE ARE CONSEQUENCES FOR SUCH THINGS."
THAT IS ONE MESSED UP FAMILY. SPEAKING OF... HOW'D THE MISSUS TAKE THE NEWS OF YOUR ASSIGNMENT?
I'D RATHER NOT TALK ABOUT IT. LET'S JUST DO OUR JOB AND ENJOY THE THOUGHT OF GRANT UP TO HIS NECK IN GARBAGE.
SKKT
I HEARD THAT!
YOU BOYS COMFORTABLE BACK THERE?
SKKT
TELL O'ROARK HE'D BETTER PRAY THIS SH!T WASHES OUT OF KEVLAR--OTHERWISE I WILL PERSONALLY KILL HIM.
ROGER THAT.

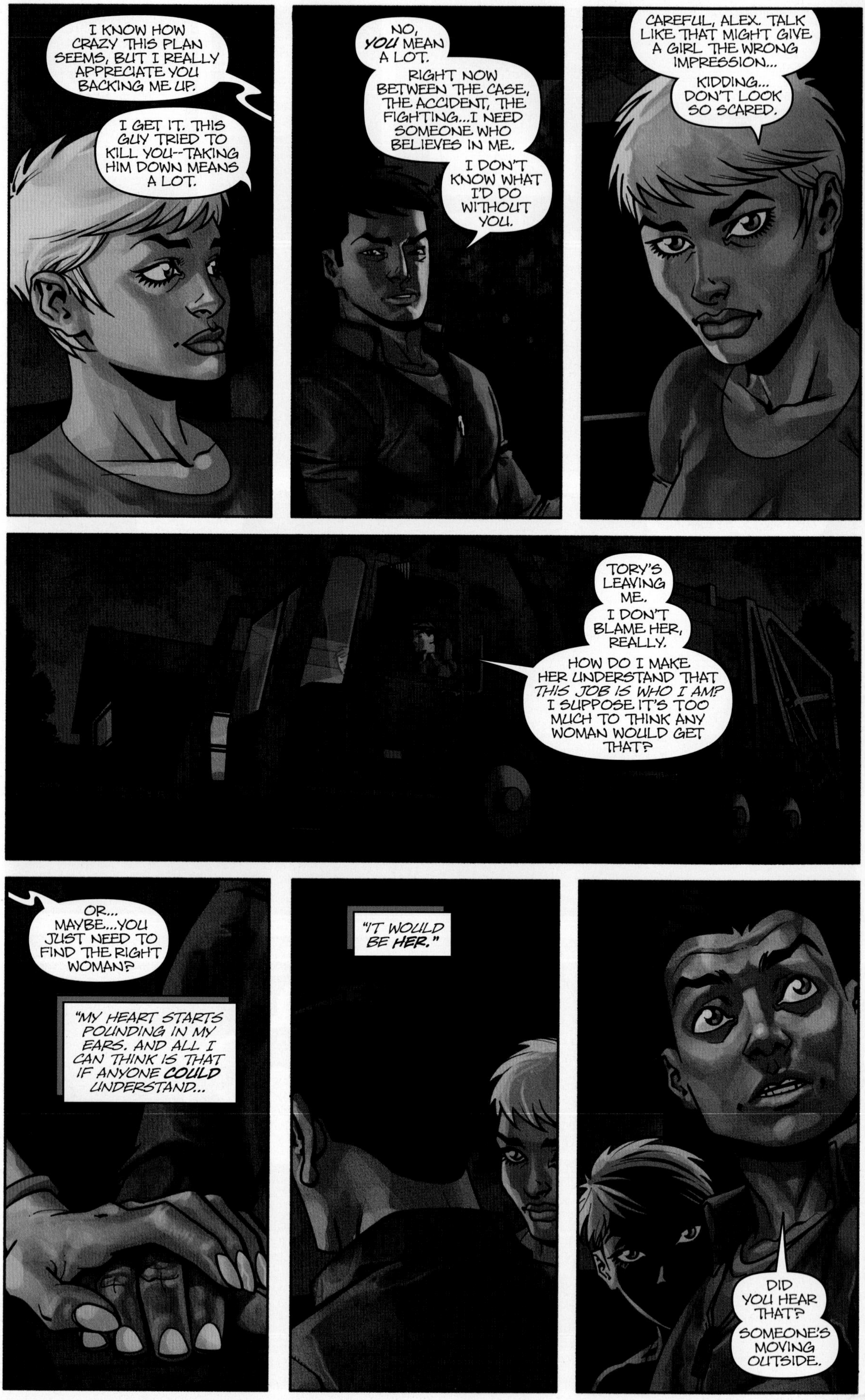
I KNOW HOW CRAZY THIS PLAN SEEMS, BUT I REALLY APPRECIATE YOU BACKING ME UP.
I GET IT. THIS GUY TRIED TO KILL YOU--TAKING HIM DOWN MEANS A LOT.
NO, YOU MEAN A LOT.
RIGHT NOW BETWEEN THE CASE, THE ACCIDENT, THE FIGHTING...I NEED SOMEONE WHO BELIEVES IN ME.
I DON'T KNOW WHAT I'D DO WITHOUT YOU.
CAREFUL, ALEX. TALK LIKE THAT MIGHT GIVE A GIRL THE WRONG IMPRESSION...
KIDDING... DON'T LOOK SO SCARED.
TORY'S LEAVING ME.
I DON'T BLAME HER, REALLY.
HOW DO I MAKE HER UNDERSTAND THAT THIS JOB IS WHO I AM? I SUPPOSE IT'S TOO MUCH TO THINK ANY WOMAN WOULD GET THAT?
OR... MAYBE...YOU JUST NEED TO FIND THE RIGHT WOMAN?
"MY HEART STARTS POUNDING IN MY EARS. AND ALL I CAN THINK IS THAT IF ANYONE COULD UNDERSTAND...
"IT WOULD BE HER."
DID YOU HEAR THAT?
SOMEONE'S MOVING OUTSIDE.

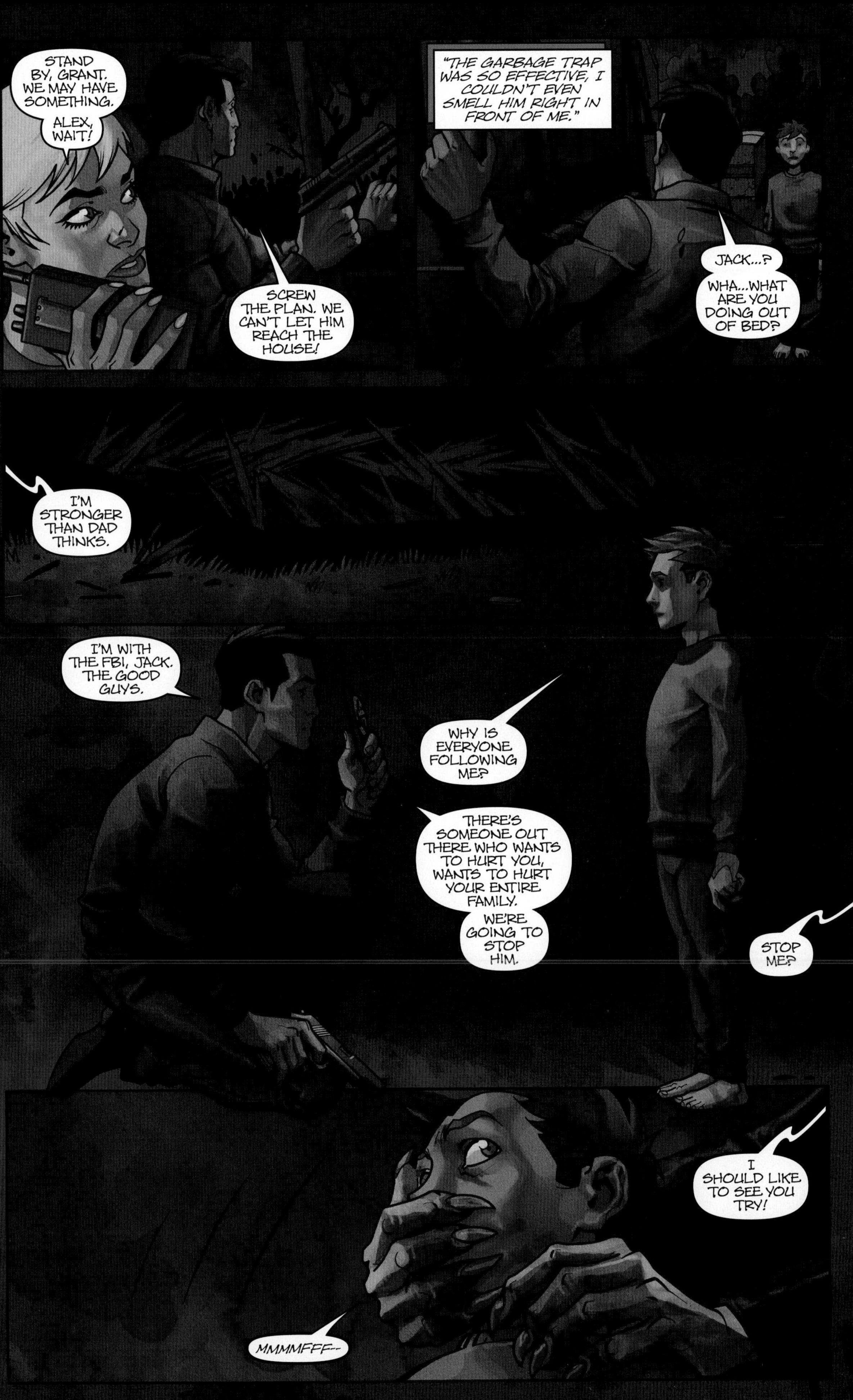
STAND BY, GRANT. WE MAY HAVE SOMETHING.
ALEX, WAIT!
SCREW THE PLAN. WE CAN'T LET HIM REACH THE HOUSE!
"THE GARBAGE TRAP WAS SO EFFECTIVE, I COULDN'T EVEN SMELL HIM RIGHT IN FRONT OF ME."
JACK...?
WHA...WHAT ARE YOU DOING OUT OF BED?
I'M STRONGER THAN DAD THINKS.
I'M WITH THE FBI, JACK. THE GOOD GUYS.
WHY IS EVERYONE FOLLOWING ME?
THERE'S SOMEONE OUT THERE WHO WANTS TO HURT YOU, WANTS TO HURT YOUR ENTIRE FAMILY.
WE'RE GOING TO STOP HIM.
STOP ME?
I SHOULD LIKE TO SEE YOU TRY!
MMMMFFF--

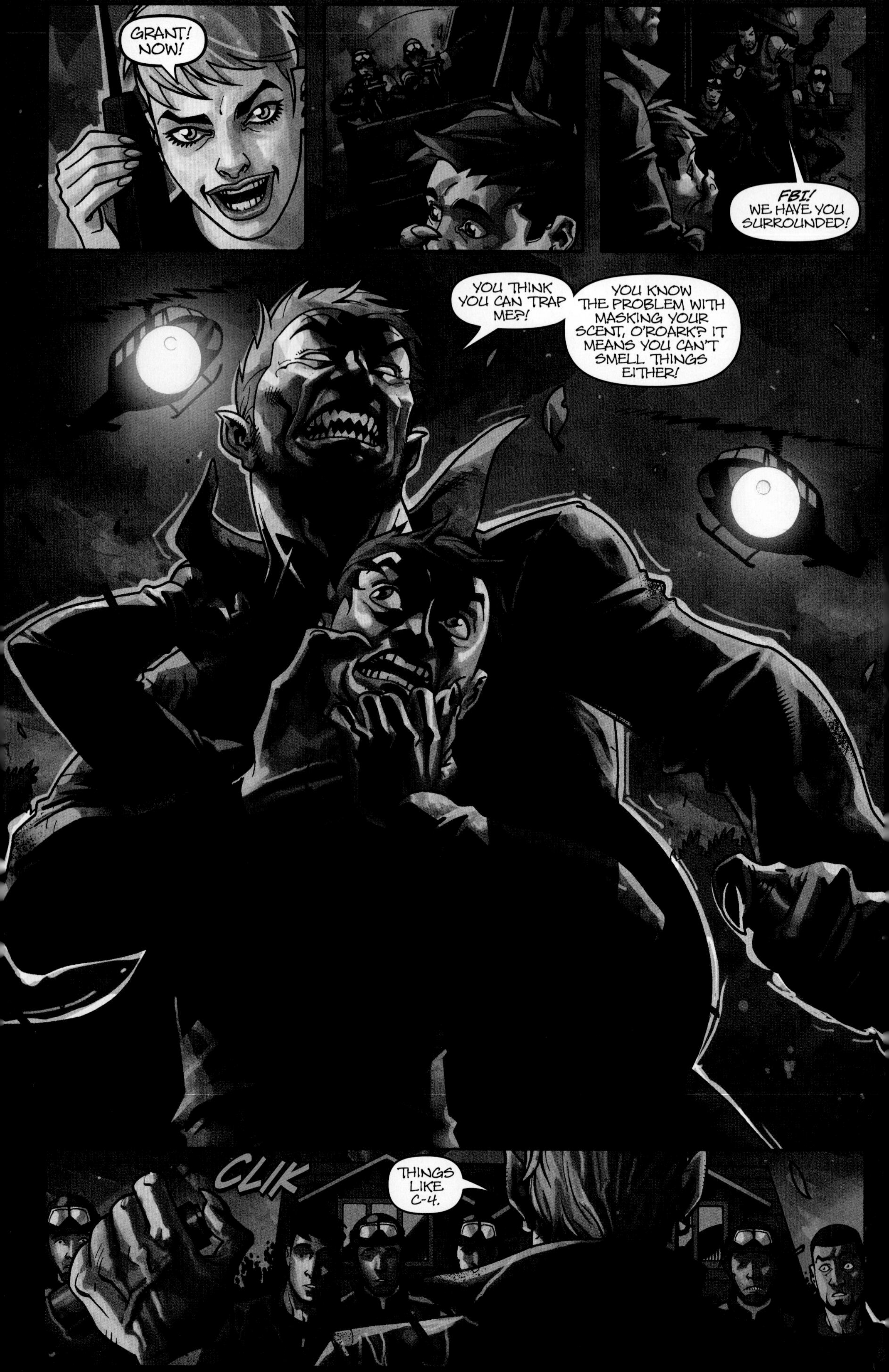
GRANT! NOW!
FBI! WE HAVE YOU SURROUNDED!
YOU THINK YOU CAN TRAP ME?!
YOU KNOW THE PROBLEM WITH MASKING YOUR SCENT, O'ROARK? IT MEANS YOU CAN'T SMELL THINGS EITHER!
CLIK
THINGS LIKE C-4.

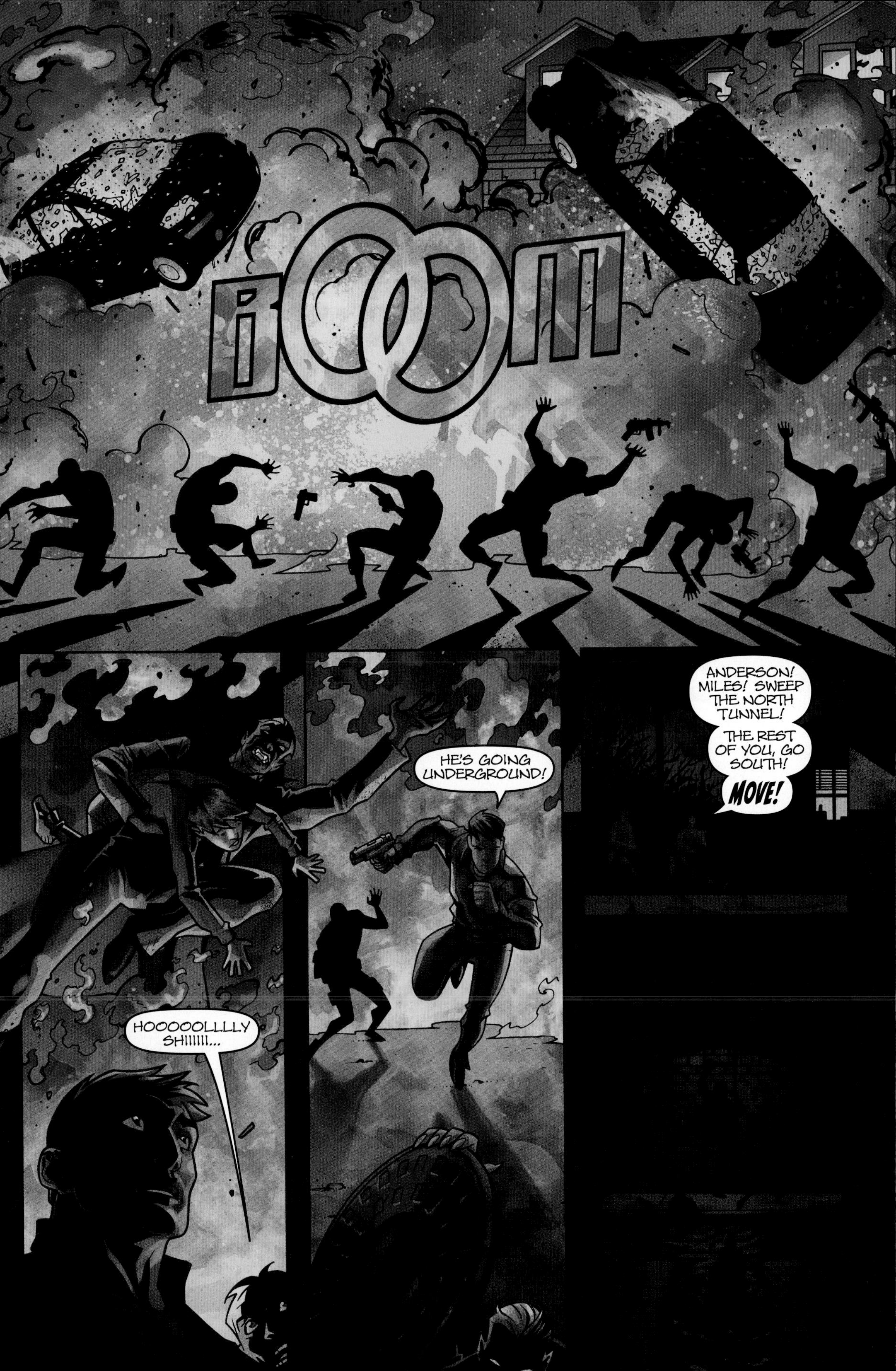
BOOM
HOOOOOLLLLLY SHIIIIII...
HE'S GOING UNDERGROUND!
ANDERSON! MILES! SWEEP THE NORTH TUNNEL!
THE REST OF YOU, GO SOUTH!
MOVE!

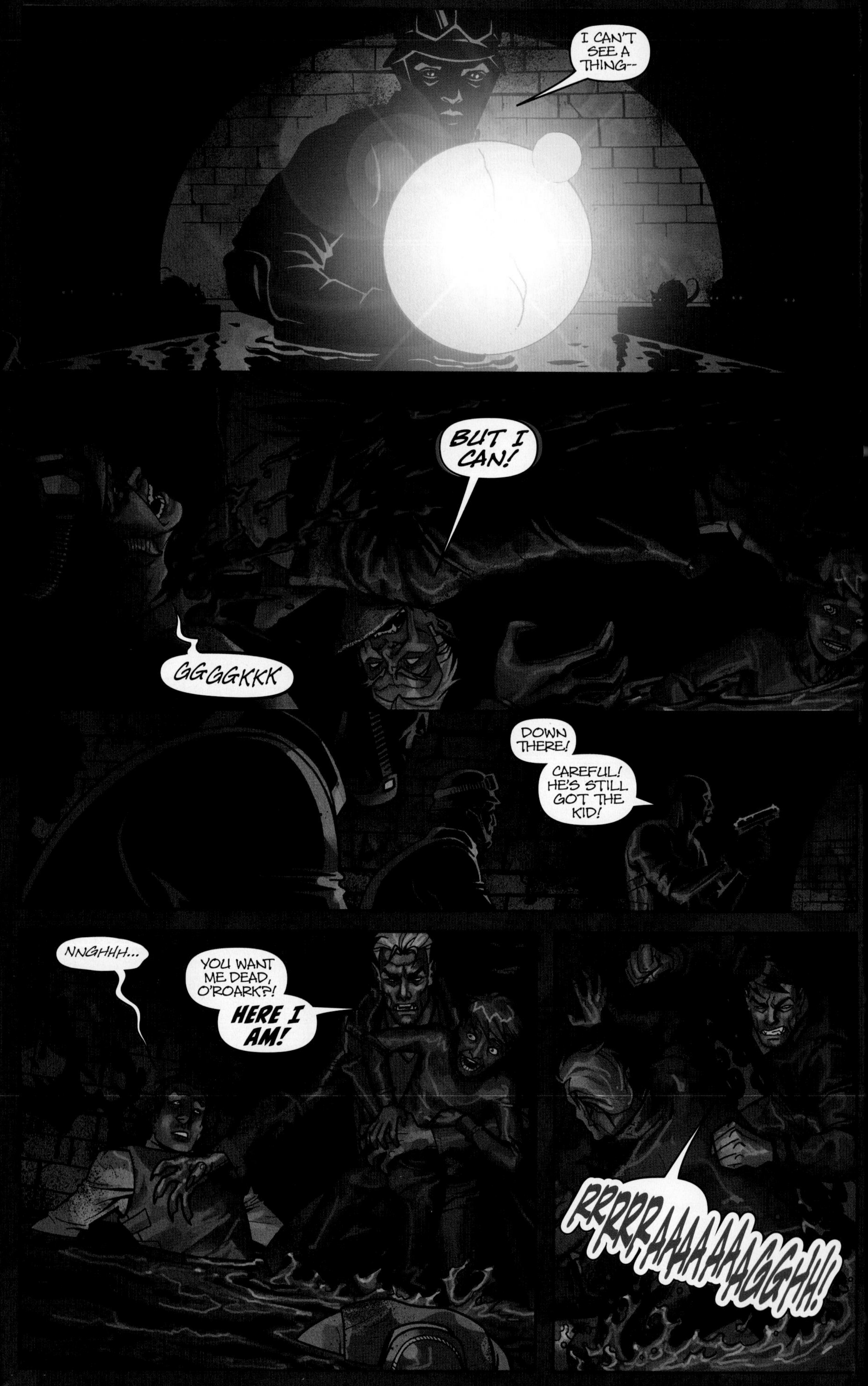
I CAN'T SEE A THING--
BUT I CAN!
GGGGKKK
DOWN THERE!
CAREFUL! HE'S STILL GOT THE KID!
NNGHHH...
YOU WANT ME DEAD, O'ROARK?!
HERE I AM!
RRRRRAAAAAAAAGGGH!!

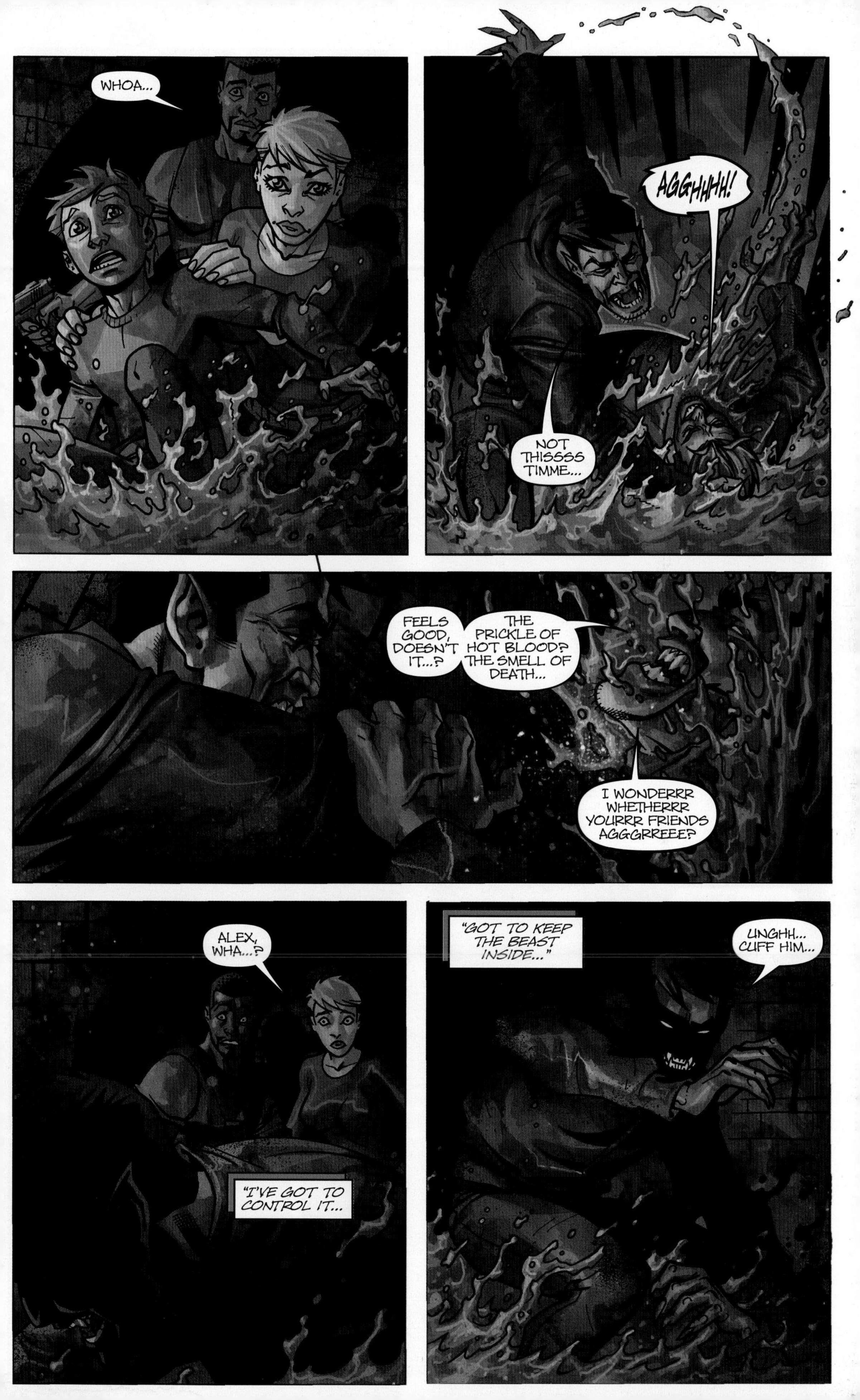
WHOA...
AGGHHHH!
NOT THISSSS TIMME...
FEELS GOOD, DOESN'T IT...?
THE PRICKLE OF HOT BLOOD? THE SMELL OF DEATH...
I WONDERRR WHETHERRR YOURRR FRIENDS AGGGRREEE?
ALEX, WHA...?
"I'VE GOT TO CONTROL IT...
"GOT TO KEEP THE BEAST INSIDE..."
UNGHH... CUFF HIM...

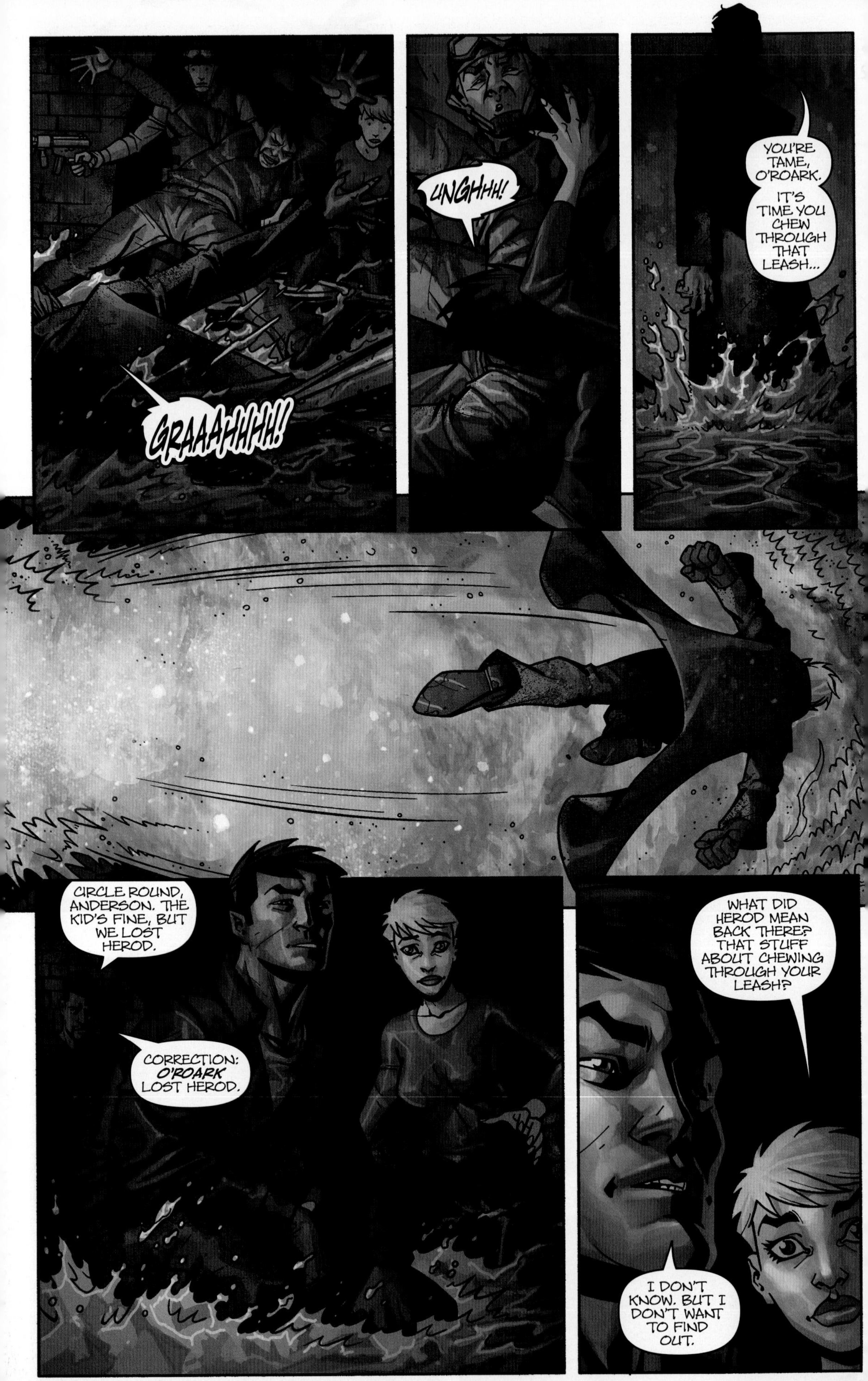
GRAAAHHHH!
UNGHHH!
YOU'RE TAME, O'ROARK.
IT'S TIME YOU CHEW THROUGH THAT LEASH...
CIRCLE ROUND, ANDERSON. THE KID'S FINE, BUT WE LOST HEROD.
CORRECTION: O'ROARK LOST HEROD.
WHAT DID HEROD MEAN BACK THERE? THAT STUFF ABOUT CHEWING THROUGH YOUR LEASH?
I DON'T KNOW. BUT I DON'T WANT TO FIND OUT.

YOU'VE REACHED SPECIAL AGENT ALEX O'ROARK. LEAVE A MESSAGE AND I'LL GET BACK TO YOU BY THE END OF THE FOLLOWING BUSINESS DAY.

BEEP

IT'S ME.

I KNOW I'M SUPPOSED TO BE MAD AT YOU. AND I STILL AM. BUT I WANTED TO LET YOU KNOW THE PATROL CAR CAME.

...THANKS FOR NOT LEAVING ME *COMPLETELY* ALONE.

WE'LL TALK WHEN YOU GET BACK.

TIT-FOR-TAT...

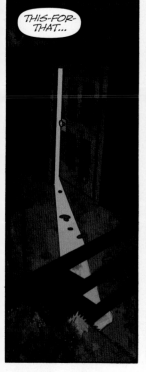

THIS-FOR-THAT...

YOU TAKE MY DOG...

WHA...?

I'LL TAKE YOUR CAT!

NO, STAY BACK...

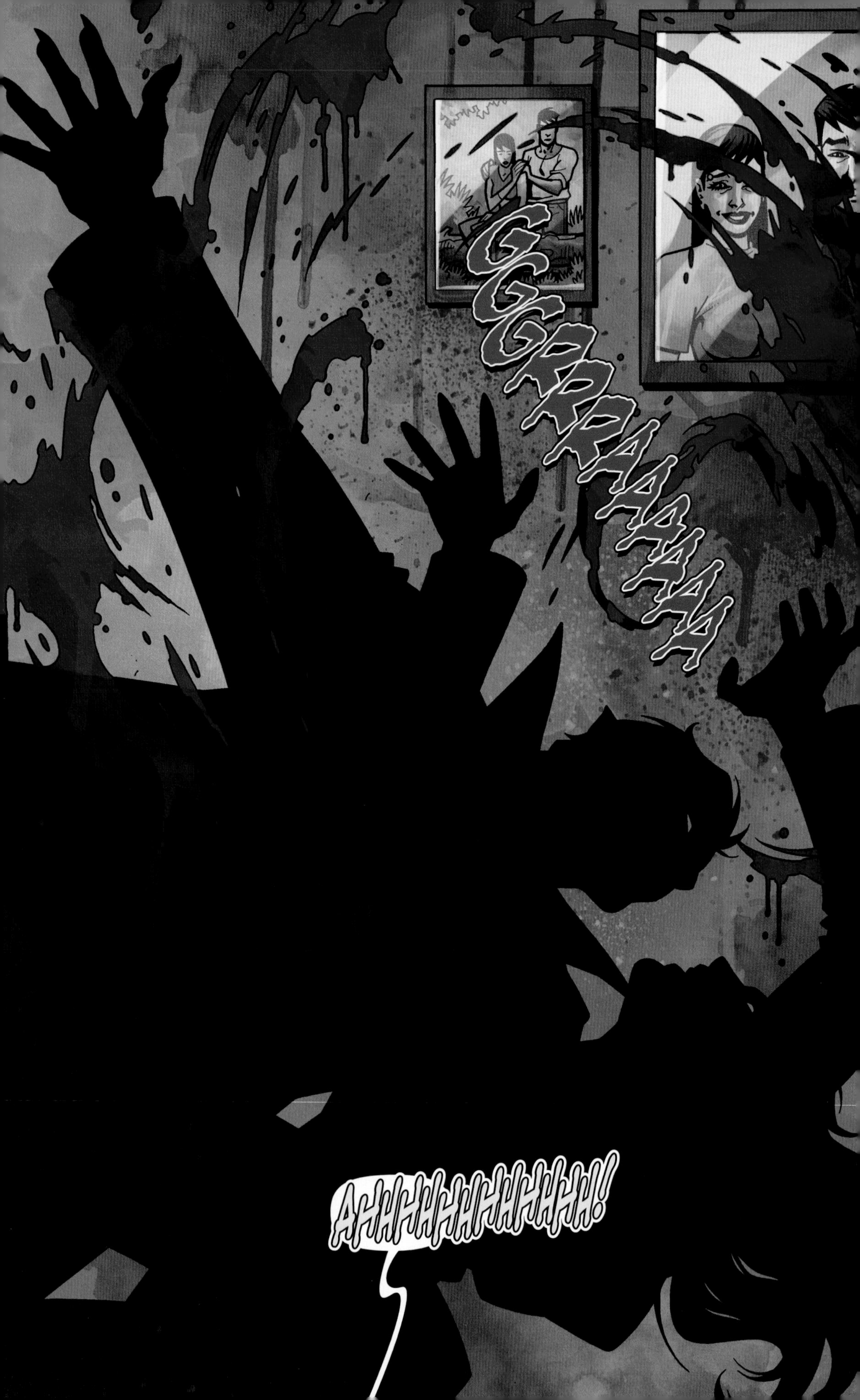
GGRRAAAAAA
AHHHHHHHHHHH!

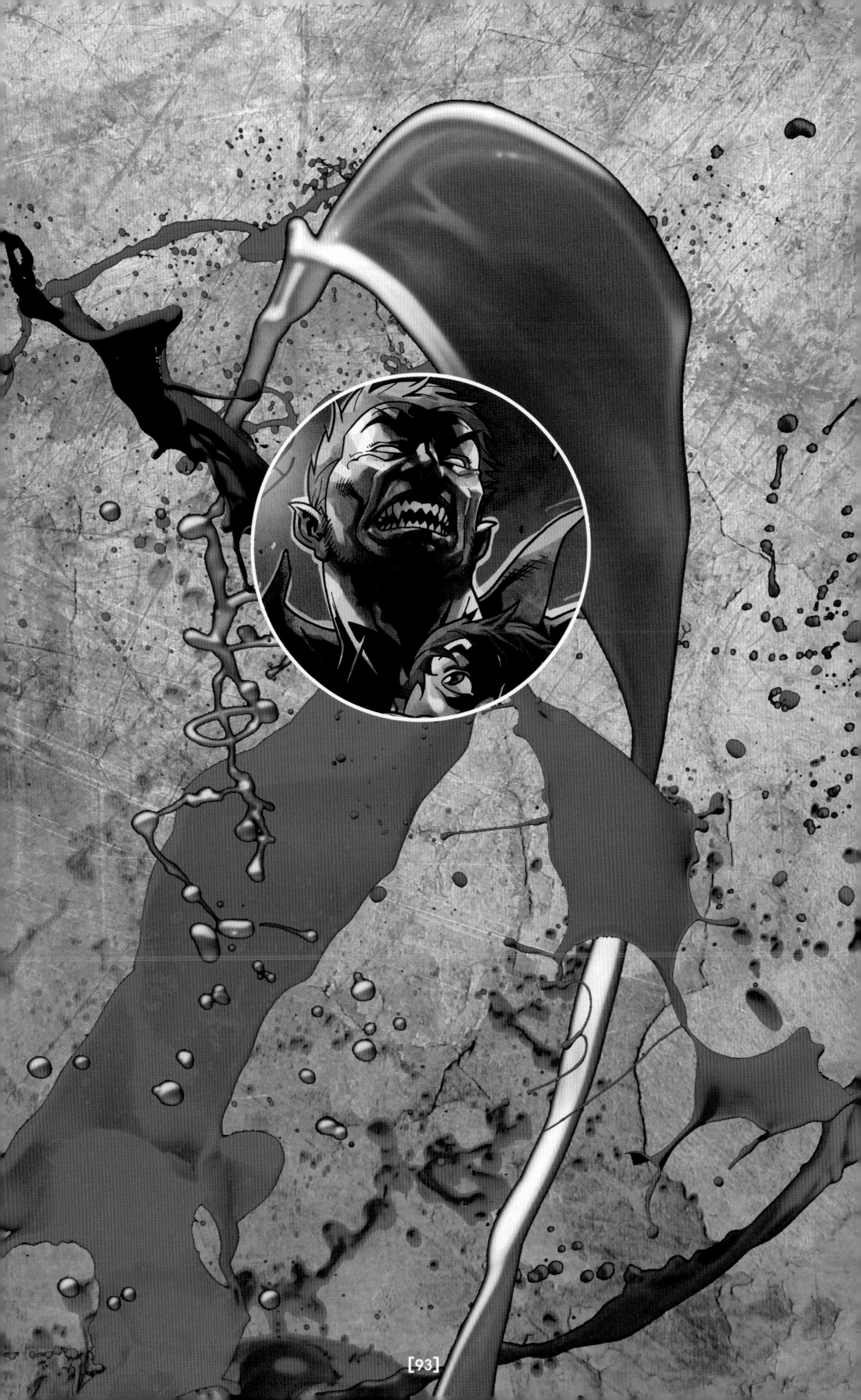

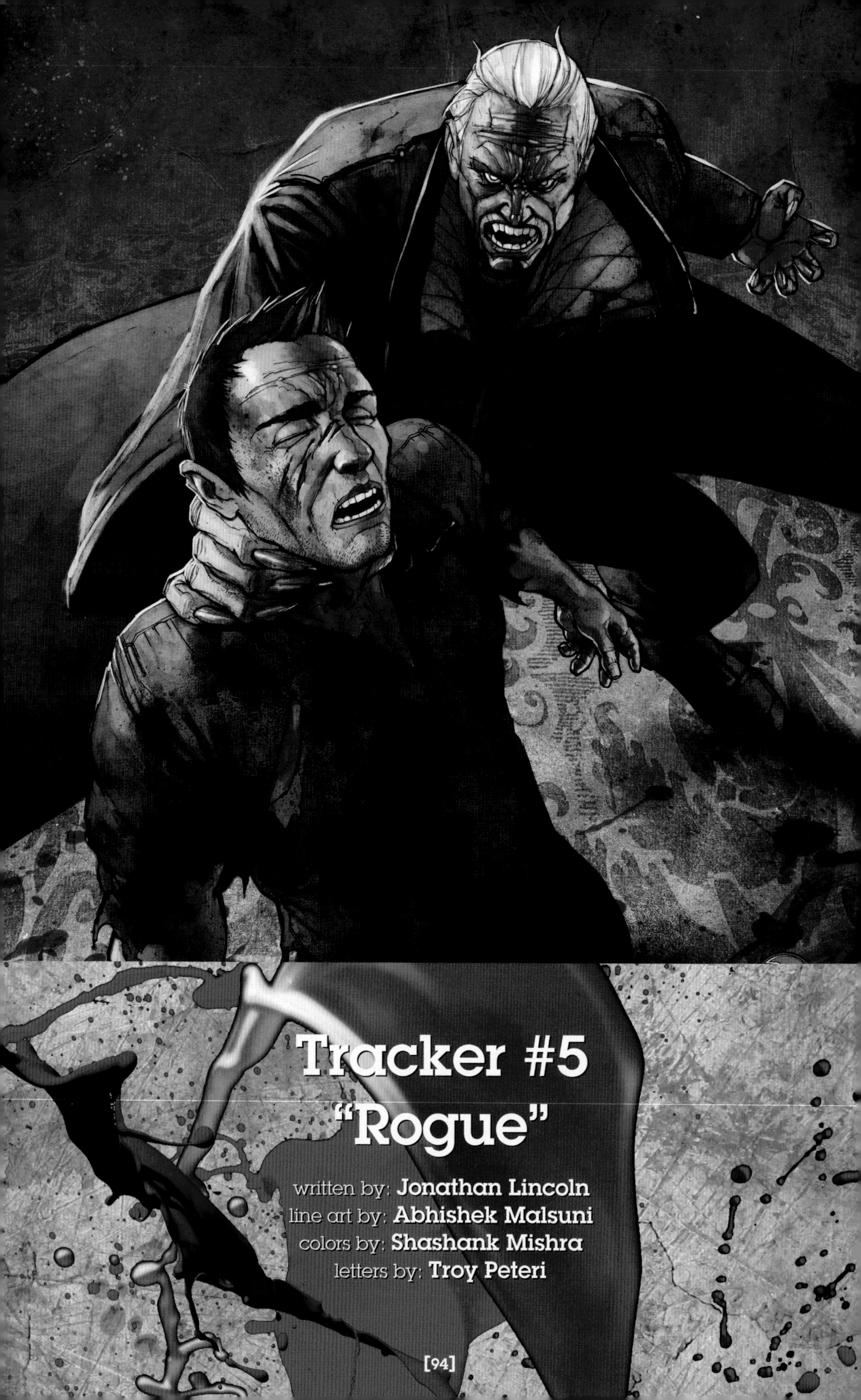

Tracker #5
"Rogue"

written by: **Jonathan Lincoln**
line art by: **Abhishek Malsuni**
colors by: **Shashank Mishra**
letters by: **Troy Peteri**

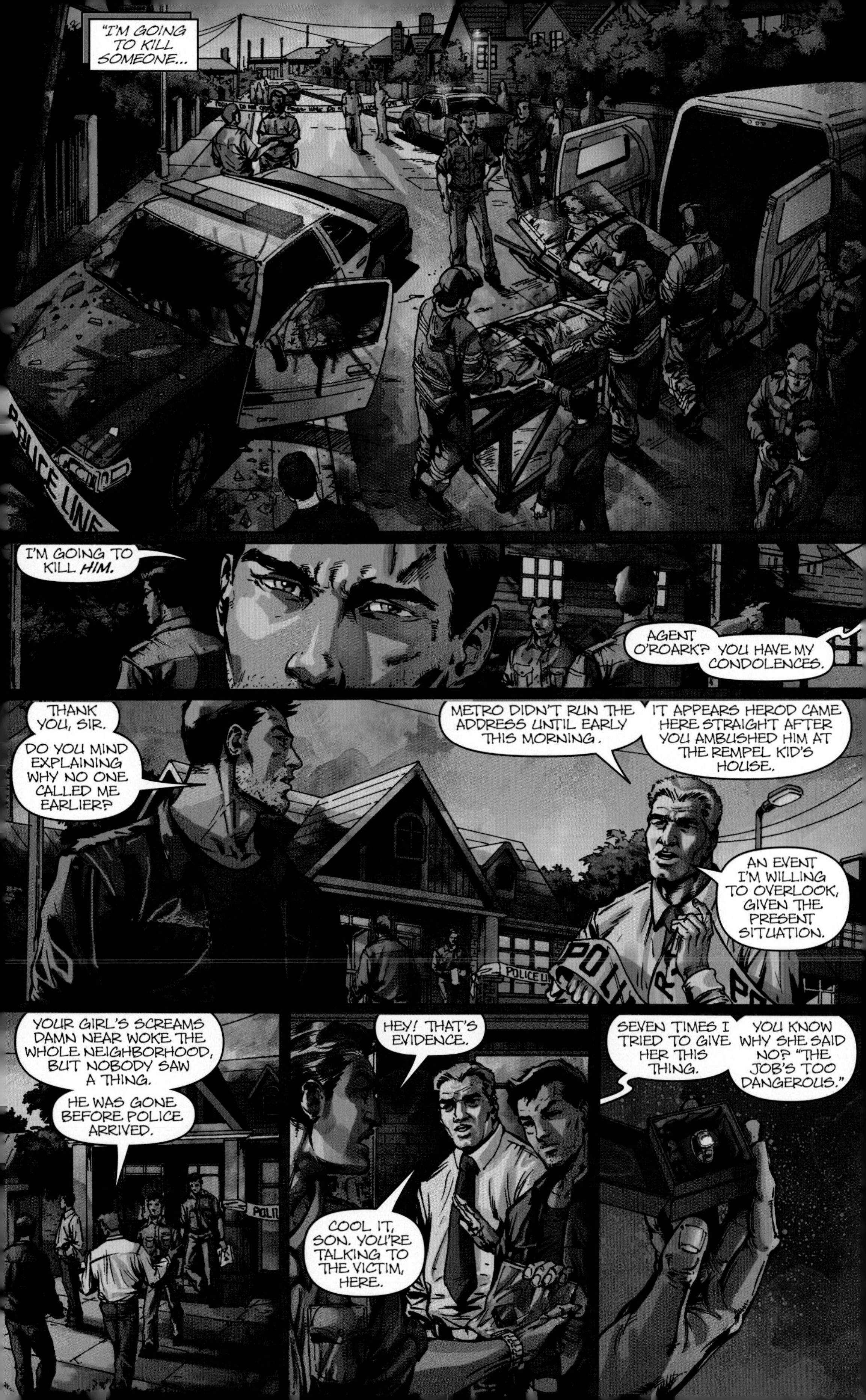
"I'M GOING TO KILL SOMEONE...
I'M GOING TO KILL *HIM.*
AGENT O'ROARK? YOU HAVE MY CONDOLENCES.
THANK YOU, SIR.
DO YOU MIND EXPLAINING WHY NO ONE CALLED ME EARLIER?
METRO DIDN'T RUN THE ADDRESS UNTIL EARLY THIS MORNING.
IT APPEARS HEROD CAME HERE STRAIGHT AFTER YOU AMBUSHED HIM AT THE REMPEL KID'S HOUSE.
AN EVENT I'M WILLING TO OVERLOOK, GIVEN THE PRESENT SITUATION.
YOUR GIRL'S SCREAMS DAMN NEAR WOKE THE WHOLE NEIGHBORHOOD, BUT NOBODY SAW A THING.
HE WAS GONE BEFORE POLICE ARRIVED.
HEY! THAT'S EVIDENCE.
COOL IT, SON. YOU'RE TALKING TO THE VICTIM, HERE.
SEVEN TIMES I TRIED TO GIVE HER THIS THING.
YOU KNOW WHY SHE SAID NO? "THE JOB'S TOO DANGEROUS."

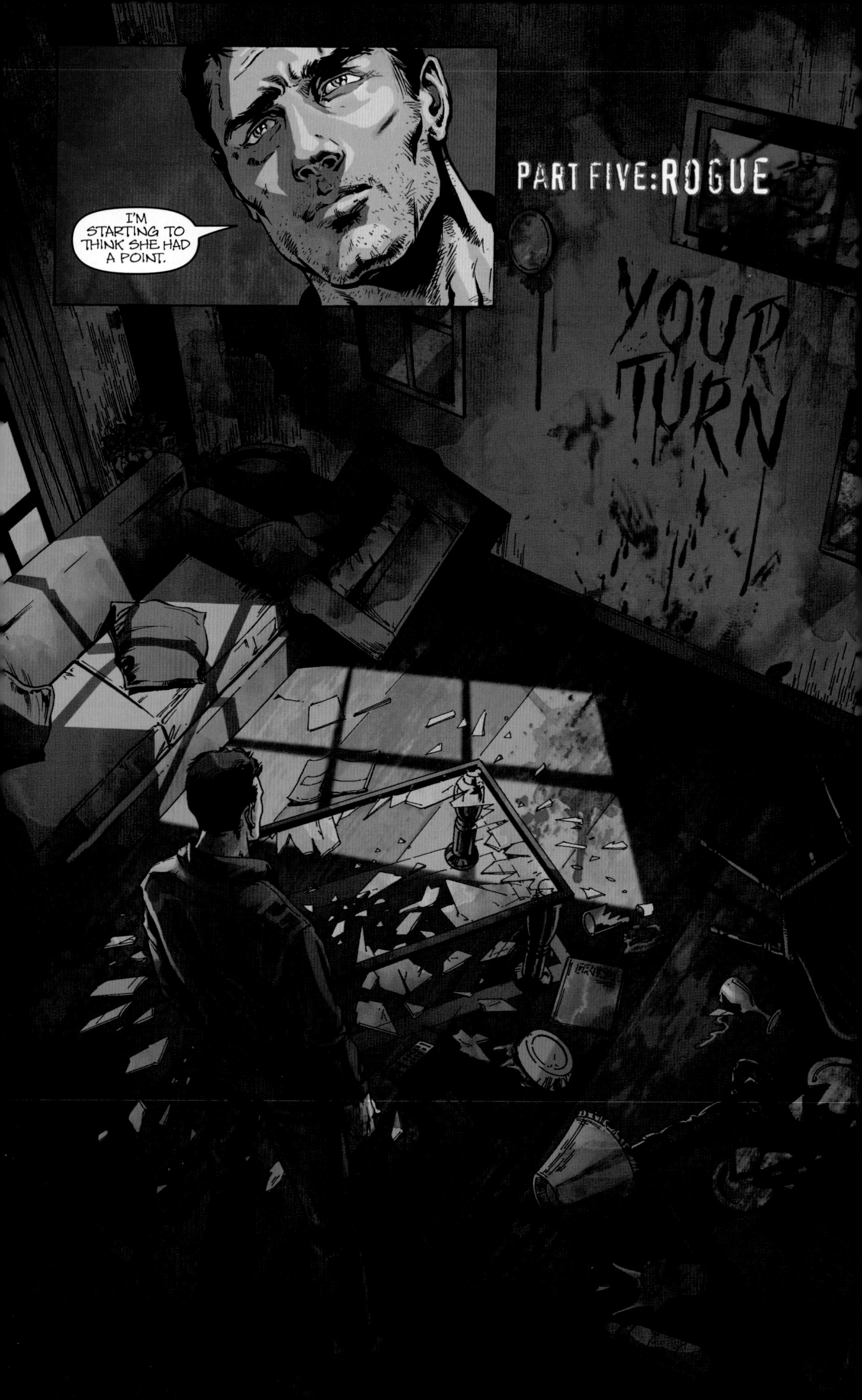
I'M STARTING TO THINK SHE HAD A POINT.
PART FIVE: ROGUE
YOUR TURN

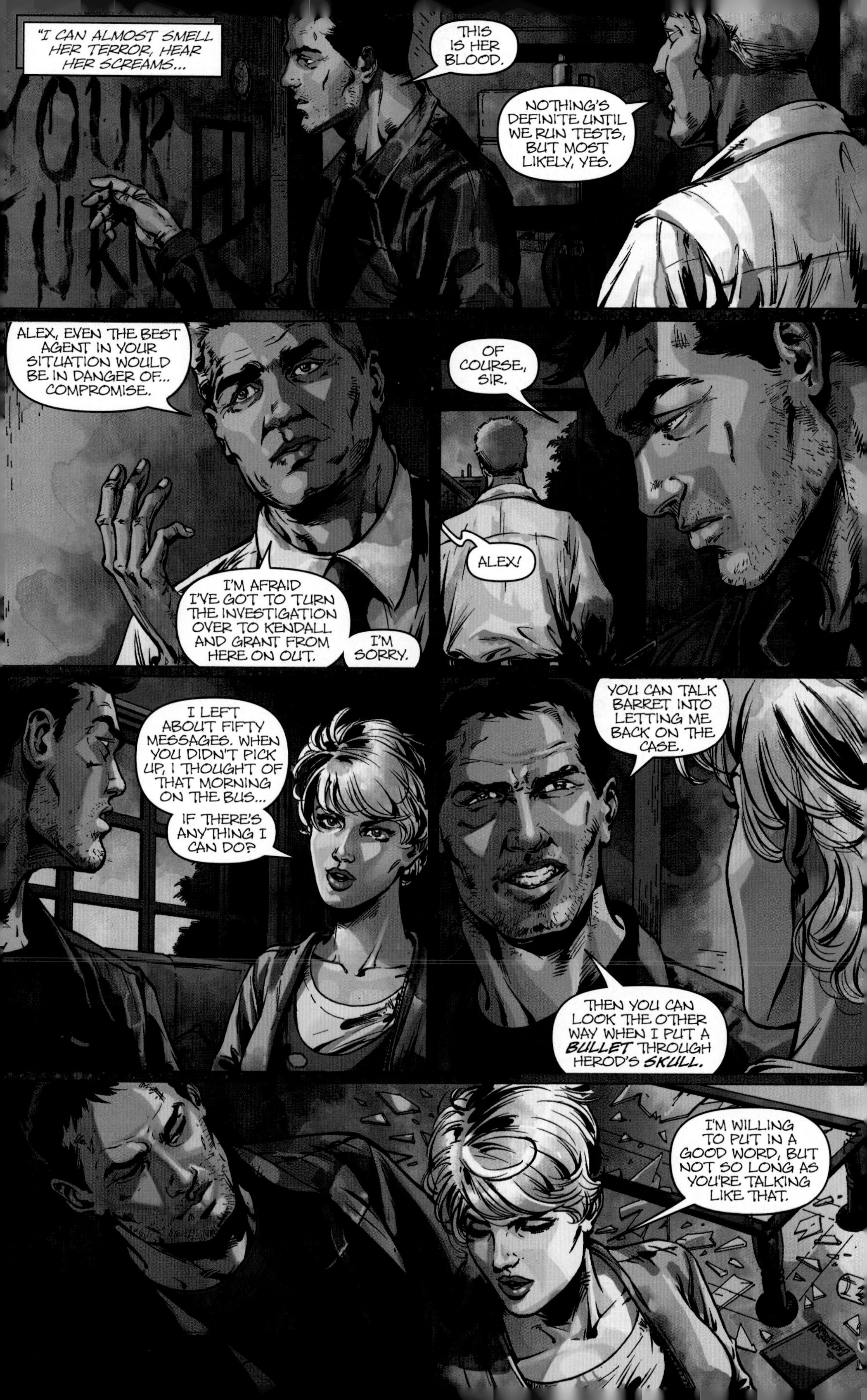
"I CAN ALMOST SMELL HER TERROR, HEAR HER SCREAMS...
THIS IS HER BLOOD.
NOTHING'S DEFINITE UNTIL WE RUN TESTS, BUT MOST LIKELY, YES.
ALEX, EVEN THE BEST AGENT IN YOUR SITUATION WOULD BE IN DANGER OF... COMPROMISE.
I'M AFRAID I'VE GOT TO TURN THE INVESTIGATION OVER TO KENDALL AND GRANT FROM HERE ON OUT.
I'M SORRY.
OF COURSE, SIR.
ALEX!
I LEFT ABOUT FIFTY MESSAGES. WHEN YOU DIDN'T PICK UP, I THOUGHT OF THAT MORNING ON THE BUS...
IF THERE'S ANYTHING I CAN DO?
YOU CAN TALK BARRET INTO LETTING ME BACK ON THE CASE.
THEN YOU CAN LOOK THE OTHER WAY WHEN I PUT A BULLET THROUGH HEROD'S SKULL.
I'M WILLING TO PUT IN A GOOD WORD, BUT NOT SO LONG AS YOU'RE TALKING LIKE THAT.

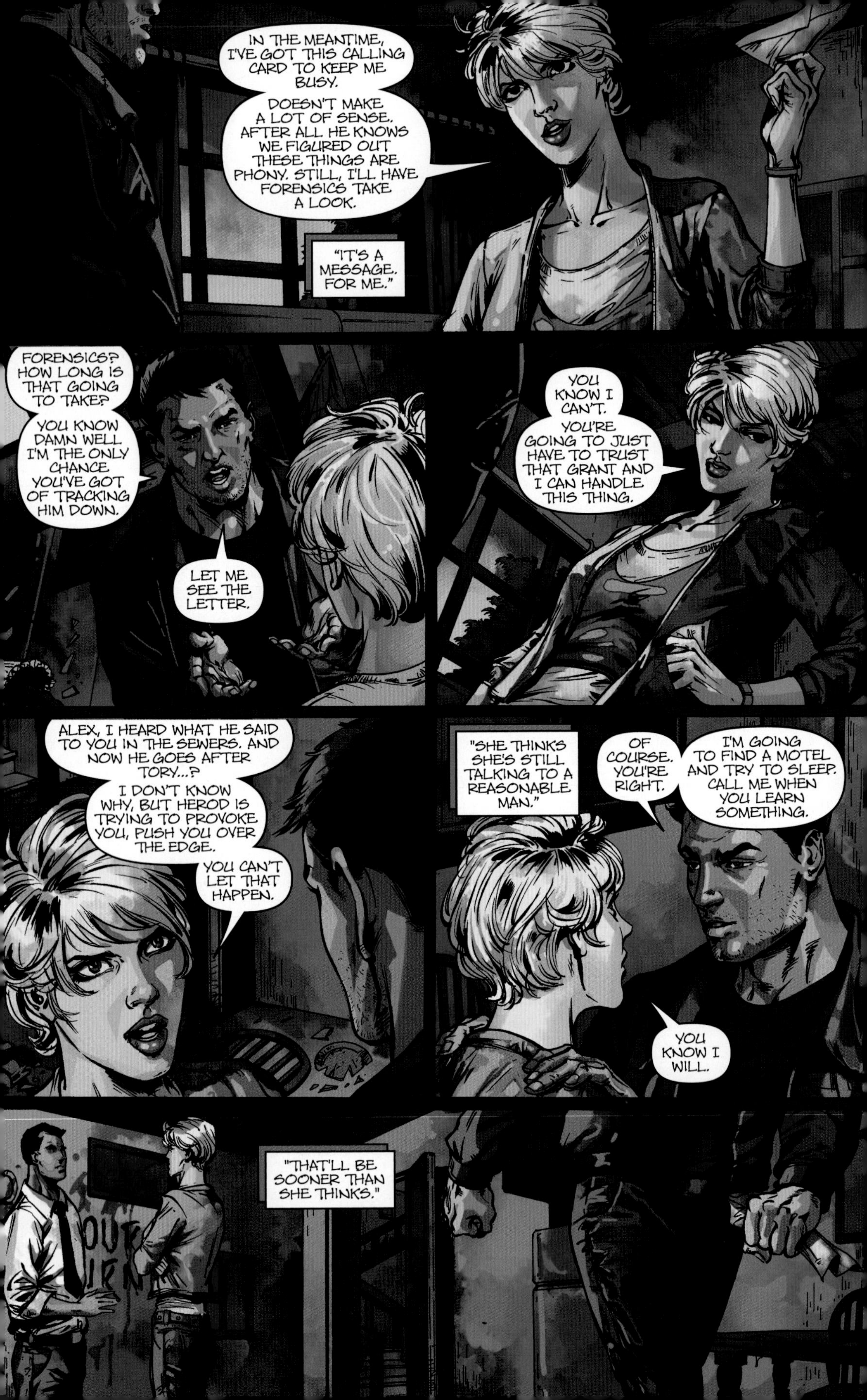
IN THE MEANTIME, I'VE GOT THIS CALLING CARD TO KEEP ME BUSY.
DOESN'T MAKE A LOT OF SENSE. AFTER ALL HE KNOWS WE FIGURED OUT THESE THINGS ARE PHONY. STILL, I'LL HAVE FORENSICS TAKE A LOOK.
"IT'S A MESSAGE. FOR ME."
FORENSICS? HOW LONG IS THAT GOING TO TAKE?
YOU KNOW DAMN WELL I'M THE ONLY CHANCE YOU'VE GOT OF TRACKING HIM DOWN.
LET ME SEE THE LETTER.
YOU KNOW I CAN'T.
YOU'RE GOING TO JUST HAVE TO TRUST THAT GRANT AND I CAN HANDLE THIS THING.
ALEX, I HEARD WHAT HE SAID TO YOU IN THE SEWERS. AND NOW HE GOES AFTER TORY...?
I DON'T KNOW WHY, BUT HEROD IS TRYING TO PROVOKE YOU, PUSH YOU OVER THE EDGE.
YOU CAN'T LET THAT HAPPEN.
"SHE THINKS SHE'S STILL TALKING TO A REASONABLE MAN."
OF COURSE. YOU'RE RIGHT.
I'M GOING TO FIND A MOTEL AND TRY TO SLEEP. CALL ME WHEN YOU LEARN SOMETHING.
YOU KNOW I WILL.
"THAT'LL BE SOONER THAN SHE THINKS."

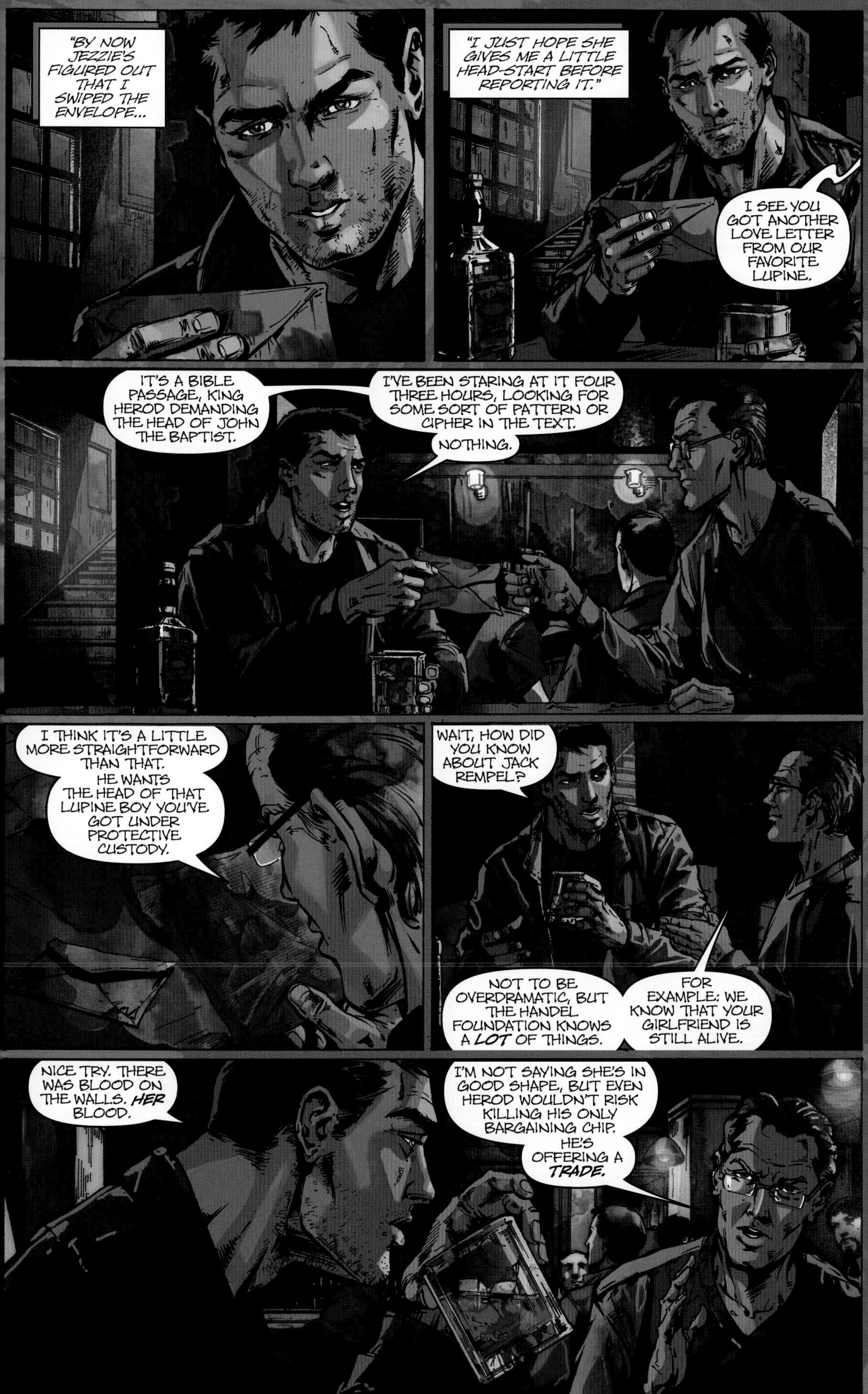
"BY NOW JEZZIE'S FIGURED OUT THAT I SWIPED THE ENVELOPE...
"I JUST HOPE SHE GIVES ME A LITTLE HEAD-START BEFORE REPORTING IT."
I SEE YOU GOT ANOTHER LOVE LETTER FROM OUR FAVORITE LUPINE.
IT'S A BIBLE PASSAGE, KING HEROD DEMANDING THE HEAD OF JOHN THE BAPTIST.
I'VE BEEN STARING AT IT FOUR THREE HOURS, LOOKING FOR SOME SORT OF PATTERN OR CIPHER IN THE TEXT.
NOTHING.
I THINK IT'S A LITTLE MORE STRAIGHTFORWARD THAN THAT.
HE WANTS THE HEAD OF THAT LUPINE BOY YOU'VE GOT UNDER PROTECTIVE CUSTODY.
WAIT, HOW DID YOU KNOW ABOUT JACK REMPEL?
NOT TO BE OVERDRAMATIC, BUT THE HANDEL FOUNDATION KNOWS A *LOT* OF THINGS.
FOR EXAMPLE: WE KNOW THAT YOUR GIRLFRIEND IS STILL ALIVE.
NICE TRY. THERE WAS BLOOD ON THE WALLS. *HER* BLOOD.
I'M NOT SAYING SHE'S IN GOOD SHAPE, BUT EVEN HEROD WOULDN'T RISK KILLING HIS ONLY BARGAINING CHIP.
HE'S OFFERING A *TRADE.*

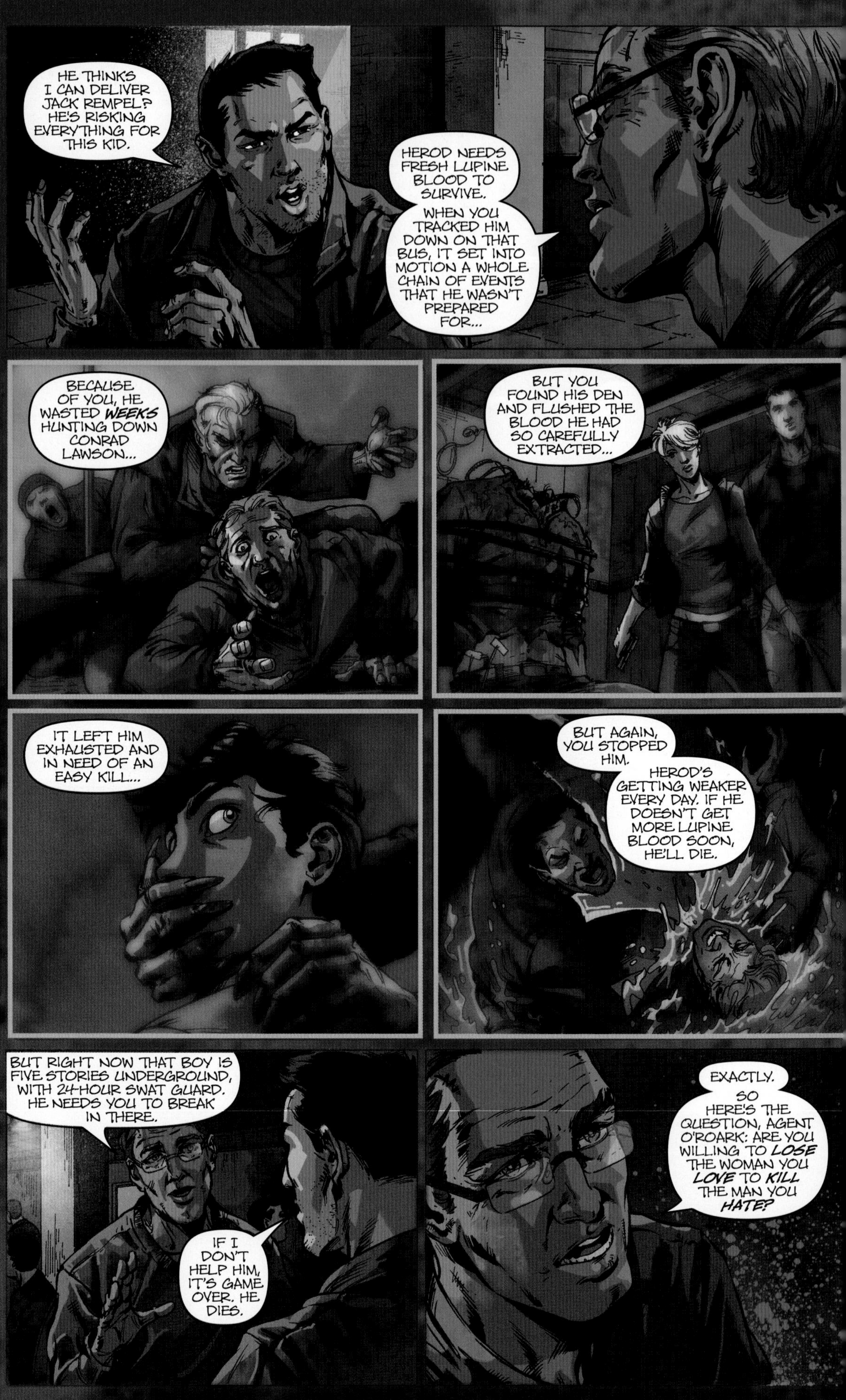

HE THINKS I CAN DELIVER JACK REMPEL? HE'S RISKING EVERYTHING FOR THIS KID.
HEROD NEEDS FRESH LUPINE BLOOD TO SURVIVE.
WHEN YOU TRACKED HIM DOWN ON THAT BUS, IT SET INTO MOTION A WHOLE CHAIN OF EVENTS THAT HE WASN'T PREPARED FOR...
BECAUSE OF YOU, HE WASTED WEEKS HUNTING DOWN CONRAD LAWSON...
BUT YOU FOUND HIS DEN AND FLUSHED THE BLOOD HE HAD SO CAREFULLY EXTRACTED...
IT LEFT HIM EXHAUSTED AND IN NEED OF AN EASY KILL...
BUT AGAIN, YOU STOPPED HIM.
HEROD'S GETTING WEAKER EVERY DAY. IF HE DOESN'T GET MORE LUPINE BLOOD SOON, HE'LL DIE.
BUT RIGHT NOW THAT BOY IS FIVE STORIES UNDERGROUND, WITH 24-HOUR SWAT GUARD. HE NEEDS YOU TO BREAK IN THERE.
IF I DON'T HELP HIM, IT'S GAME OVER. HE DIES.
EXACTLY.
SO HERE'S THE QUESTION, AGENT O'ROARK: ARE YOU WILLING TO LOSE THE WOMAN YOU LOVE TO KILL THE MAN YOU HATE?

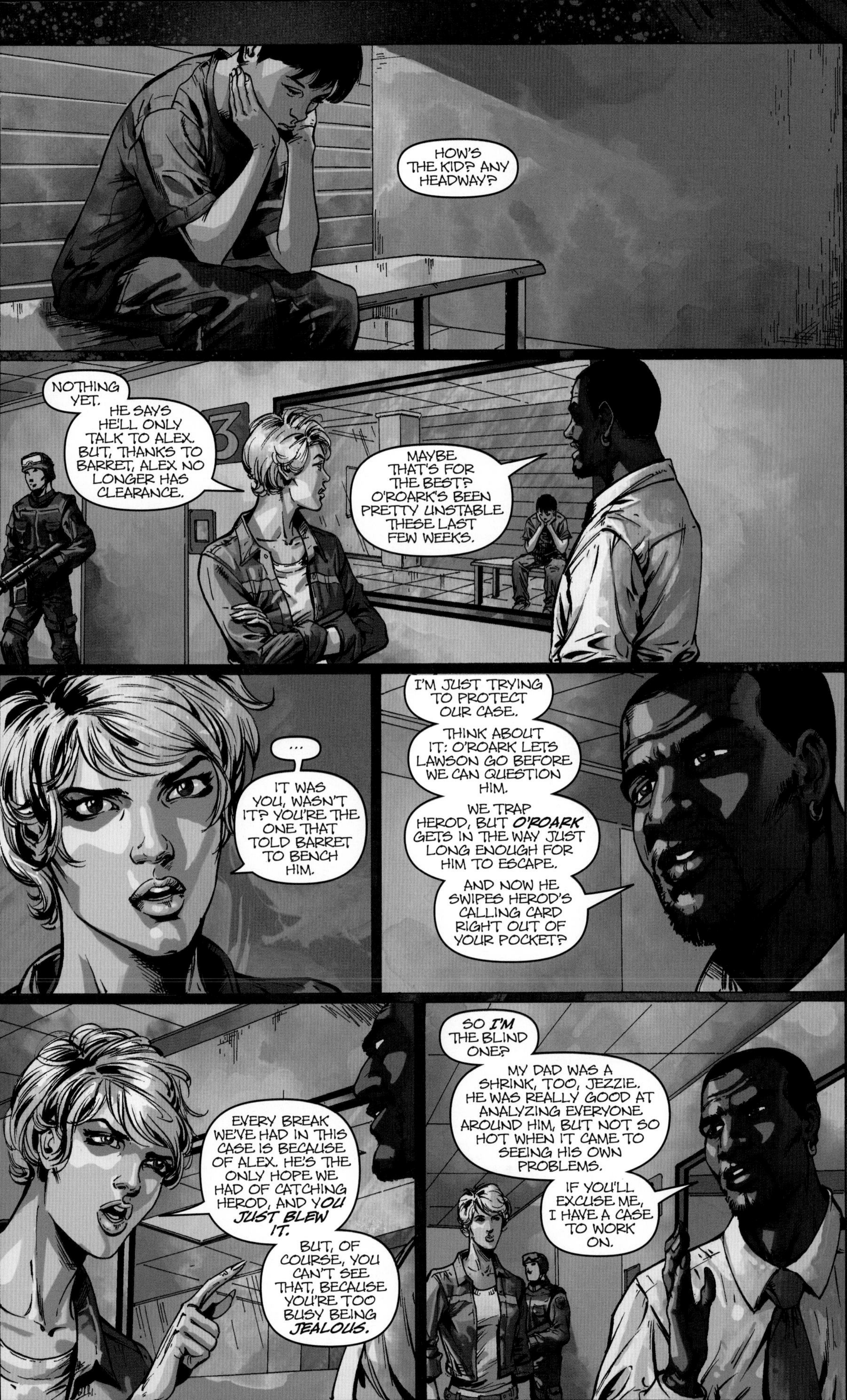

HOW'S THE KID? ANY HEADWAY?
NOTHING YET.
HE SAYS HE'LL ONLY TALK TO ALEX. BUT, THANKS TO BARRET, ALEX NO LONGER HAS CLEARANCE.
MAYBE THAT'S FOR THE BEST? O'ROARK'S BEEN PRETTY UNSTABLE THESE LAST FEW WEEKS.
...
IT WAS YOU, WASN'T IT? YOU'RE THE ONE THAT TOLD BARRET TO BENCH HIM.
I'M JUST TRYING TO PROTECT OUR CASE.
THINK ABOUT IT: O'ROARK LETS LAWSON GO BEFORE WE CAN QUESTION HIM.
WE TRAP HEROD, BUT O'ROARK GETS IN THE WAY JUST LONG ENOUGH FOR HIM TO ESCAPE.
AND NOW HE SWIPES HEROD'S CALLING CARD RIGHT OUT OF YOUR POCKET?
EVERY BREAK WE'VE HAD IN THIS CASE IS BECAUSE OF ALEX. HE'S THE ONLY HOPE WE HAD OF CATCHING HEROD, AND YOU JUST BLEW IT.
BUT, OF COURSE, YOU CAN'T SEE THAT, BECAUSE YOU'RE TOO BUSY BEING JEALOUS.
SO I'M THE BLIND ONE?
MY DAD WAS A SHRINK, TOO, JEZZIE. HE WAS REALLY GOOD AT ANALYZING EVERYONE AROUND HIM, BUT NOT SO HOT WHEN IT CAME TO SEEING HIS OWN PROBLEMS.
IF YOU'LL EXCUSE ME, I HAVE A CASE TO WORK ON.

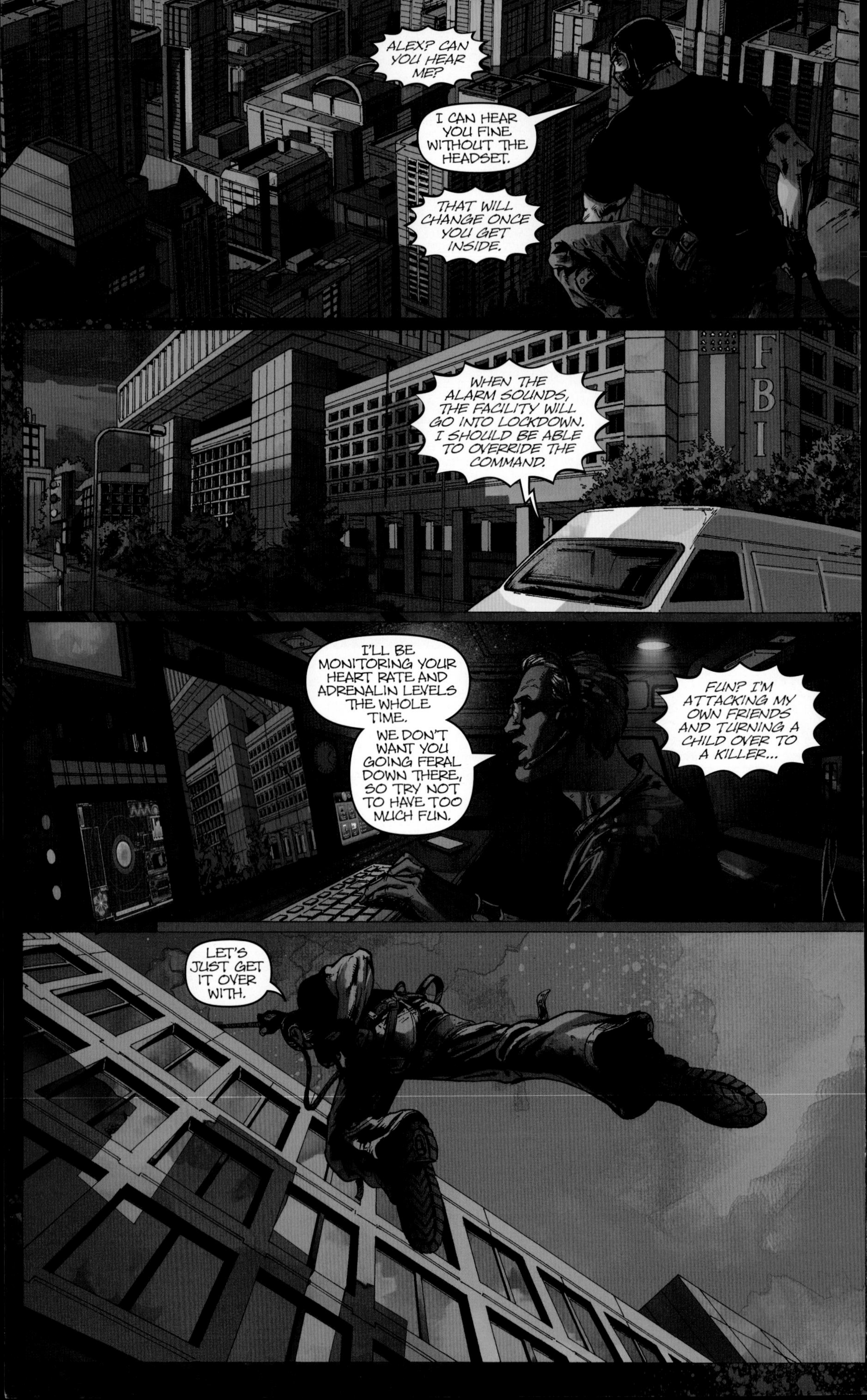
ALEX? CAN YOU HEAR ME?
I CAN HEAR YOU FINE WITHOUT THE HEADSET.
THAT WILL CHANGE ONCE YOU GET INSIDE.
F B I
WHEN THE ALARM SOUNDS, THE FACILITY WILL GO INTO LOCKDOWN. I SHOULD BE ABLE TO OVERRIDE THE COMMAND.
I'LL BE MONITORING YOUR HEART RATE AND ADRENALIN LEVELS THE WHOLE TIME.
WE DON'T WANT YOU GOING FERAL DOWN THERE, SO TRY NOT TO HAVE TOO MUCH FUN.
FUN? I'M ATTACKING MY OWN FRIENDS AND TURNING A CHILD OVER TO A KILLER...
LET'S JUST GET IT OVER WITH.

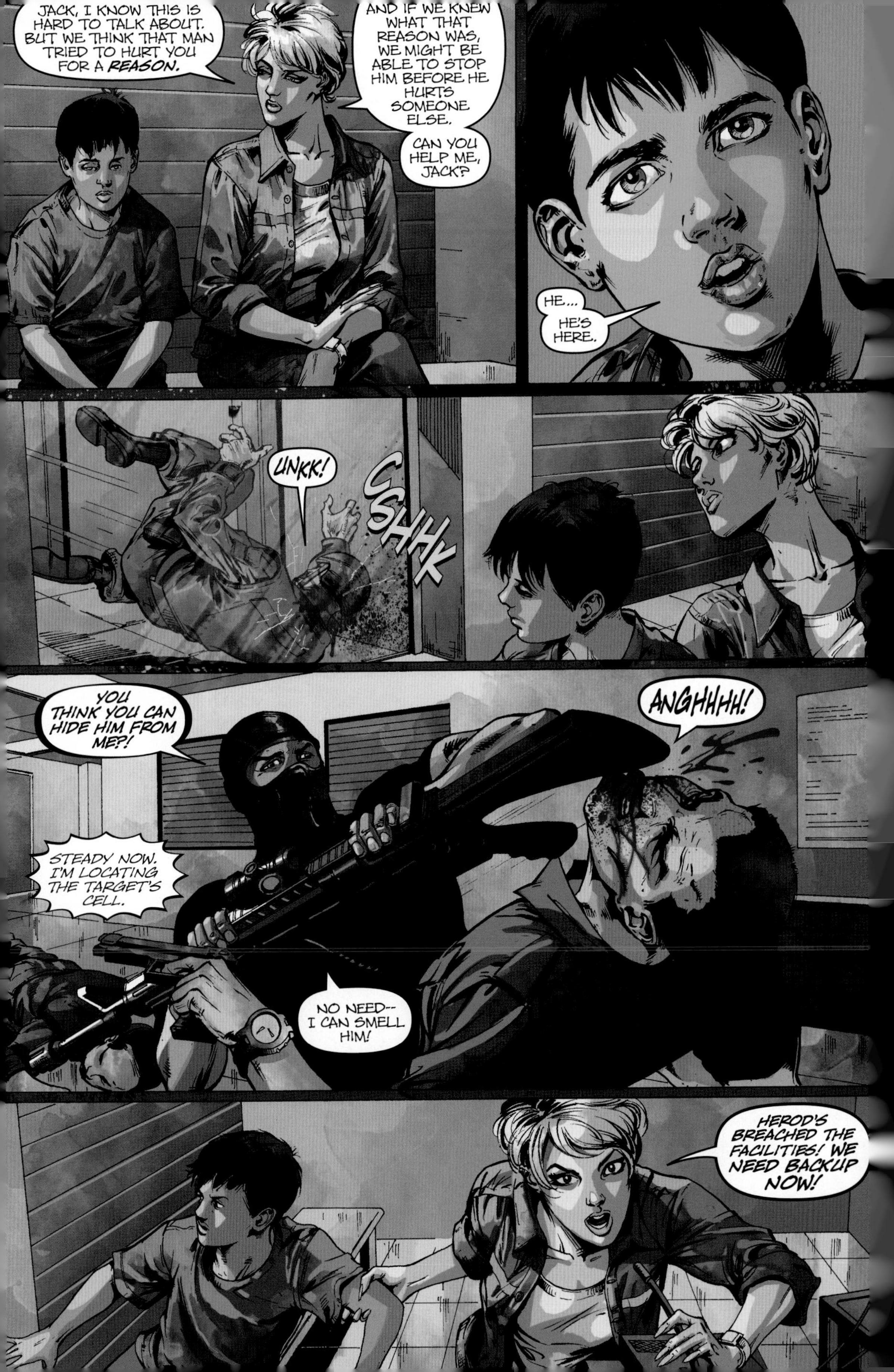
JACK, I KNOW THIS IS HARD TO TALK ABOUT. BUT WE THINK THAT MAN TRIED TO HURT YOU FOR A REASON.
AND IF WE KNEW WHAT THAT REASON WAS, WE MIGHT BE ABLE TO STOP HIM BEFORE HE HURTS SOMEONE ELSE.
CAN YOU HELP ME, JACK?
HE... HE'S HERE.
UNKK!
CSHHK
YOU THINK YOU CAN HIDE HIM FROM ME?!
ANGHHHH!
STEADY NOW. I'M LOCATING THE TARGET'S CELL.
NO NEED-- I CAN SMELL HIM!
HEROD'S BREACHED THE FACILITIES! WE NEED BACKUP NOW!

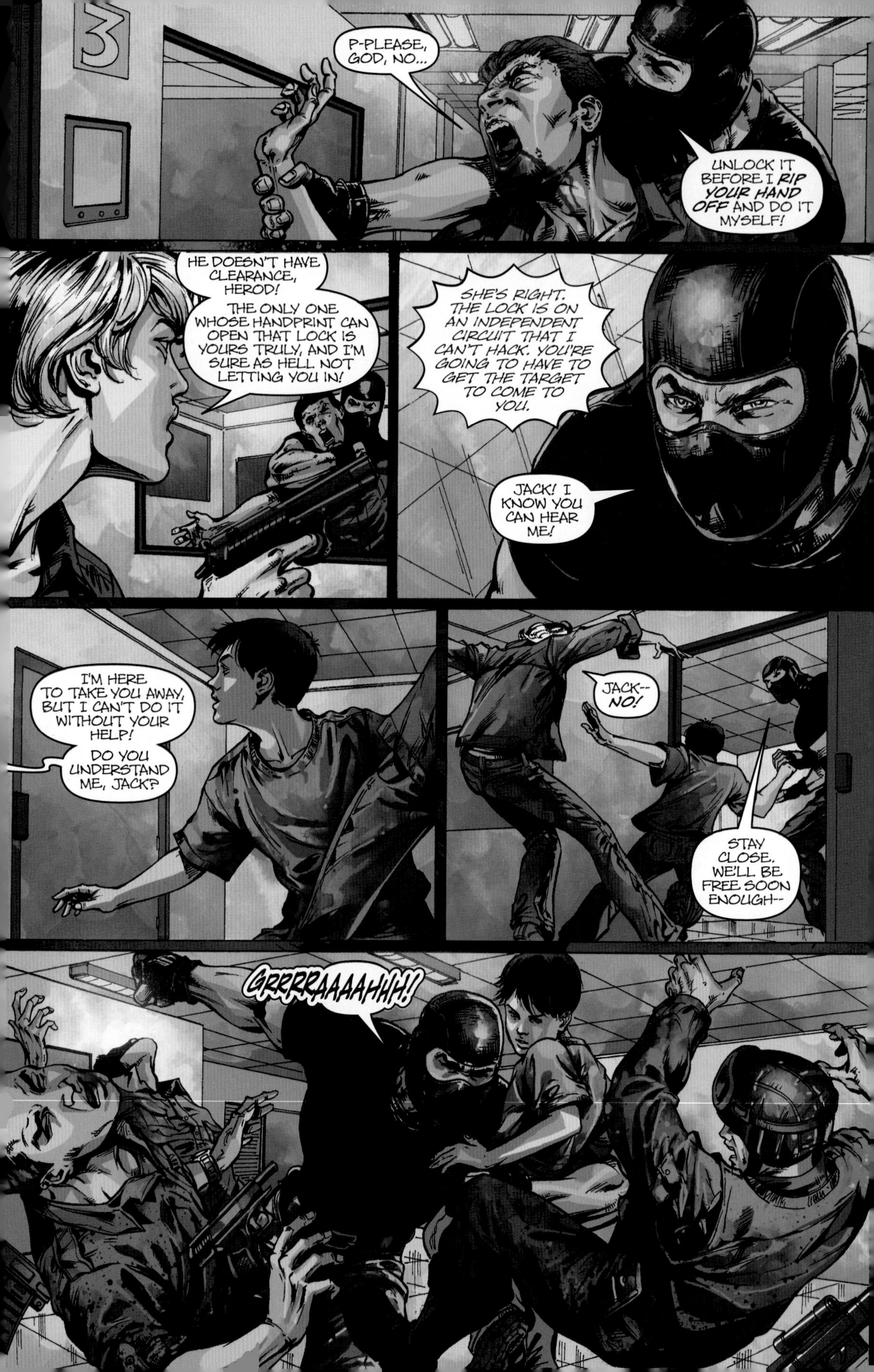
3
P-PLEASE, GOD, NO...
UNLOCK IT BEFORE I **RIP YOUR HAND OFF** AND DO IT MYSELF!
HE DOESN'T HAVE CLEARANCE, HEROD!
THE ONLY ONE WHOSE HANDPRINT CAN OPEN THAT LOCK IS YOURS TRULY, AND I'M SURE AS HELL NOT LETTING YOU IN!
SHE'S RIGHT. THE LOCK IS ON AN INDEPENDENT CIRCUIT THAT I CAN'T HACK. YOU'RE GOING TO HAVE TO GET THE TARGET TO COME TO YOU.
JACK! I KNOW YOU CAN HEAR ME!
I'M HERE TO TAKE YOU AWAY, BUT I CAN'T DO IT WITHOUT YOUR HELP!
DO YOU UNDERSTAND ME, JACK?
JACK-- **NO!**
STAY CLOSE. WE'LL BE FREE SOON ENOUGH--
GRRRRAAAAHHH!!

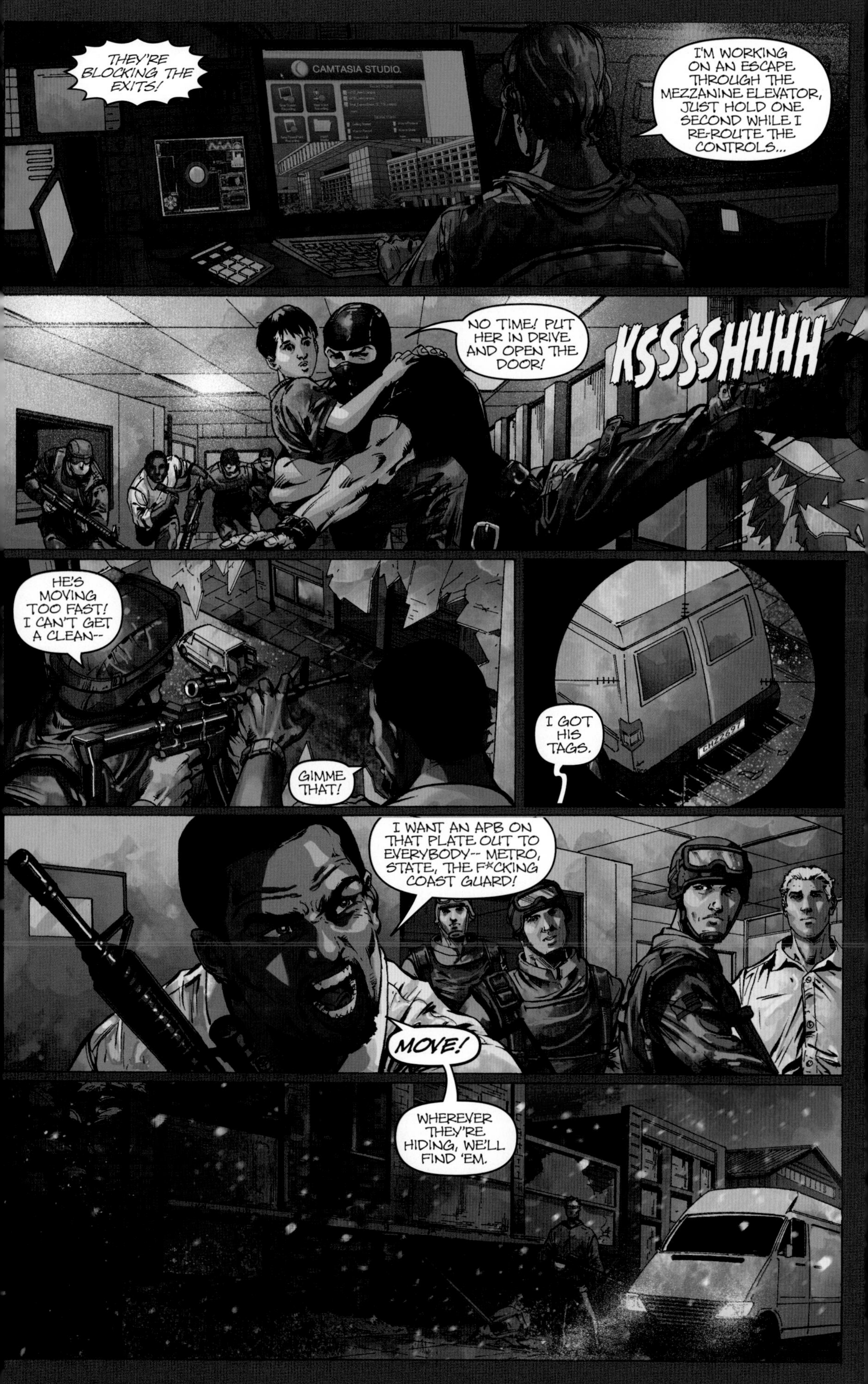
THEY'RE BLOCKING THE EXITS!
CAMTASIA STUDIO.
I'M WORKING ON AN ESCAPE THROUGH THE MEZZANINE ELEVATOR, JUST HOLD ONE SECOND WHILE I RE-ROUTE THE CONTROLS...
NO TIME! PUT HER IN DRIVE AND OPEN THE DOOR!
KSSSSHHHH
HE'S MOVING TOO FAST! I CAN'T GET A CLEAN--
GIMME THAT!
I GOT HIS TAGS.
I WANT AN APB ON THAT PLATE OUT TO EVERYBODY-- METRO, STATE, THE F*CKING COAST GUARD!
MOVE!
WHEREVER THEY'RE HIDING, WE'LL FIND 'EM.

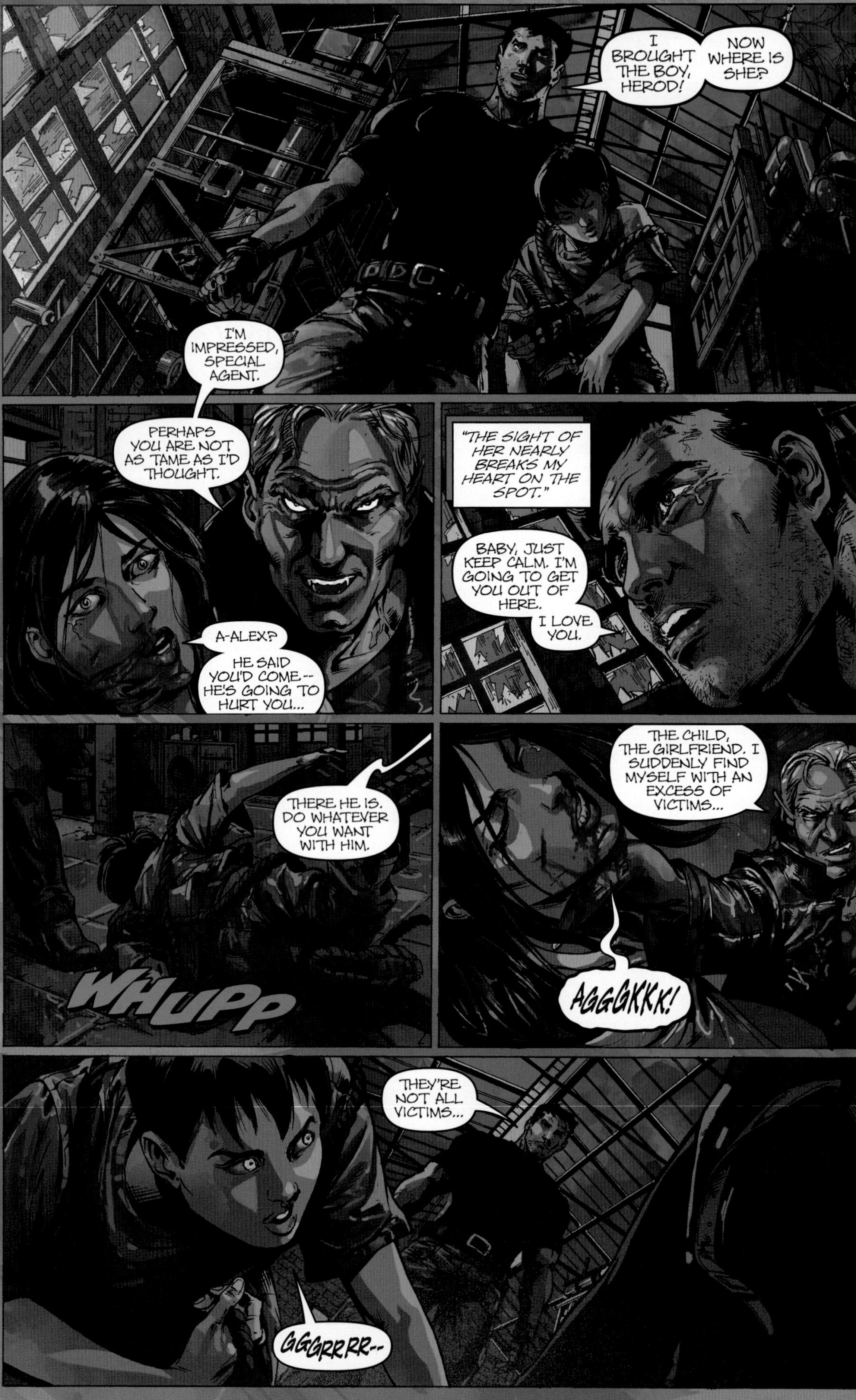
I BROUGHT THE BOY, HEROD!
NOW WHERE IS SHE?
I'M IMPRESSED, SPECIAL AGENT.
PERHAPS YOU ARE NOT AS TAME AS I'D THOUGHT.
A-ALEX?
HE SAID YOU'D COME-- HE'S GOING TO HURT YOU...
"THE SIGHT OF HER NEARLY BREAKS MY HEART ON THE SPOT."
BABY, JUST KEEP CALM. I'M GOING TO GET YOU OUT OF HERE.
I LOVE YOU.
THERE HE IS. DO WHATEVER YOU WANT WITH HIM.
WHUPP
THE CHILD, THE GIRLFRIEND. I SUDDENLY FIND MYSELF WITH AN EXCESS OF VICTIMS...
AGGGKKK!
THEY'RE NOT ALL VICTIMS...
GGGRRRR--

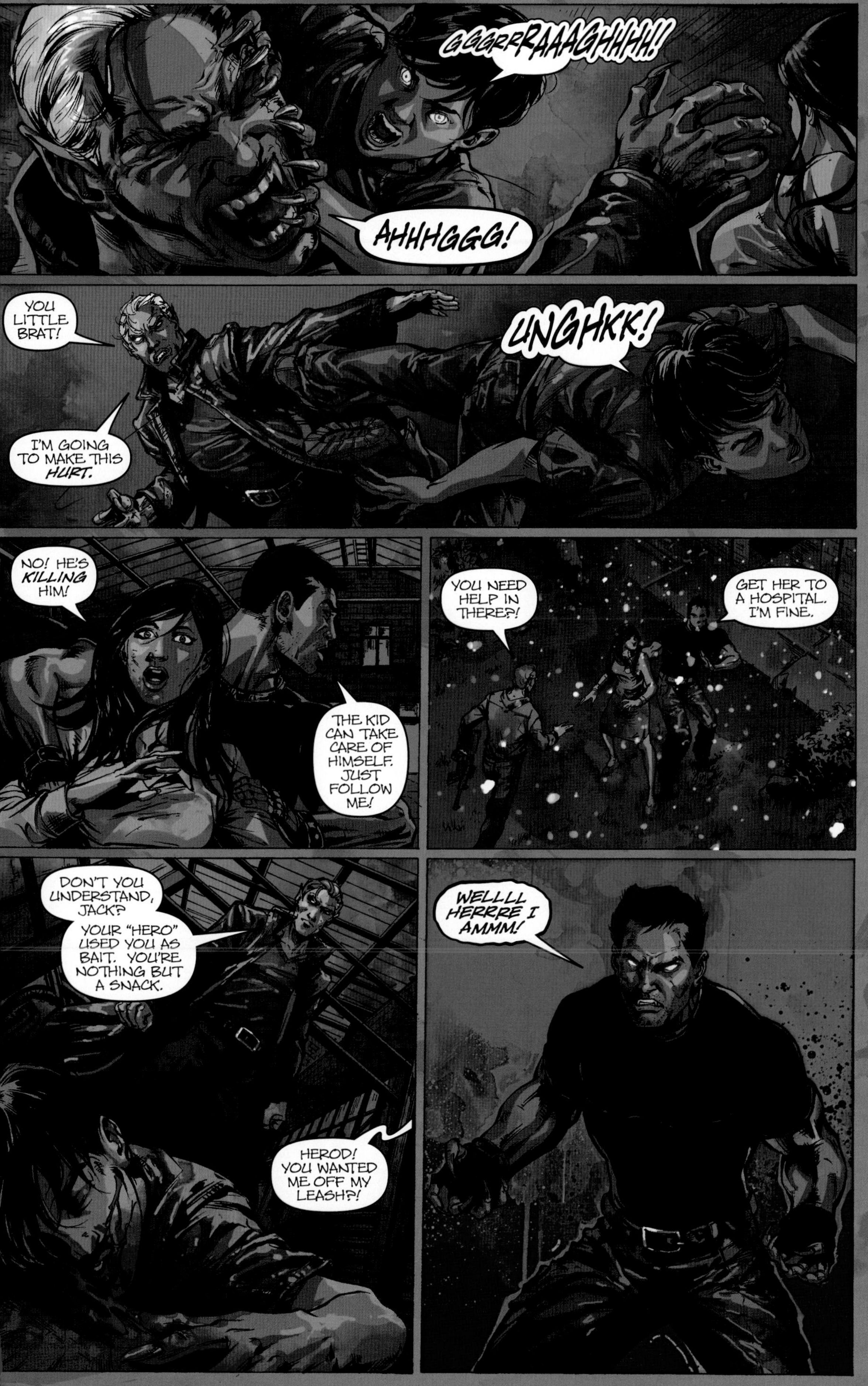
GGGRRRAAAGHHHH!
AHHHGGG!
YOU LITTLE BRAT!
UNGHKK!
I'M GOING TO MAKE THIS *HURT.*
NO! HE'S *KILLING* HIM!
THE KID CAN TAKE CARE OF HIMSELF. JUST FOLLOW ME!
YOU NEED HELP IN THERE?!
GET HER TO A HOSPITAL. I'M FINE.
DON'T YOU UNDERSTAND, JACK?
YOUR "HERO" USED YOU AS BAIT. YOU'RE NOTHING BUT A SNACK.
HEROD! YOU WANTED ME OFF MY LEASH?!
WELLLL HERRRE I AMMM!

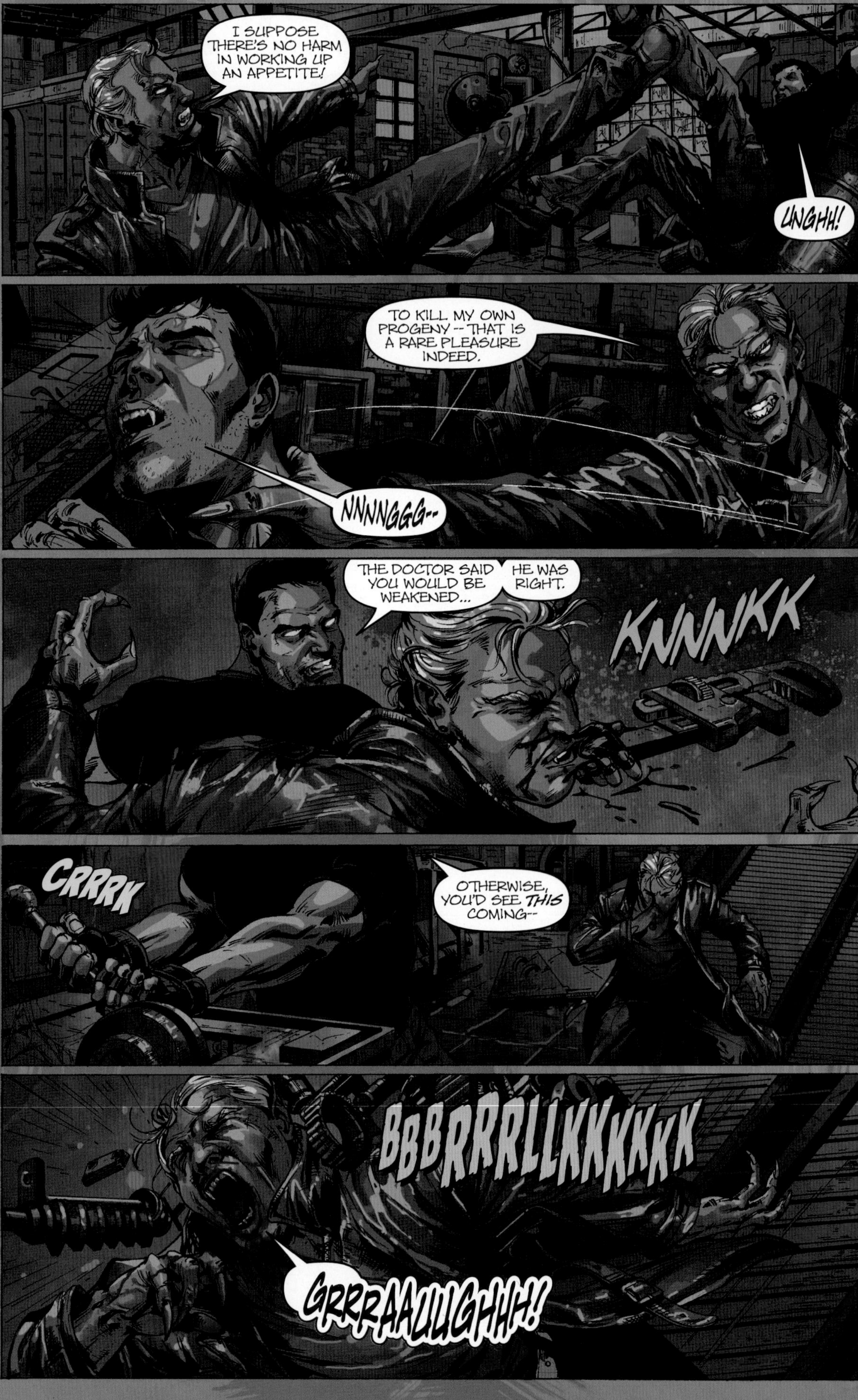
I SUPPOSE THERE'S NO HARM IN WORKING UP AN APPETITE!
UNGHH!
TO KILL MY OWN PROGENY -- THAT IS A RARE PLEASURE INDEED.
NNNNGGG--
THE DOCTOR SAID YOU WOULD BE WEAKENED...
HE WAS RIGHT.
KNNNKK
CRRRK
OTHERWISE, YOU'D SEE THIS COMING--
BBBRRRLLKKKKKK
GRRRAAUUGHHH!

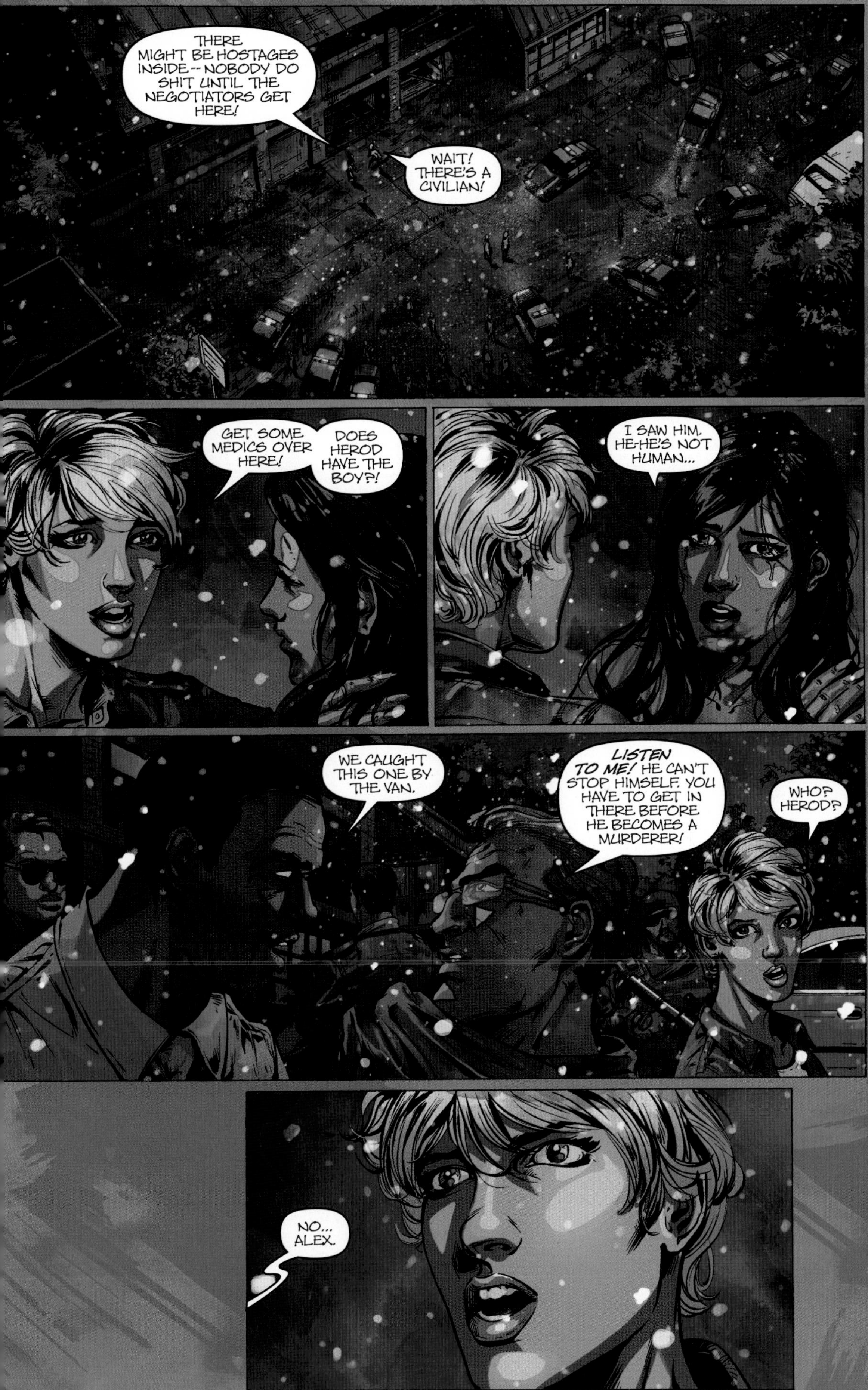
THERE MIGHT BE HOSTAGES INSIDE--NOBODY DO SHIT UNTIL THE NEGOTIATORS GET HERE!
WAIT! THERE'S A CIVILIAN!
GET SOME MEDICS OVER HERE!
DOES HEROD HAVE THE BOY?!
I SAW HIM. HE-HE'S NOT HUMAN...
WE CAUGHT THIS ONE BY THE VAN.
LISTEN TO ME! HE CAN'T STOP HIMSELF. YOU HAVE TO GET IN THERE BEFORE HE BECOMES A MURDERER!
WHO? HEROD?
NO... ALEX.

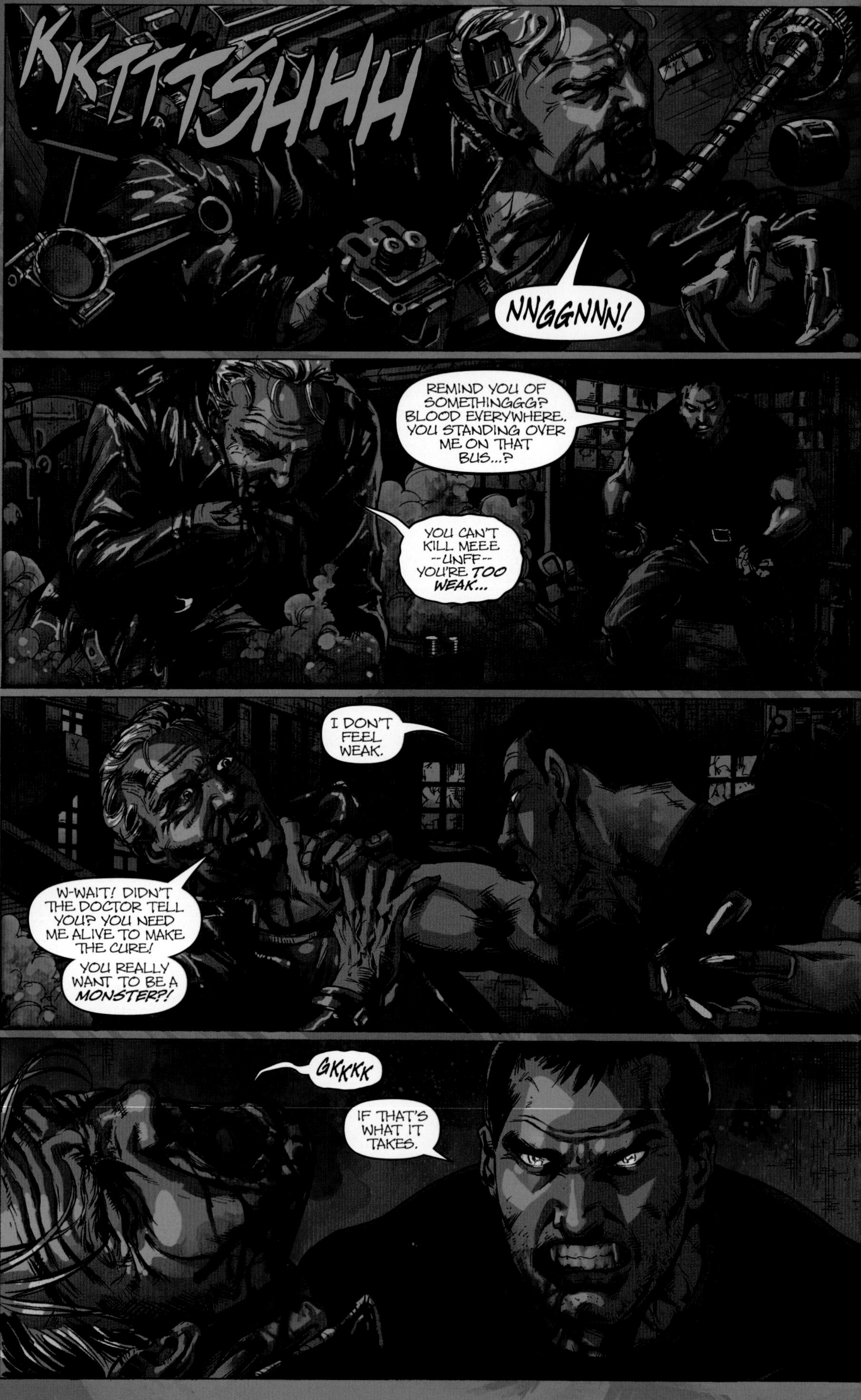
KKTTTSHHH
NNGGNNN!
REMIND YOU OF SOMETHINGGG? BLOOD EVERYWHERE. YOU STANDING OVER ME ON THAT BUS...?
YOU CAN'T KILL MEEE --UNFF-- YOU'RE TOO WEAK...
I DON'T FEEL WEAK.
W-WAIT! DIDN'T THE DOCTOR TELL YOU? YOU NEED ME ALIVE TO MAKE THE CURE!
YOU REALLY WANT TO BE A MONSTER?!
GKKKK
IF THAT'S WHAT IT TAKES.

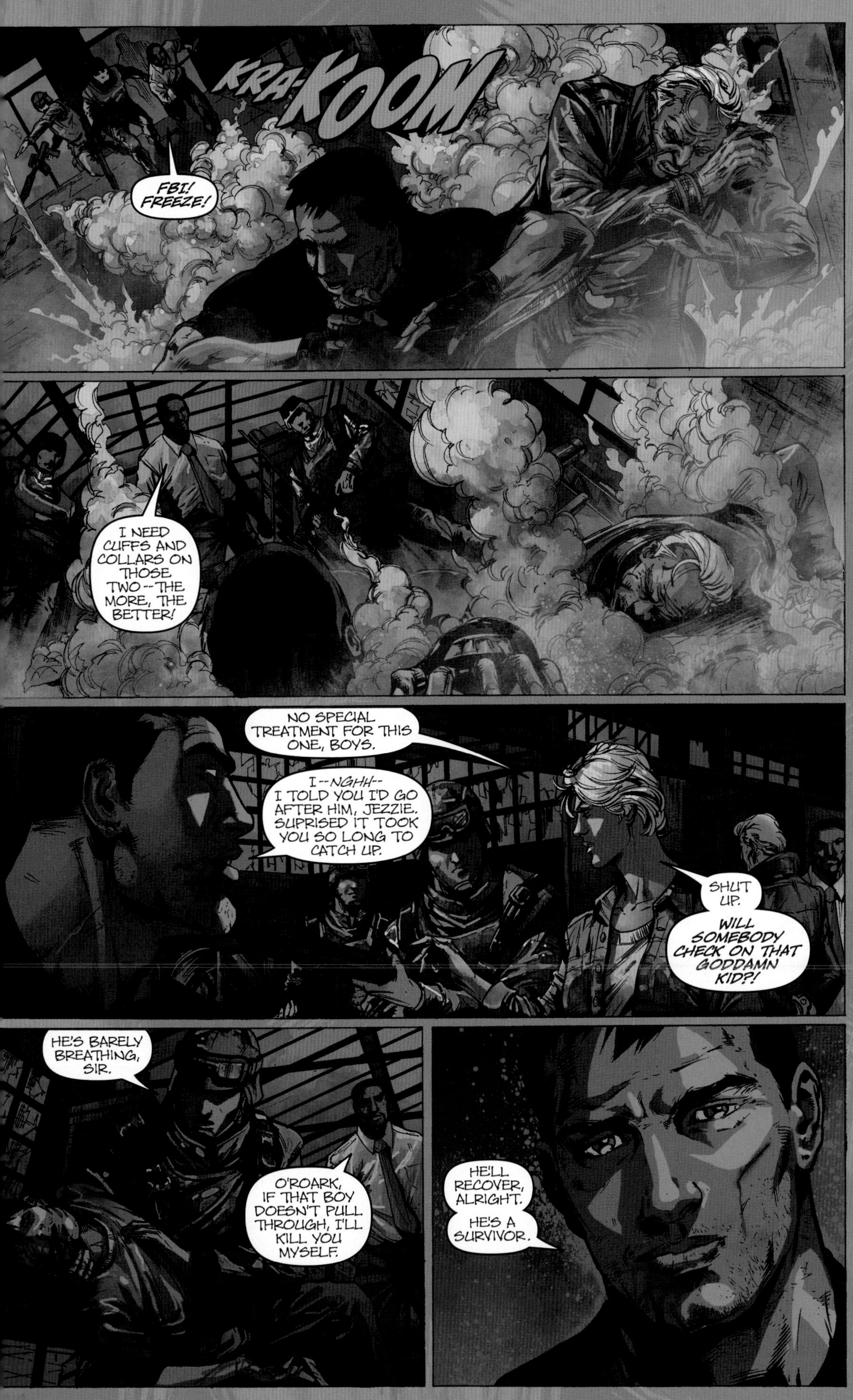
KRA-KOOM
FBI! FREEZE!
I NEED CUFFS AND COLLARS ON THOSE TWO--THE MORE, THE BETTER!
NO SPECIAL TREATMENT FOR THIS ONE, BOYS.
I--NGHH-- I TOLD YOU I'D GO AFTER HIM, JEZZIE. SUPRISED IT TOOK YOU SO LONG TO CATCH UP.
SHUT UP.
WILL SOMEBODY CHECK ON THAT GODDAMN KID?!
HE'S BARELY BREATHING, SIR.
O'ROARK, IF THAT BOY DOESN'T PULL THROUGH, I'LL KILL YOU MYSELF.
HE'LL RECOVER, ALRIGHT.
HE'S A SURVIVOR.

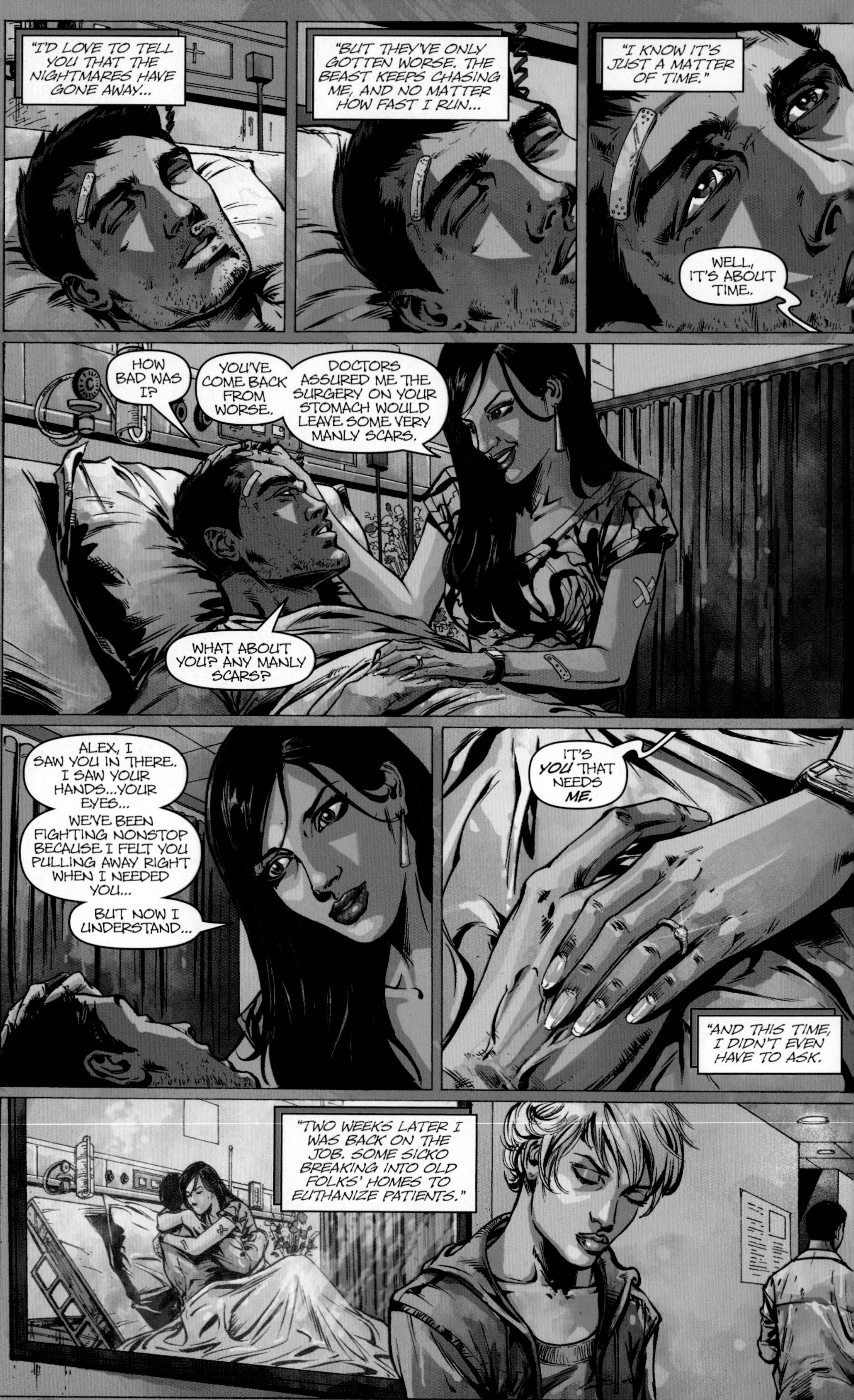
"I'D LOVE TO TELL YOU THAT THE NIGHTMARES HAVE GONE AWAY...
"BUT THEY'VE ONLY GOTTEN WORSE. THE BEAST KEEPS CHASING ME, AND NO MATTER HOW FAST I RUN...
"I KNOW IT'S JUST A MATTER OF TIME."
WELL, IT'S ABOUT TIME.
HOW BAD WAS I?
YOU'VE COME BACK FROM WORSE.
DOCTORS ASSURED ME THE SURGERY ON YOUR STOMACH WOULD LEAVE SOME VERY MANLY SCARS.
WHAT ABOUT YOU? ANY MANLY SCARS?
ALEX, I SAW YOU IN THERE. I SAW YOUR HANDS...YOUR EYES...
WE'VE BEEN FIGHTING NONSTOP BECAUSE I FELT YOU PULLING AWAY RIGHT WHEN I NEEDED YOU...
BUT NOW I UNDERSTAND...
IT'S YOU THAT NEEDS ME.
"AND THIS TIME, I DIDN'T EVEN HAVE TO ASK.
"TWO WEEKS LATER I WAS BACK ON THE JOB. SOME SICKO BREAKING INTO OLD FOLKS' HOMES TO EUTHANIZE PATIENTS."

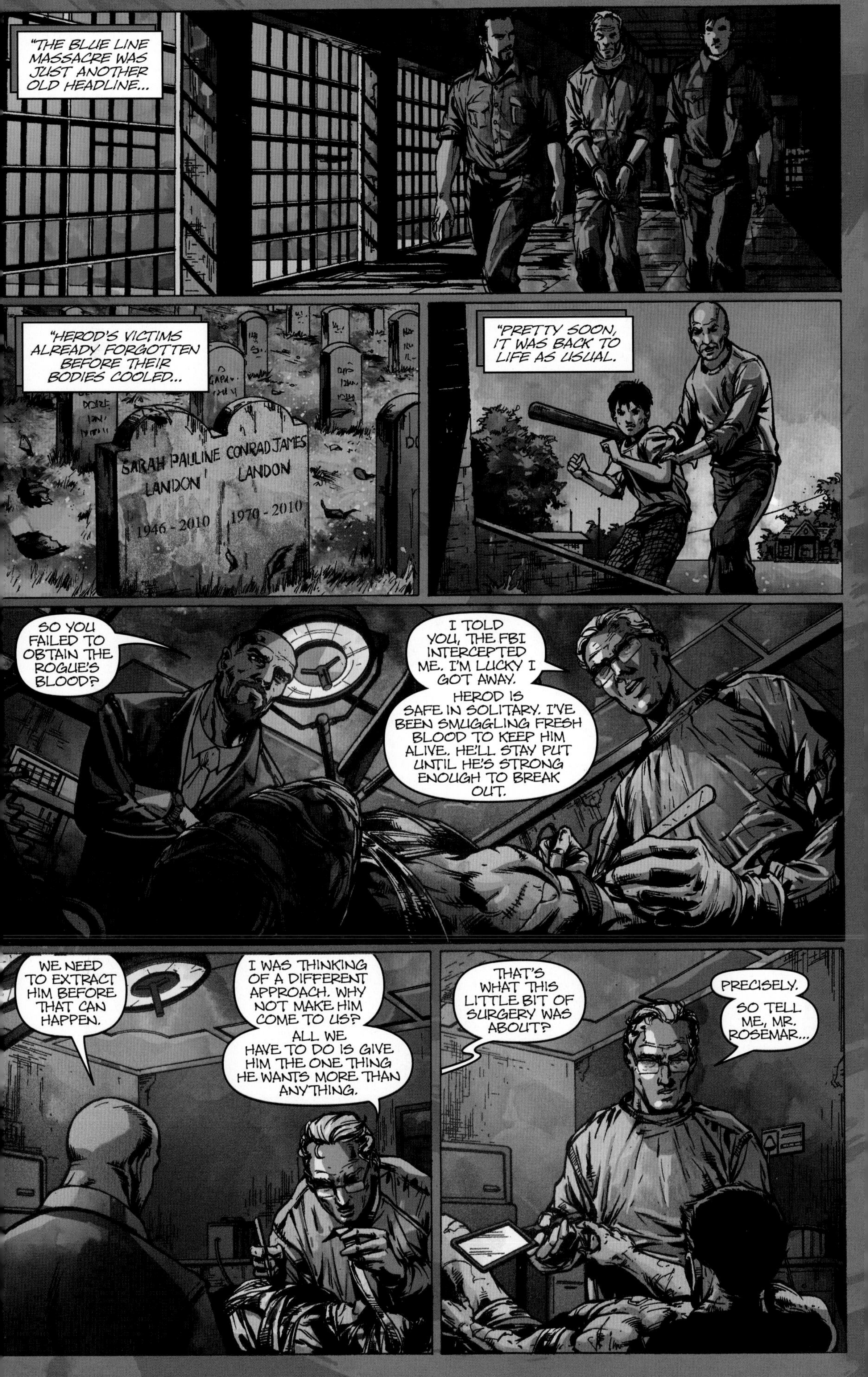
"THE BLUE LINE MASSACRE WAS JUST ANOTHER OLD HEADLINE...
"HEROD'S VICTIMS ALREADY FORGOTTEN BEFORE THEIR BODIES COOLED...
SARAH PAULINE LANDON 1946 - 2010
CONRAD JAMES LANDON 1970 - 2010
"PRETTY SOON, IT WAS BACK TO LIFE AS USUAL.
SO YOU FAILED TO OBTAIN THE ROGUE'S BLOOD?
I TOLD YOU, THE FBI INTERCEPTED ME. I'M LUCKY I GOT AWAY.
HEROD IS SAFE IN SOLITARY. I'VE BEEN SMUGGLING FRESH BLOOD TO KEEP HIM ALIVE. HE'LL STAY PUT UNTIL HE'S STRONG ENOUGH OUT TO BREAK OUT.
WE NEED TO EXTRACT HIM BEFORE THAT CAN HAPPEN.
I WAS THINKING OF A DIFFERENT APPROACH. WHY NOT MAKE HIM COME TO US?
ALL WE HAVE TO DO IS GIVE HIM THE ONE THING HE WANTS MORE THAN ANYTHING.
THAT'S WHAT THIS LITTLE BIT OF SURGERY WAS ABOUT?
PRECISELY.
SO TELL ME, MR. ROSEMAR...

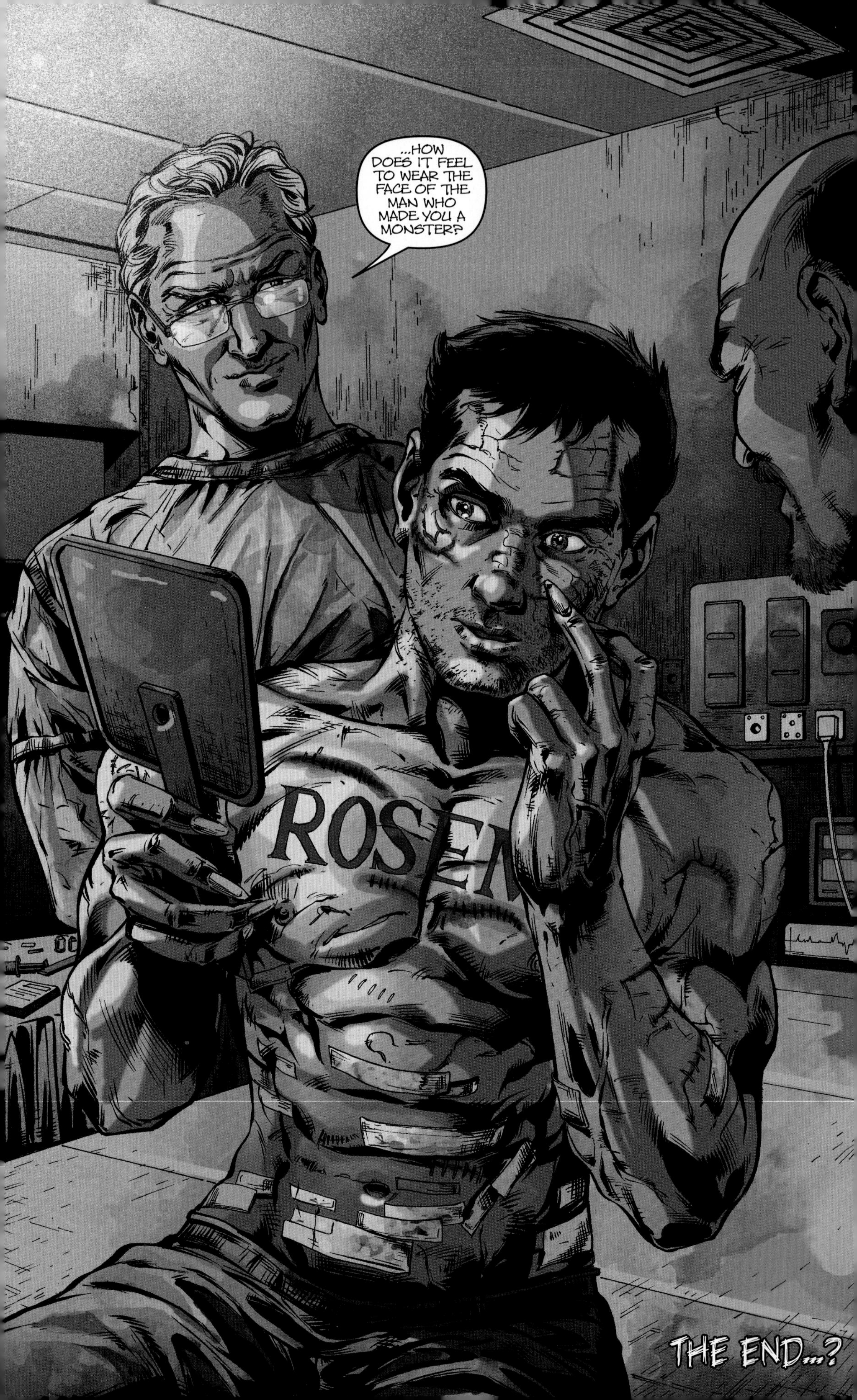
...HOW DOES IT FEEL TO WEAR THE FACE OF THE MAN WHO MADE YOU A MONSTER?
ROSEN
THE END...?

TRACKER™

COVER & DESIGN GALLERY

TRACKER

San Diego Comic-Con
Issue #0, cover process: **Francis Tsai**

Left: **Initial Color Rough**

Below: **First draft Colors**

Facing page: **Final art**

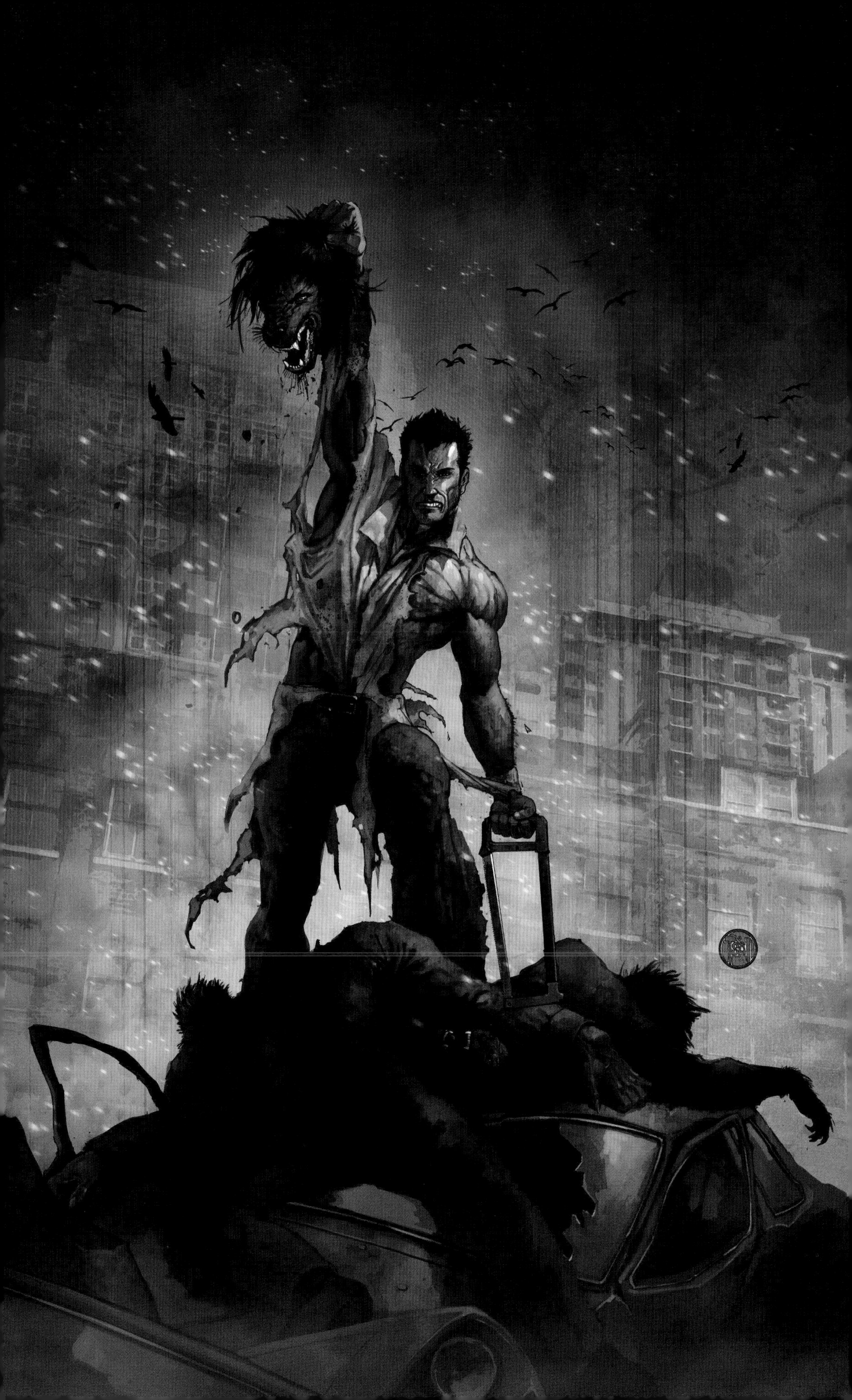

TRACKER™

Issue #1, cover A process: **Francis Tsai**

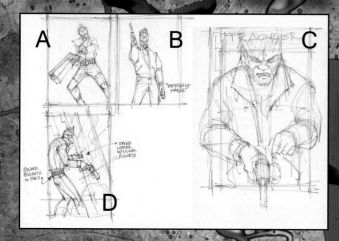

A
B
C
D
TRACKER
"WEREWOLF HANDS"
SPEED LOADER W/SILVER BULLETS
SILVER BULLETS IN BELT

above: **Initial thumbnail layouts**

above right: **First Thumbnail comp**

Right: **Revised thumbnail**

Facing page: **Final art**

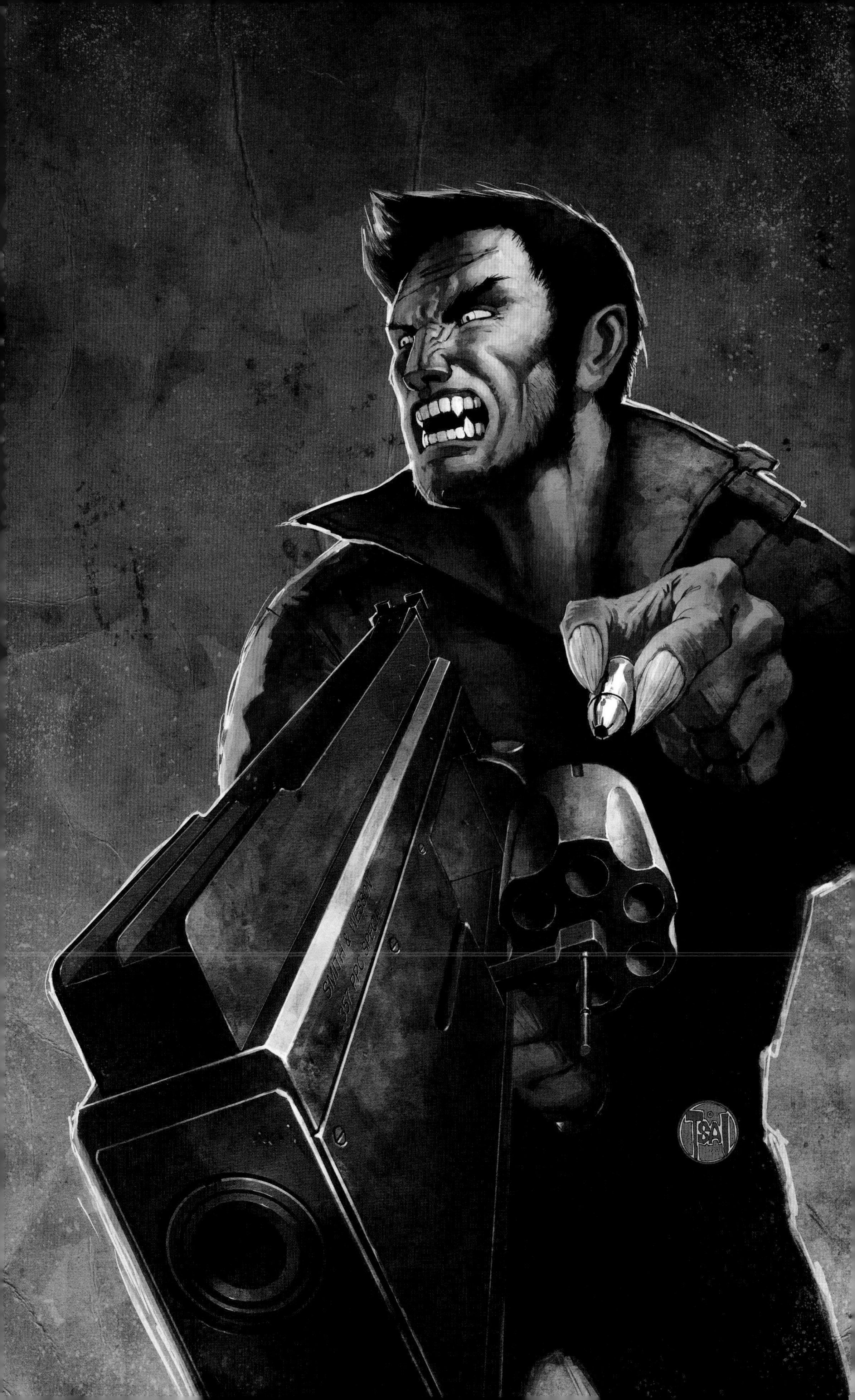

SMITH & WESSON
357 PPC SPECIAL
TSAI

TRACKER™

Issue #1, cover B process:
Darick Robertson & JD Smith

Left: **Thumbnail concept reference by Filip Sablik**

Lower left: **Initial Thumbnail from Darick Robertson**

Below: **Line art by Darick Robertson**

Facing page: **Final art by Darick Robertson & JD Smith**

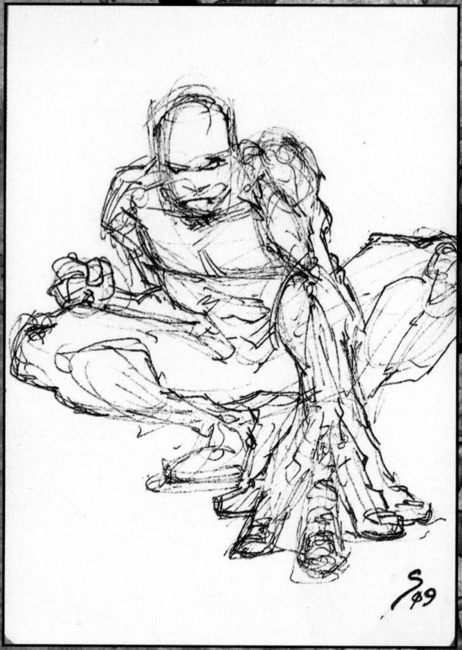

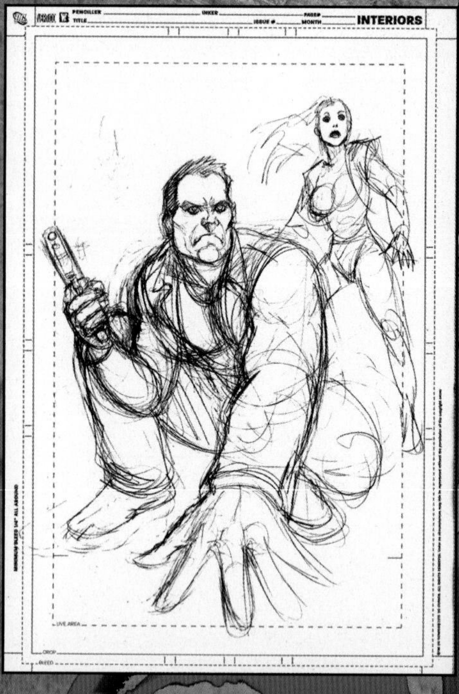
INTERIORS

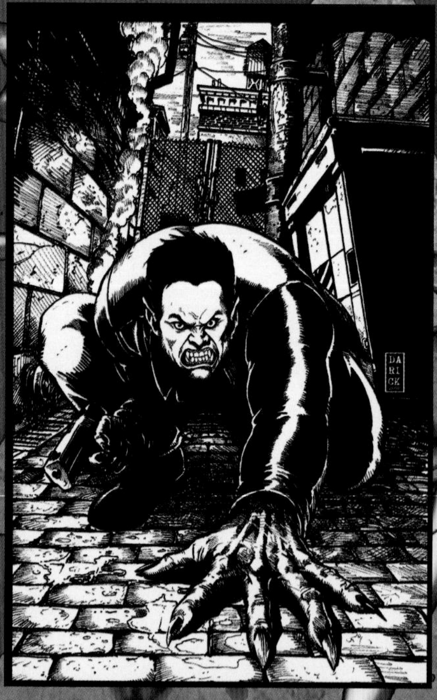

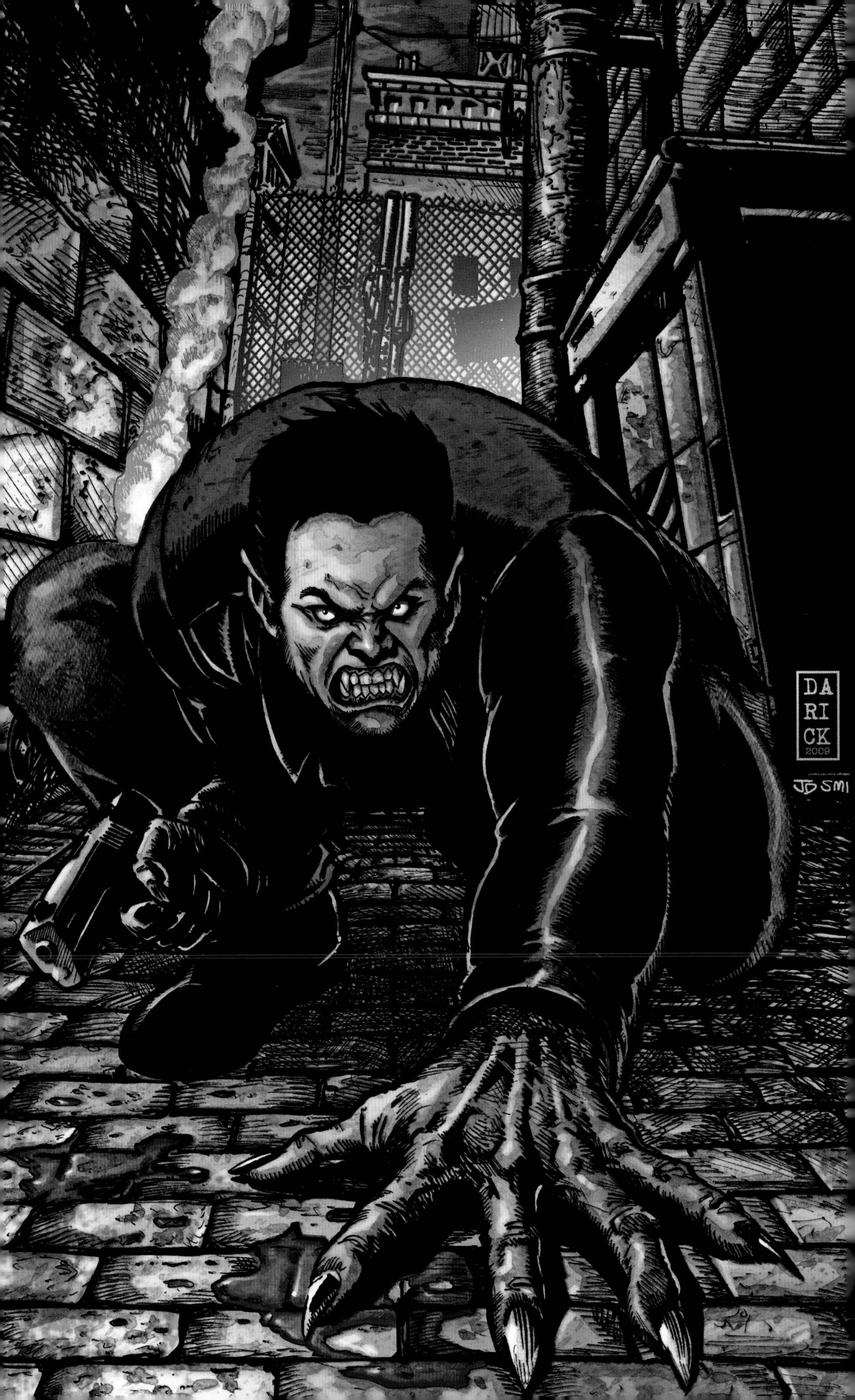
DA
RI
CK
2009
JB SMI

TRACKER

ISSUE #2, COVER PROCESS: FRANCIS TSAI

LEFT: INITIAL THUMBNAIL CONCEPT

LOWER LEFT: REVISED THUMBNAIL CONCEPT

BELOW: COLOR ROUGH FIRST DRAFT

FACING PAGE: FINAL ART BY FRANCIS TSAI

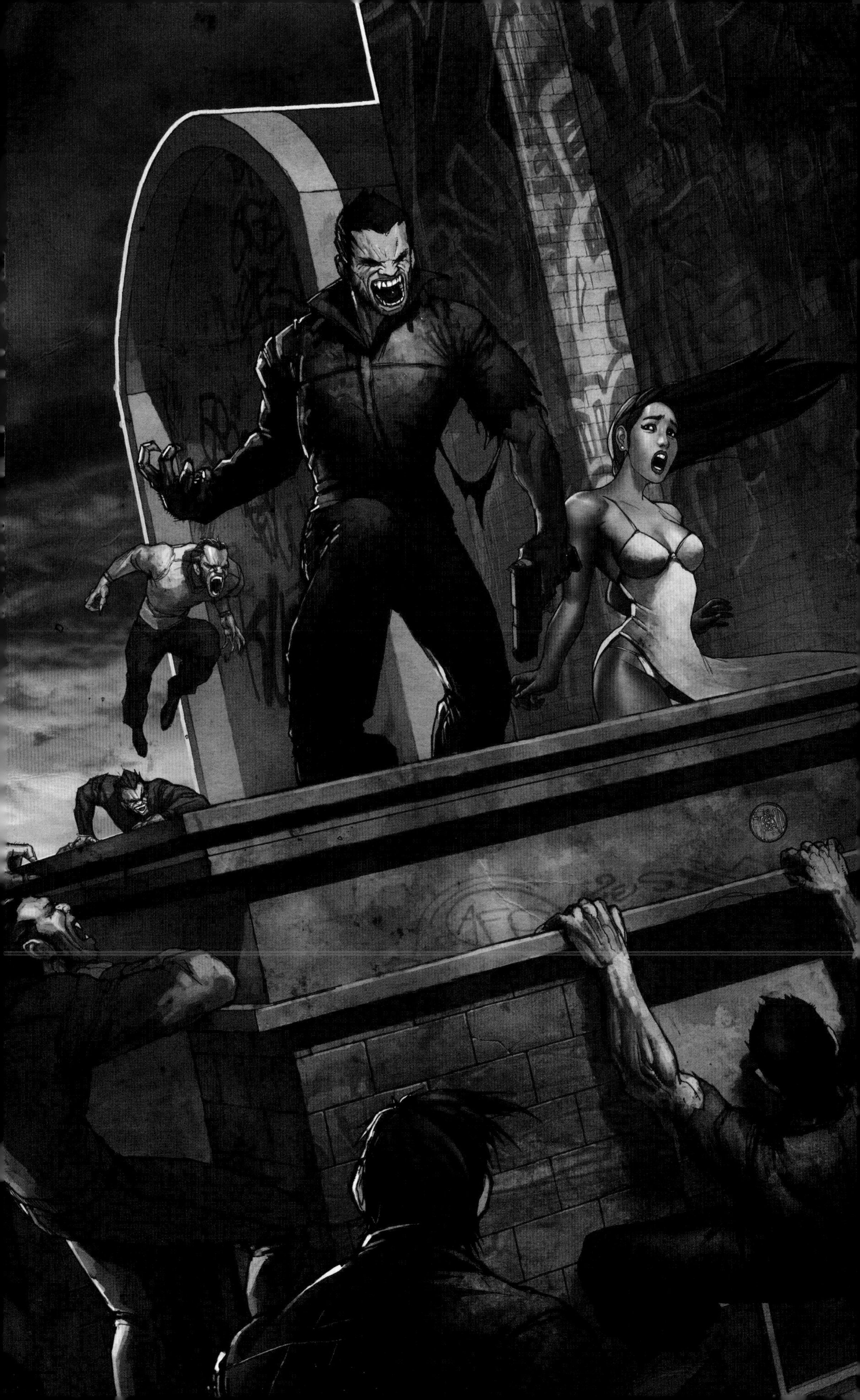

TRACKER™

Issue #3, cover process: **Francis Tsai**

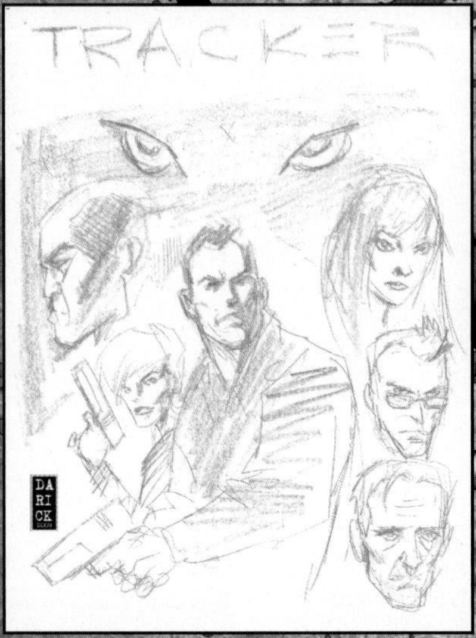
TRACKER

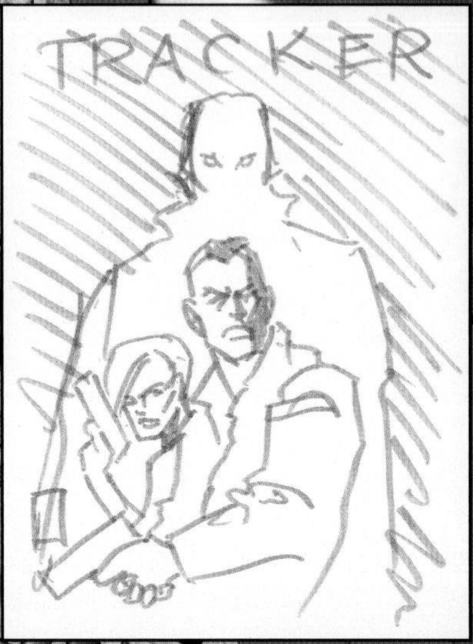
TRACKER

Above: **Initial Thumbnail concepts**

Below: **Color Roughs First Draft**

Facing page: **Final art by Francis Tsai**

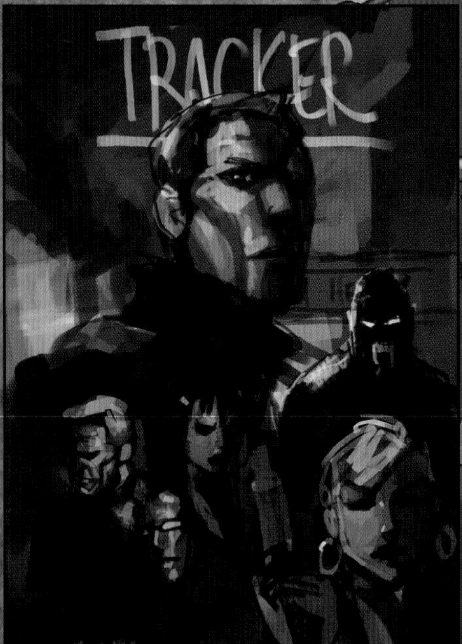
TRACKER

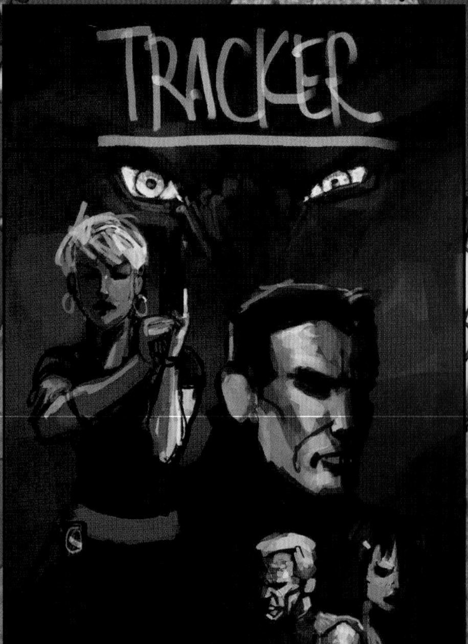
TRACKER

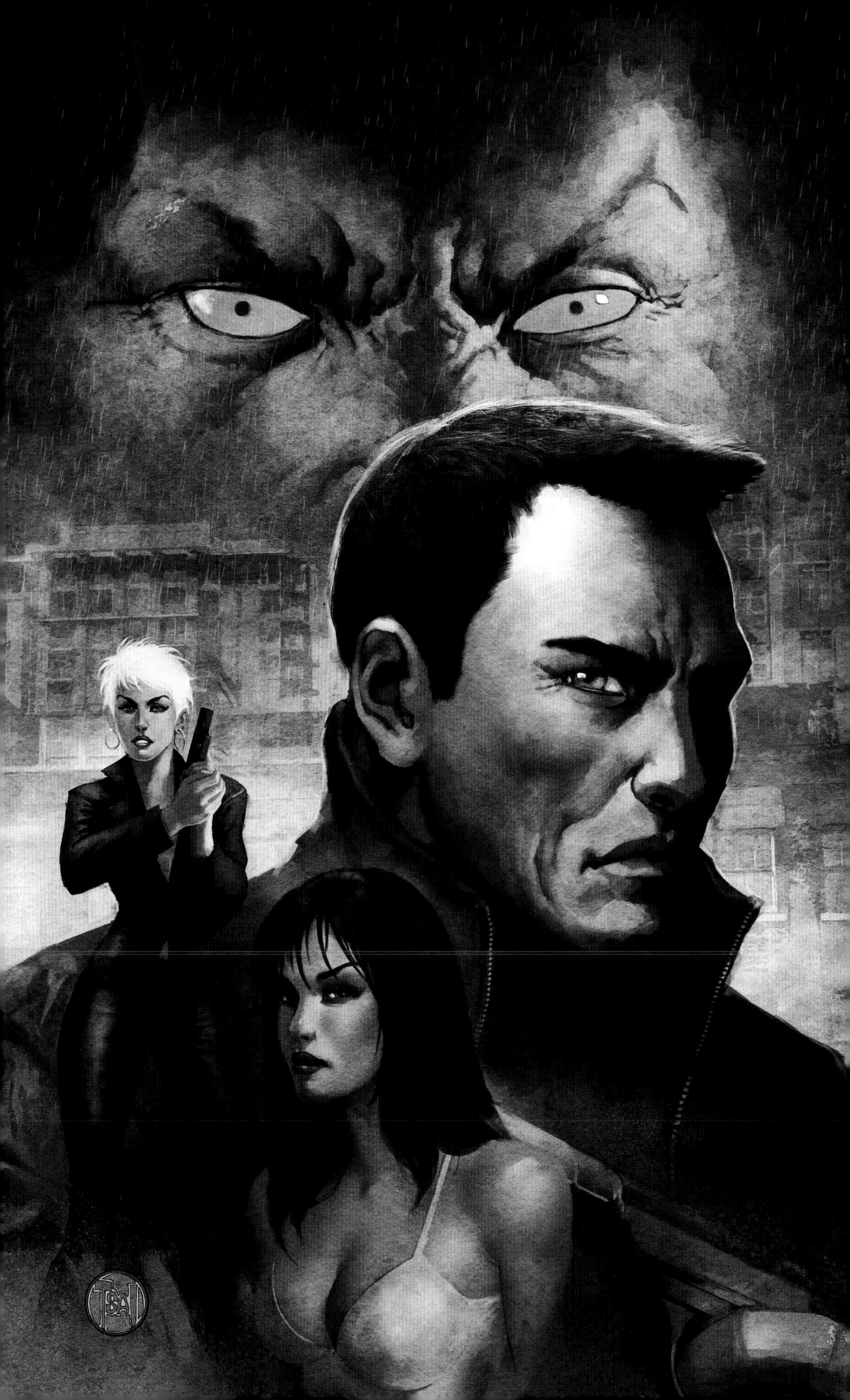

TRACKER™

Issue #4, cover process: **Francis Tsai**

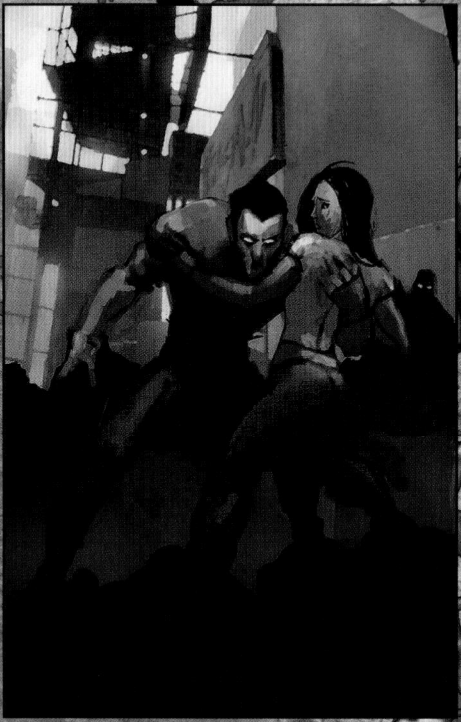

Left: **Initial Thumbnail concept**

Below: **Color Rough First Draft**

Facing page: **Final art by Francis Tsai**

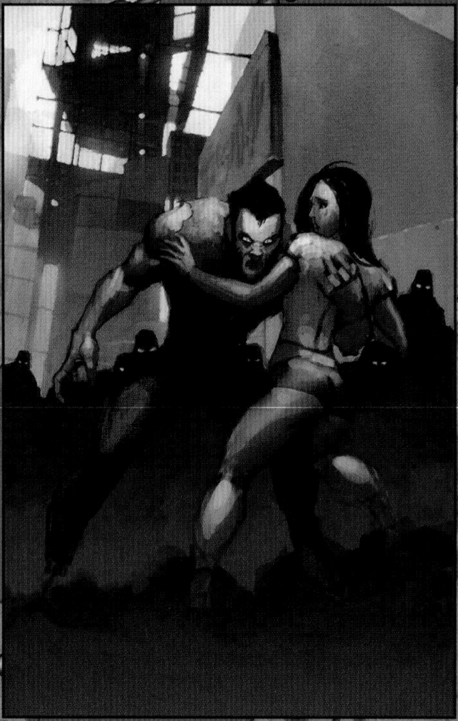

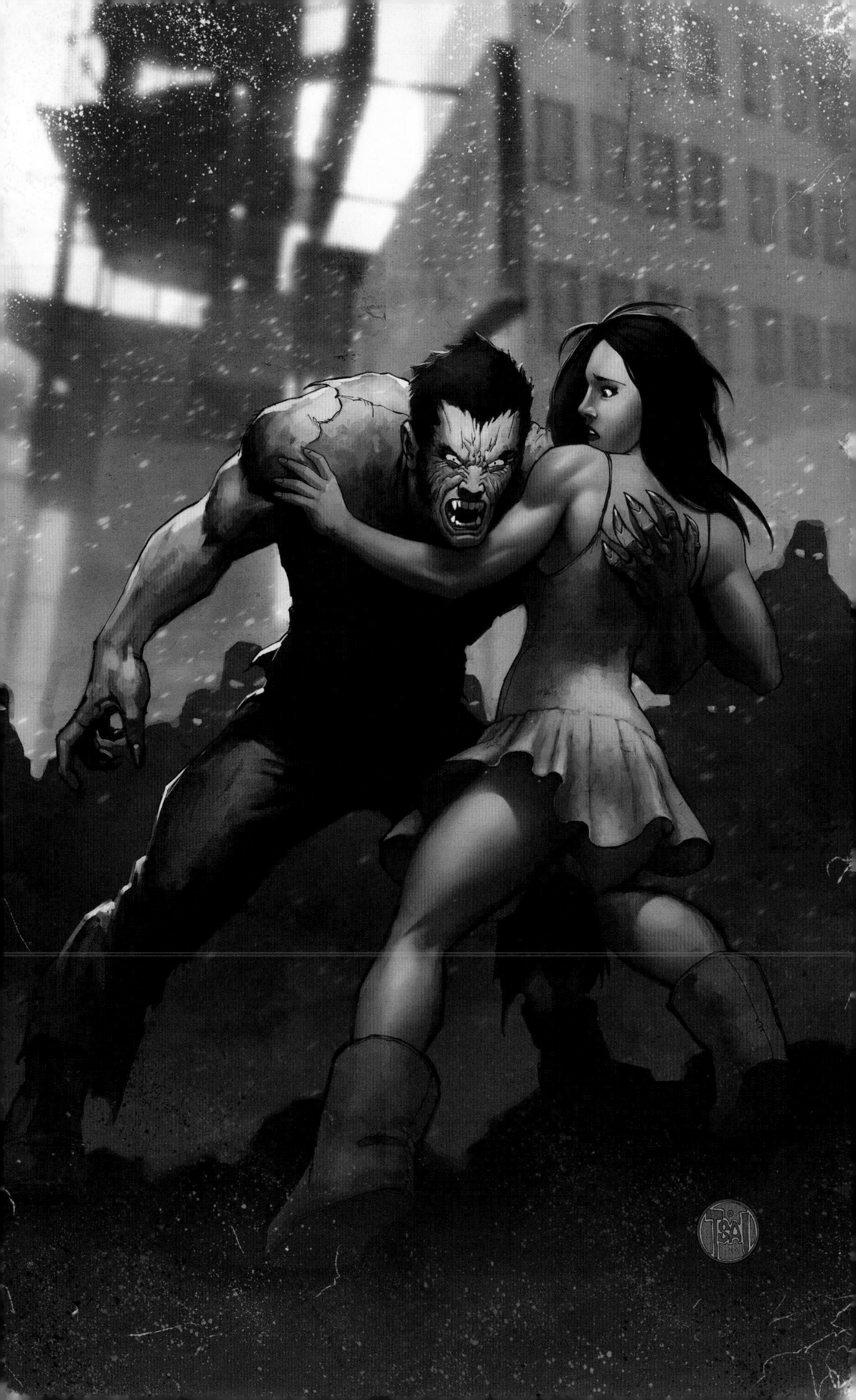

TRACKER™

Issue #5, cover process: **Francis Tsai**

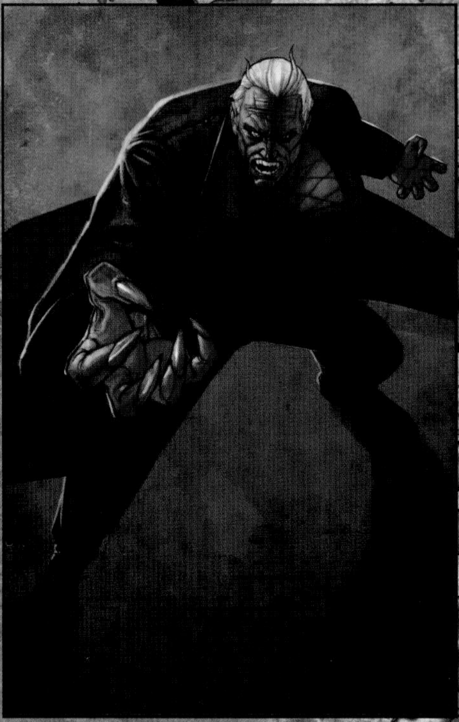

Left: **Color concept**

Below: **Revised color draft**

Facing page: **Final art by Francis Tsai**

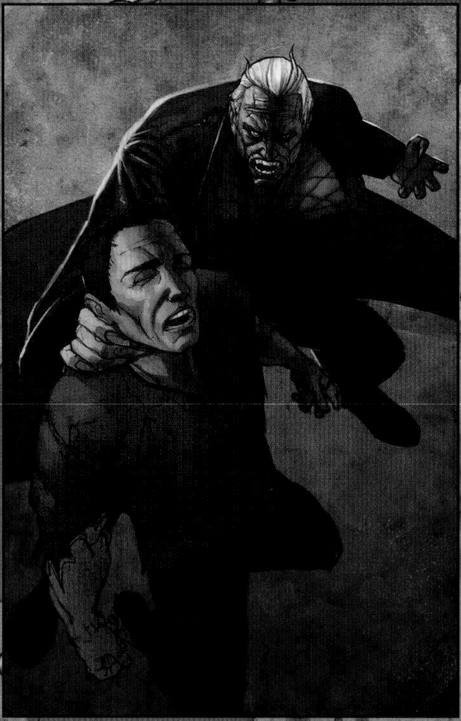

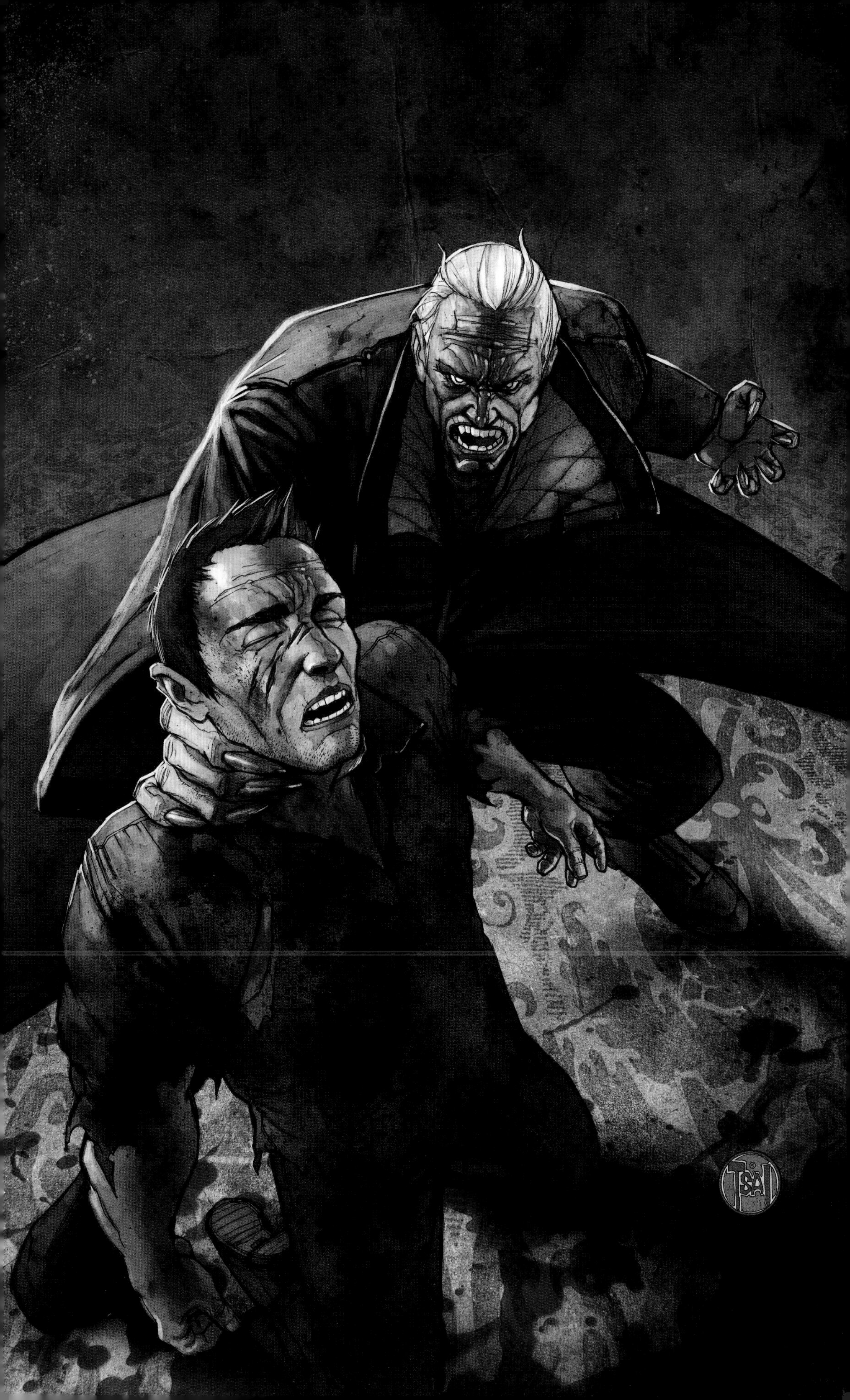

TRACKER™

CHARACTER BIOS & SKETCHES

FROM THE 2009 SAN DIEGO COMIC-CON TRACKER PREVIEW

ART BY FRANCIS TSAI

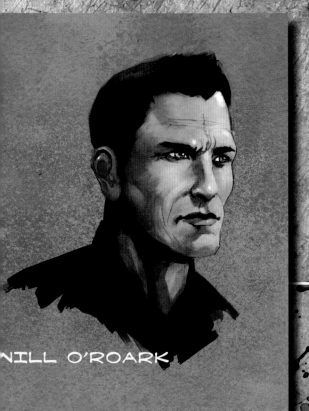

WILL O'ROARK

ALEJANDRO (ALEX) O'ROARK
★ ★ ★ ★ ★

A FEDERAL AGENT WHO SPECIALIZES IN TRACKING. HE GREW UP POOR, THE SON OF A LATINA MOTHER AND AN ABUSIVE IRISH FATHER. ALEX FOUGHT TOOTH-AND-NAIL TO GET WHERE HE IS TODAY; HE'S PROUD OF HIS CAREER. BUT ALL THIS CHANGES WHEN A CASE LEADS HIM INTO THE GAPING MAW OF A WEREWOLF—RIPPING HIS NEAT LITTLE LIFE TO SHREDS.

EDITOR'S NOTE: ALEX WAS ORIGINALLY CALLED "WILL" IN THE FIRST DRAFT OF THE SCRIPT

TORY REYES

ALEX'S LONGTIME GIRLFRIEND. SHE'S THE HOTTEST THIRD-GRADE TEACHER YOU'VE EVER SEEN, AND THERE'S NO QUESTION EVERY BOY IN HER CLASSROOM IS HOPELESSLY IN LOVE WITH HER. ALEX IS CRAZY ABOUT HER TOO—BUT TORY REFUSES TO SETTLE DOWN UNLESS HE'S WILLING TO RETIRE HIS WEAPON.

TORY REYES

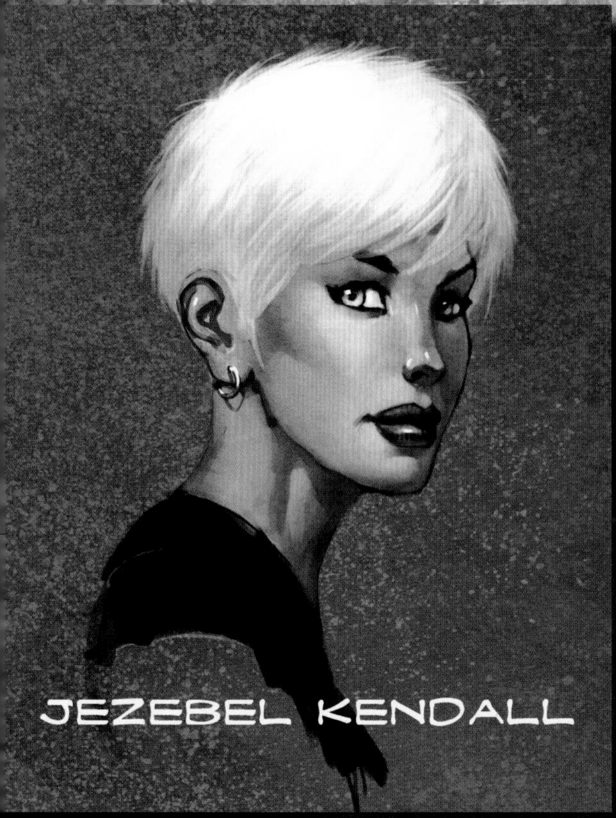
JEZEBEL KENDALL

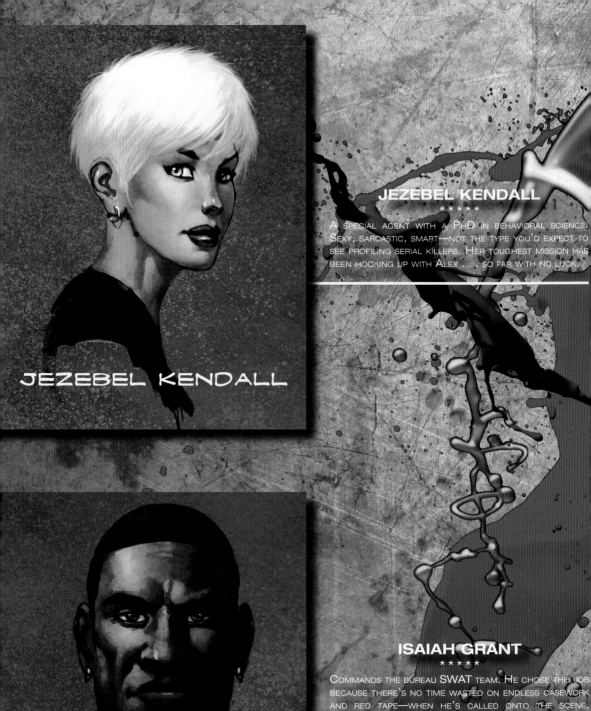

JEZEBEL KENDALL

* * * * *

A special agent with a PhD in behavioral science. Sexy, sarcastic, smart—not the type you'd expect to see profiling serial killers. Her toughest mission has been hooking up with Alex . . . so far with no luck.

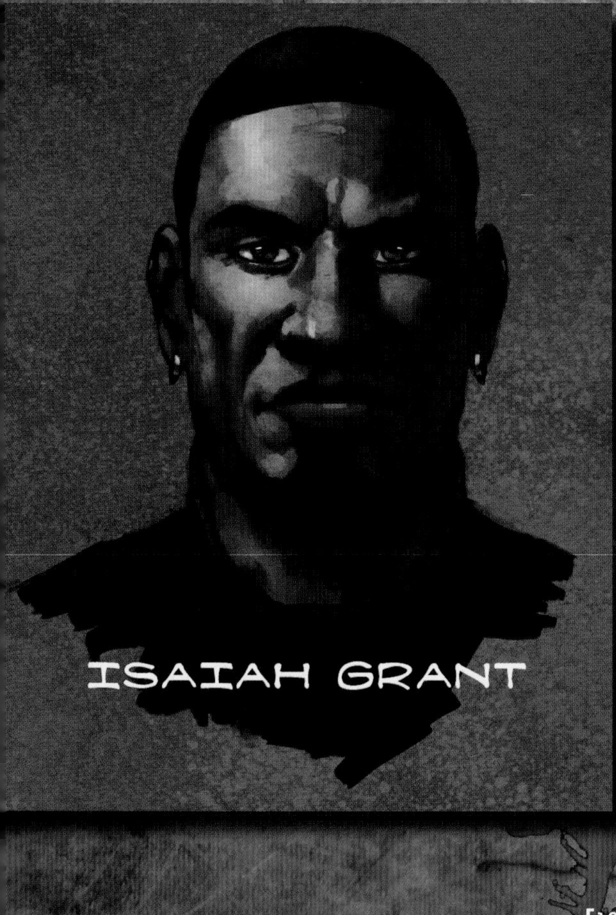
ISAIAH GRANT

ISAIAH GRANT

* * * * *

Commands the bureau SWAT team. He chose this job because there's no time wasted on endless casework and red tape—when he's called onto the scene, someone's going to die. He's an ambitious prick who wouldn't hesitate to throw a guy under the bus if it meant promotion, especially if that guy is Alex.

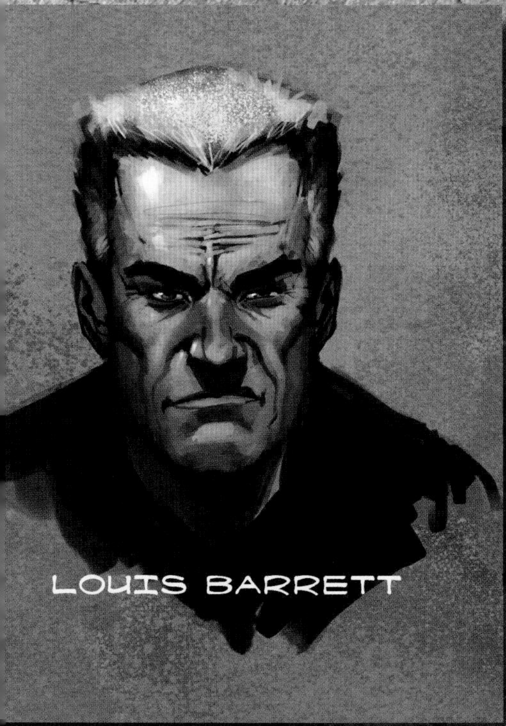
LOUIS BARRETT

LOUIS BARRETT

* * * * *

A former sniper for the FBI's Hostage Rescue Team—the meanest, toughest group of agents in the world. He was there at Ruby Ridge, Waco, and countless other missions he's not at liberty to discuss. He's got the bureau slogan ("fidelity, bravery, integrity") tattooed on his ass and won't stand for even a hint of misconduct.

DR. CYRIL TUCKER

* * * * *

A werewolf researcher for a shadowy organization called the Handel Foundation. He signed up thinking he was going to save the world, but has since learned he might be destroying it. He knows more about lycanthropy than any man alive, and he may even have the cure. He becomes Alex's go-to-guy for all things werewolf. But crossing his employers would be a deadly mistake, which makes him a dubious ally for Alex.

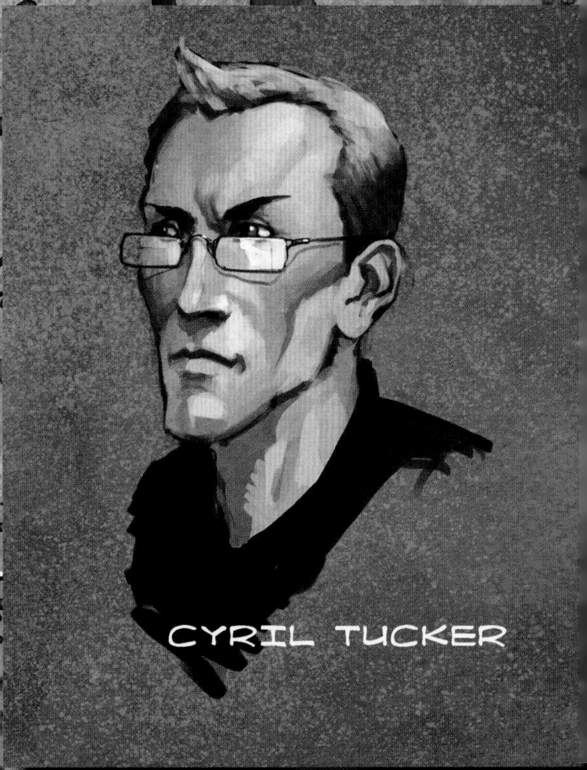
CYRIL TUCKER

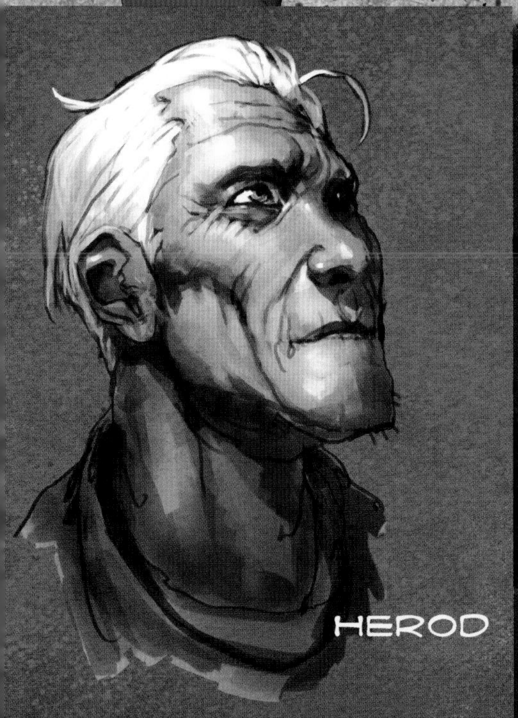
HEROD

HEROD

* * * * *

The FBI's deadliest serial killer on record. Nobody alive has ever seen his face . . . he also happens to be a werewolf. Over the years, Herod has learned how to exercise incredible control over his feral state, making him the most dangerous combination: a calculating sociopath with vicious killer instincts. He's Hannibal Lecter with fangs.

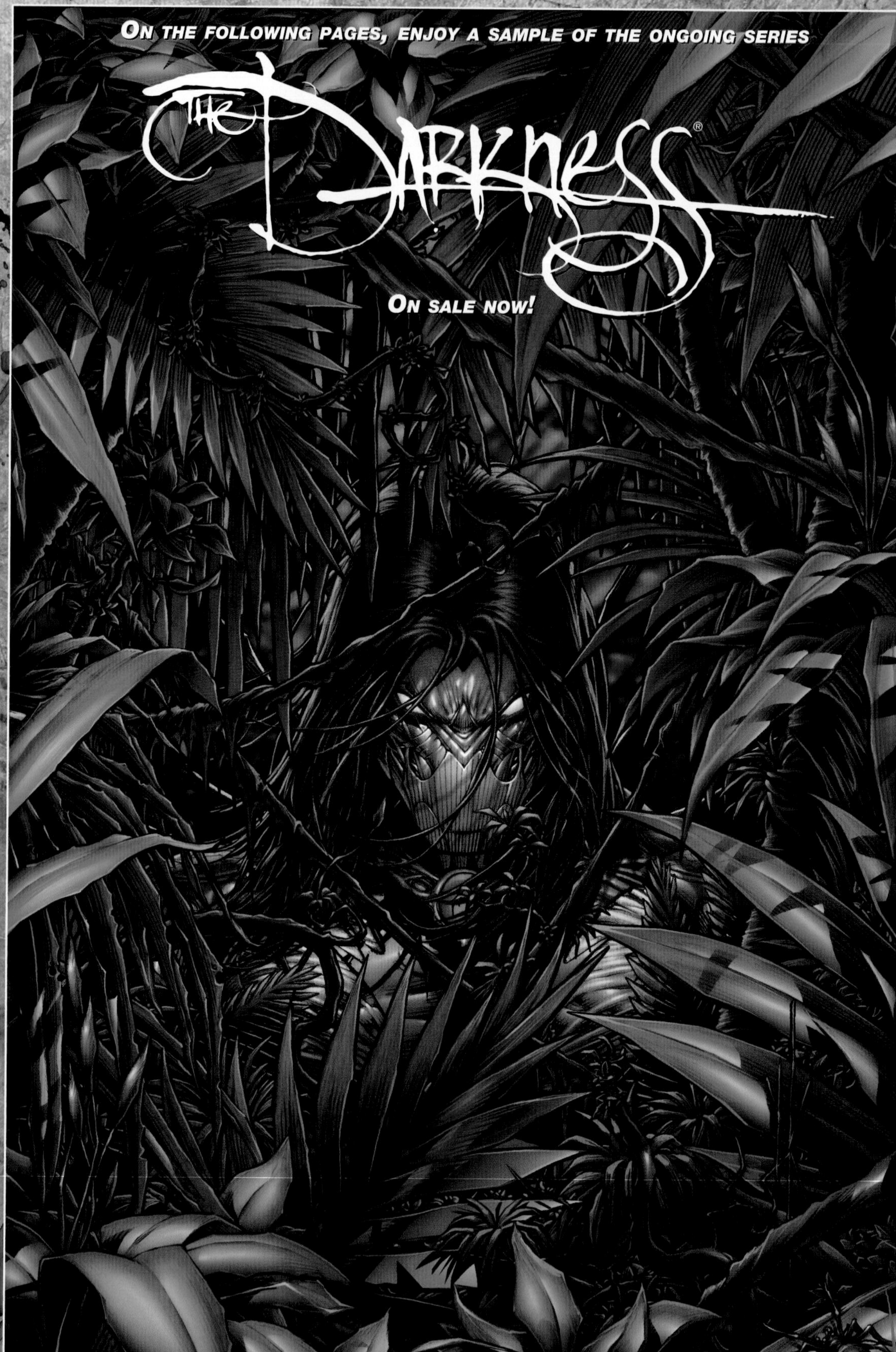
ON THE FOLLOWING PAGES, ENJOY A SAMPLE OF THE ONGOING SERIES
THE DARKNESS®
ON SALE NOW!
ART BY: DALE KEOWN

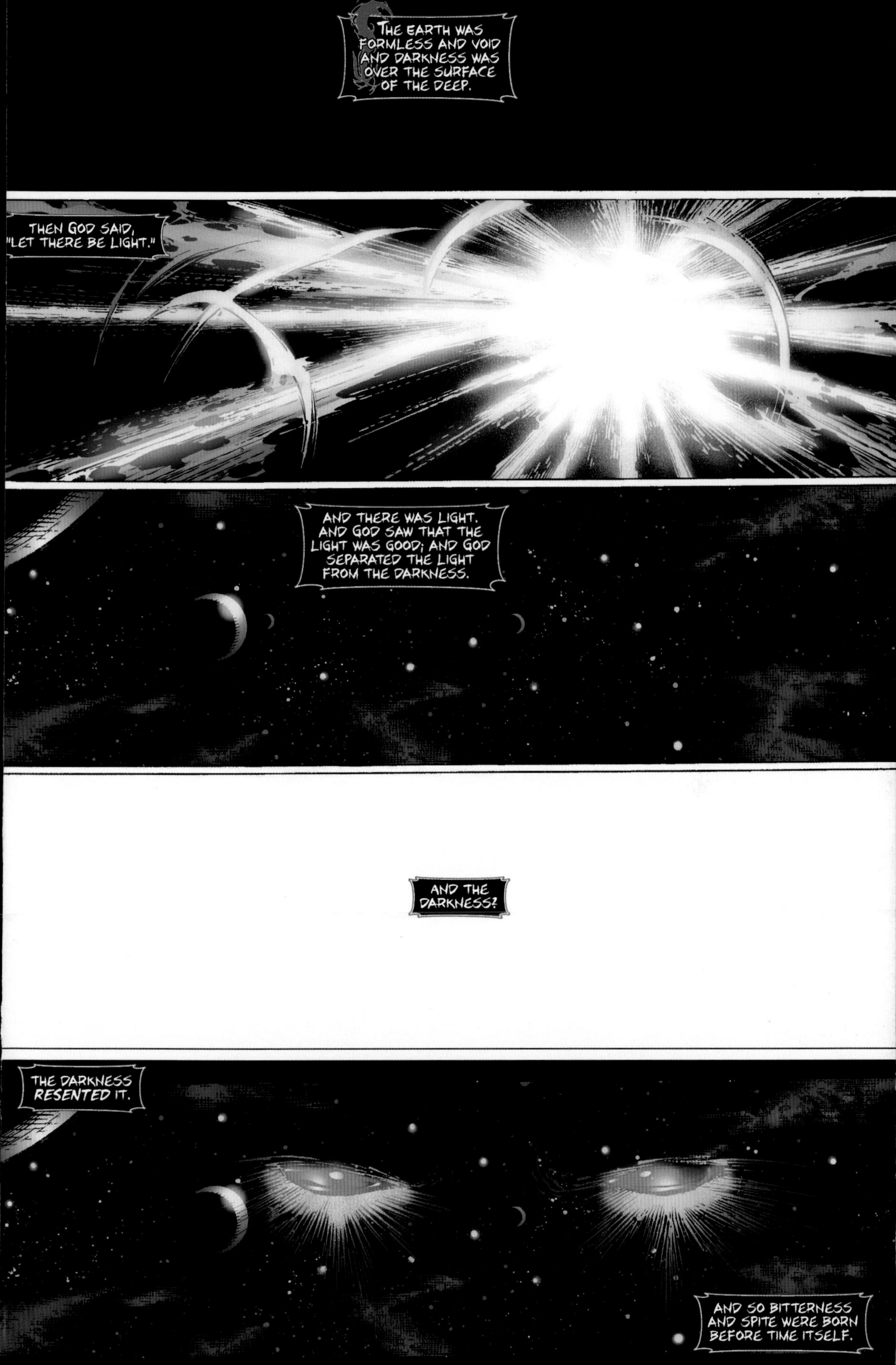
THE EARTH WAS FORMLESS AND VOID AND DARKNESS WAS OVER THE SURFACE OF THE DEEP.
THEN GOD SAID, "LET THERE BE LIGHT."
AND THERE WAS LIGHT. AND GOD SAW THAT THE LIGHT WAS GOOD; AND GOD SEPARATED THE LIGHT FROM THE DARKNESS.
AND THE DARKNESS?
THE DARKNESS RESENTED IT.
AND SO BITTERNESS AND SPITE WERE BORN BEFORE TIME ITSELF.

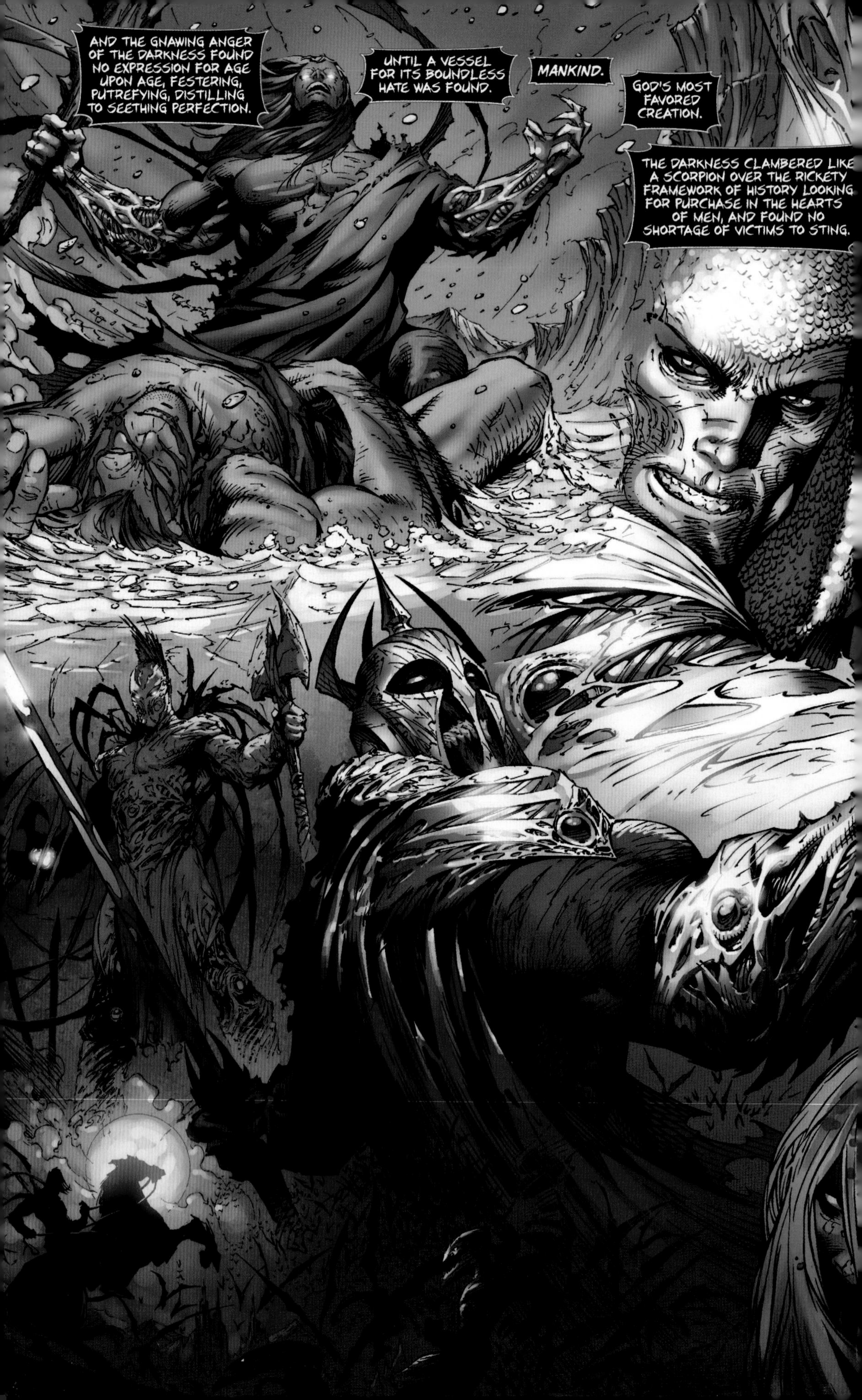
AND THE GNAWING ANGER OF THE DARKNESS FOUND NO EXPRESSION FOR AGE UPON AGE, FESTERING, PUTREFYING, DISTILLING TO SEETHING PERFECTION.
UNTIL A VESSEL FOR ITS BOUNDLESS HATE WAS FOUND.
MANKIND.
GOD'S MOST FAVORED CREATION.
THE DARKNESS CLAMBERED LIKE A SCORPION OVER THE RICKETY FRAMEWORK OF HISTORY LOOKING FOR PURCHASE IN THE HEARTS OF MEN, AND FOUND NO SHORTAGE OF VICTIMS TO STING.

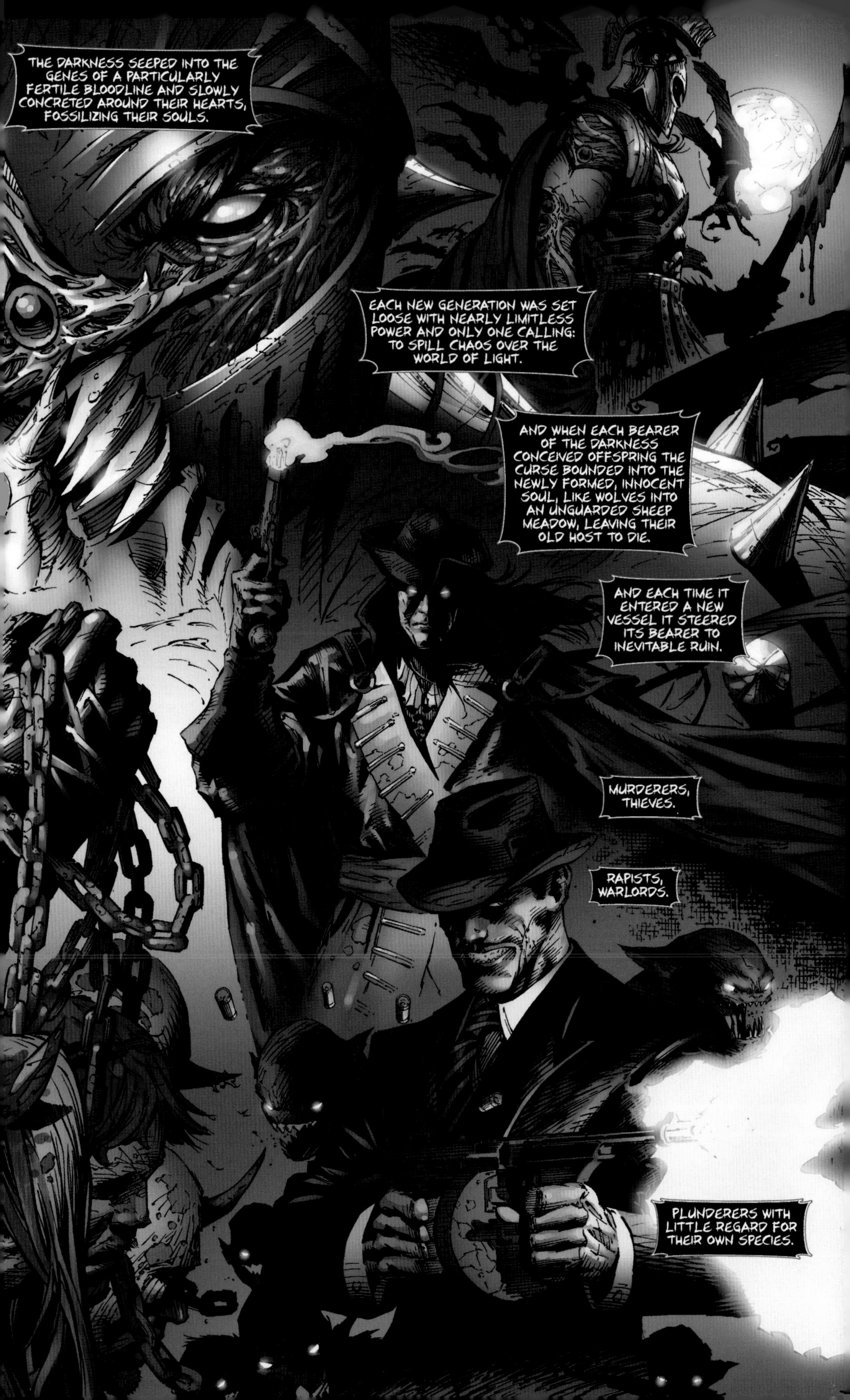

THE DARKNESS SEEPED INTO THE GENES OF A PARTICULARLY FERTILE BLOODLINE AND SLOWLY CONCRETED AROUND THEIR HEARTS, FOSSILIZING THEIR SOULS.
EACH NEW GENERATION WAS SET LOOSE WITH NEARLY LIMITLESS POWER AND ONLY ONE CALLING: TO SPILL CHAOS OVER THE WORLD OF LIGHT.
AND WHEN EACH BEARER OF THE DARKNESS CONCEIVED OFFSPRING THE CURSE BOUNDED INTO THE NEWLY FORMED, INNOCENT SOUL, LIKE WOLVES INTO AN UNGUARDED SHEEP MEADOW, LEAVING THEIR OLD HOST TO DIE.
AND EACH TIME IT ENTERED A NEW VESSEL IT STEERED ITS BEARER TO INEVITABLE RUIN.
MURDERERS, THIEVES.
RAPISTS, WARLORDS.
PLUNDERERS WITH LITTLE REGARD FOR THEIR OWN SPECIES.

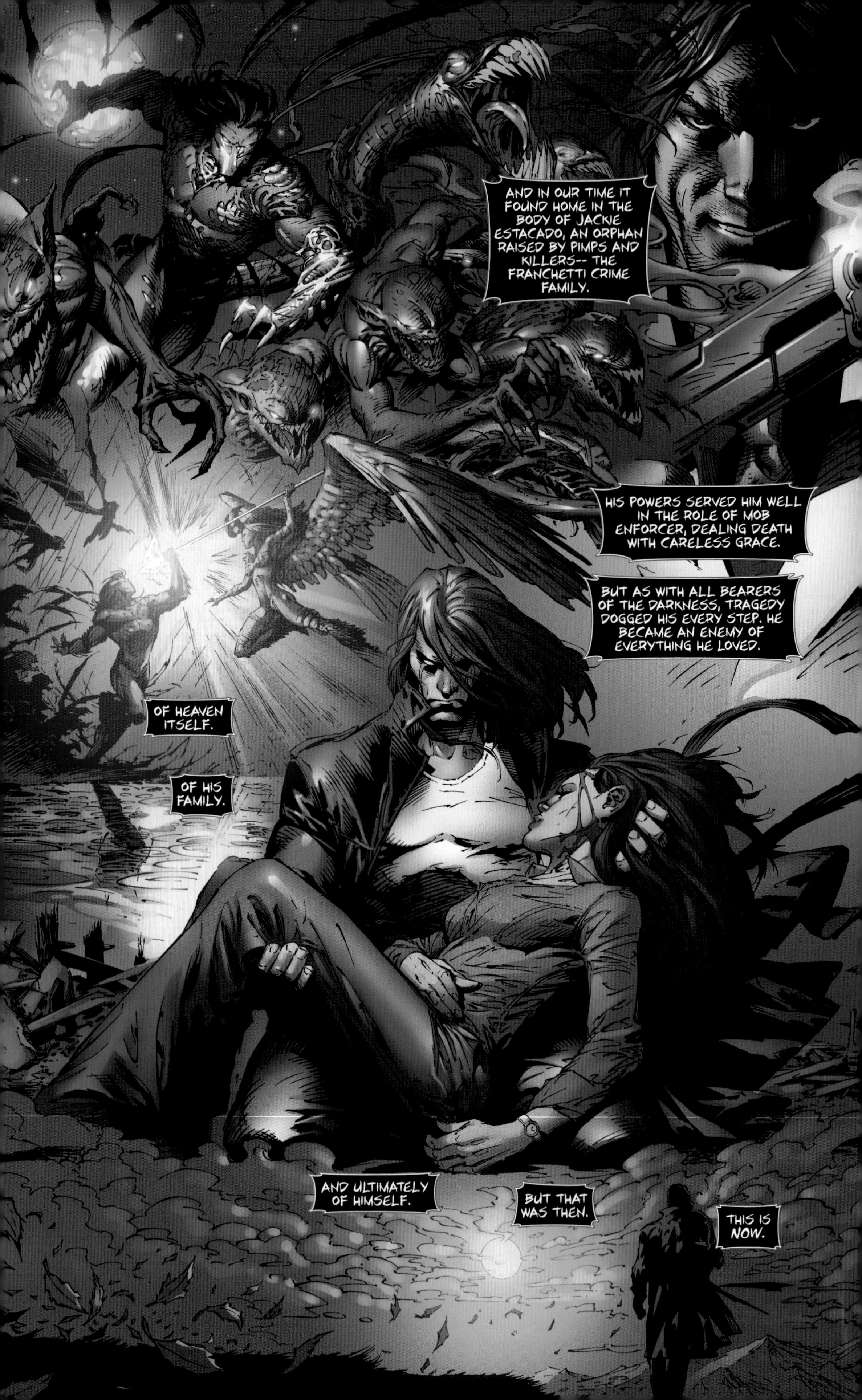
AND IN OUR TIME IT FOUND HOME IN THE BODY OF JACKIE ESTACADO, AN ORPHAN RAISED BY PIMPS AND KILLERS-- THE FRANCHETTI CRIME FAMILY.
HIS POWERS SERVED HIM WELL IN THE ROLE OF MOB ENFORCER, DEALING DEATH WITH CARELESS GRACE.
BUT AS WITH ALL BEARERS OF THE DARKNESS, TRAGEDY DOGGED HIS EVERY STEP. HE BECAME AN ENEMY OF EVERYTHING HE LOVED.
OF HEAVEN ITSELF.
OF HIS FAMILY.
AND ULTIMATELY OF HIMSELF.
BUT THAT WAS THEN.
THIS IS NOW.

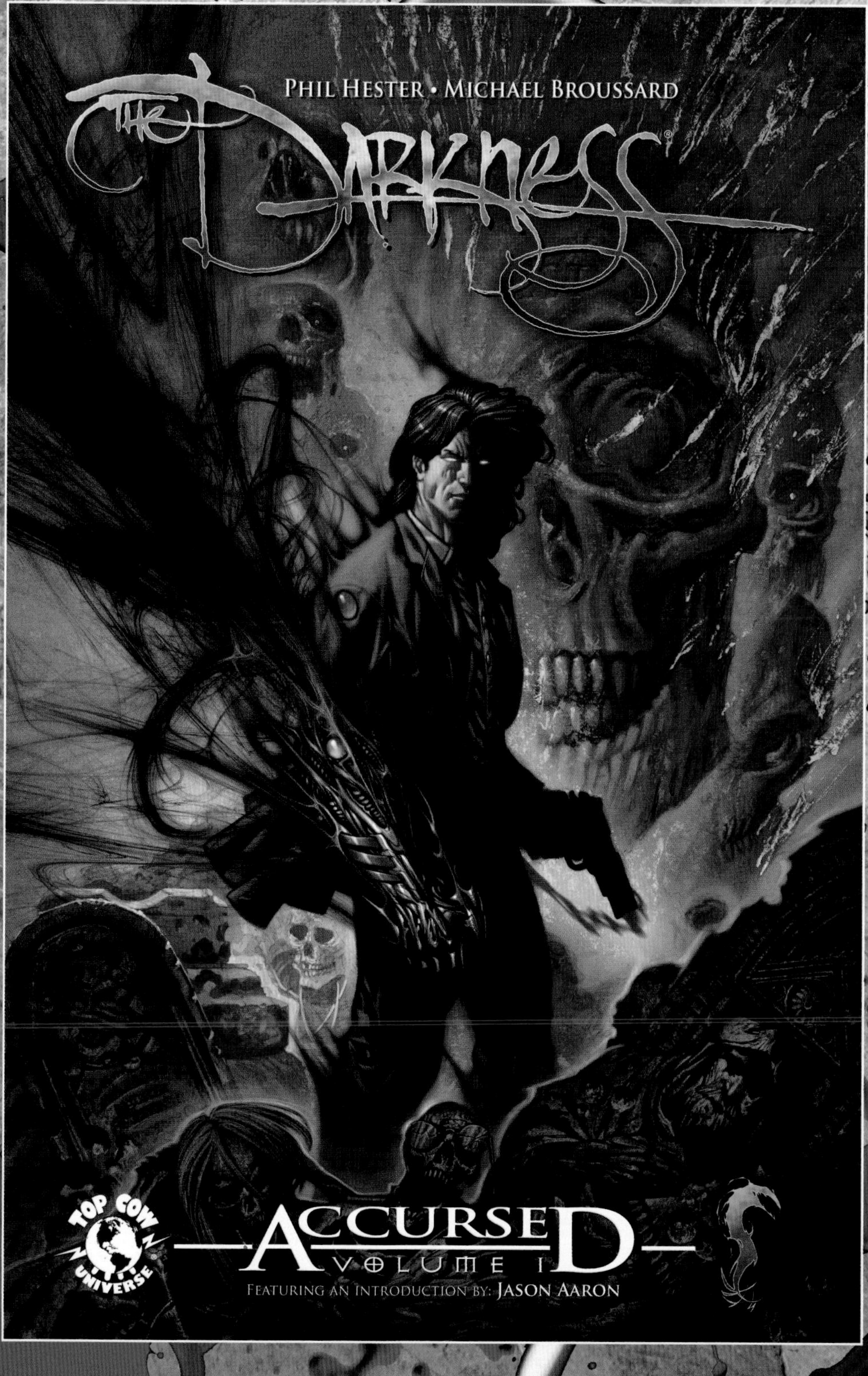
PHIL HESTER • MICHAEL BROUSSARD
THE DARKNESS
ACCURSED
VOLUME I
FEATURING AN INTRODUCTION BY: JASON AARON
TOP COW UNIVERSE

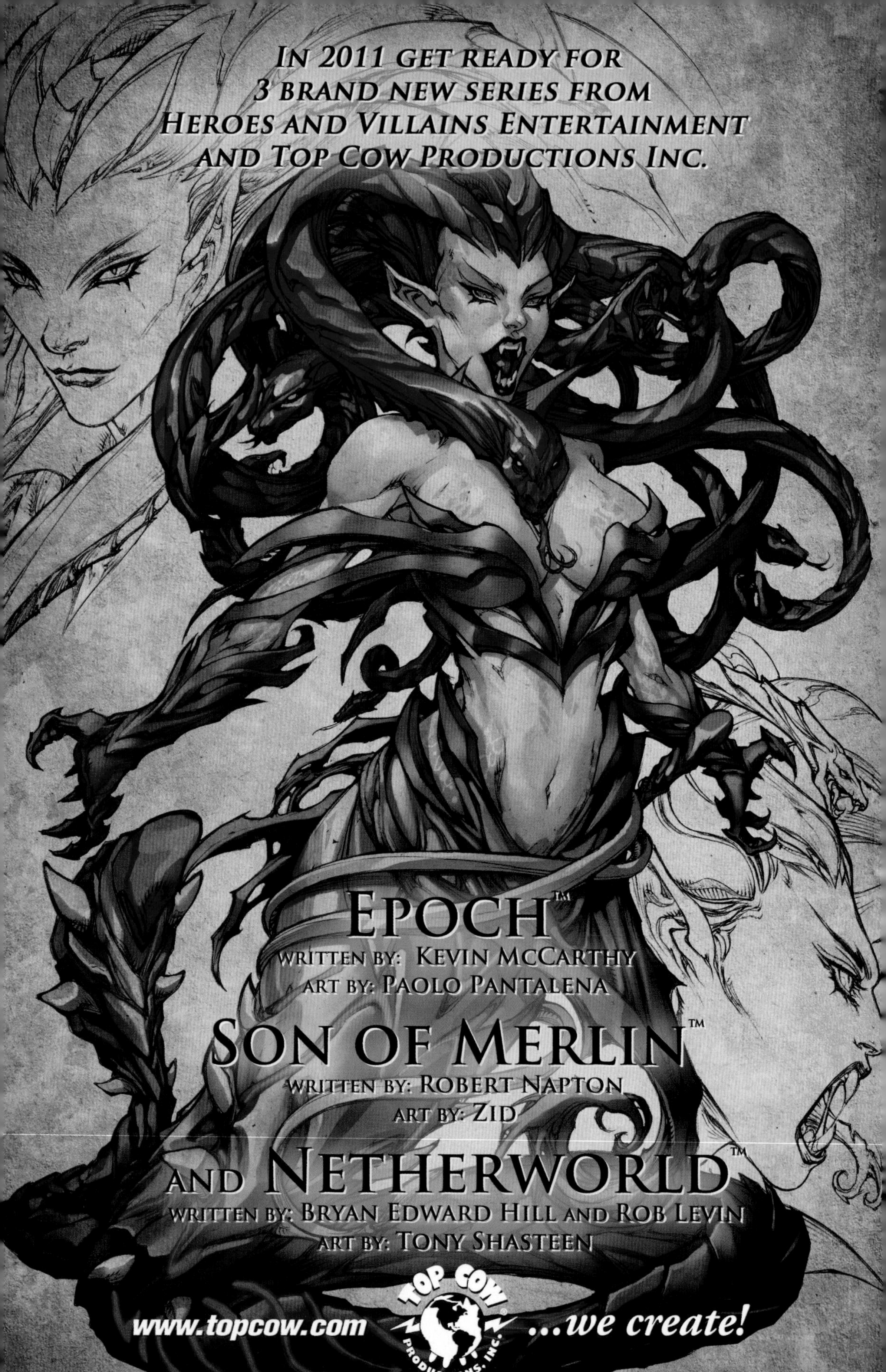
In 2011 get ready for
3 brand new series from
Heroes and Villains Entertainment
and Top Cow Productions Inc.
Epoch™
written by: Kevin McCarthy
art by: Paolo Pantalena
Son of Merlin™
written by: Robert Napton
art by: Zid
and Netherworld™
written by: Bryan Edward Hill and Rob Levin
art by: Tony Shasteen
www.topcow.com
Top Cow Productions, Inc.
...we create!

RICK LOVERD • JEREMY HAUN
BERSERKER
DIVIDE
FEATURING AN INTRODUCTION BY: MILO VENTIMIGLIA AND RUSS CUNDIFF

RON MARZ • STJEPAN SEJIC
WITCHBLADE
REDEMPTION VOLUME 1
FEATURING AN INTRODUCTION BY: TODD MCFARLANE

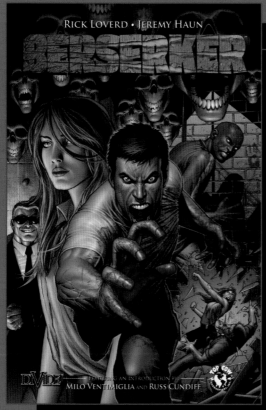

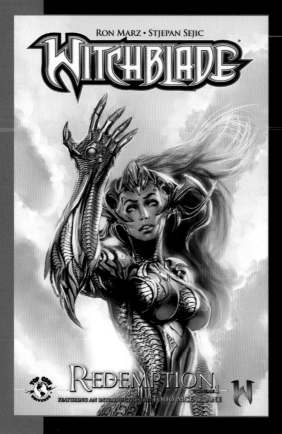

Jump into the Top Cow Universe with The Darkness!

PHIL HESTER • MICHAEL BROUSSARD
The Darkness
ACCURSED
VOLUME 1
FEATURING AN INTRODUCTION BY: JASON AARON

The Darkness

Accursed vol.1

written by:
Phil Hester

pencils by:
Michael Broussard

Mafia hitman Jackie Estacado was both blessed and cursed on his 21st birthday when he became the bearer of The Darkness, an elemental force that allows those who wield it access to an otherwordly dimension and control over the demons who dwell there. Forces for good in the world rise up to face Jackie and the evil his gift represents, but there is one small problem. In this story...they are the bad guys.

Now's your chance to read "Empire," the first storyline by the new creative team of **Phil Hester** (*Firebreather, Green Arrow*) and **Michael Broussard** (*Unholy Union*) that marked the shocking return of *The Darkness* to the Top Cow Universe!

Book Market Edtion
(ISBN: 978-1-58240-958-0) $9.99

PHIL HESTER • JORGE LUCAS
The Darkness
ACCURSED
VOLUME 2

The Darkness

Accursed vol.2

written by: Phil Hester

pencils by: Jorge Lucas, Michael Broussard, Joe Benitez, Dale Keown and more!

Collects *The Darkness* volume 3 #7-10 and the double-sized *The Darkness* #75 (issue #11 before the Legacy Numbering took effect), plus a cover gallery and behind-the-scenes extras!

(ISBN: 978-1-58240-044-4) $9.99

PHIL HESTER • MICHAEL BROUSSARD
The Darkness
ACCURSED
VOLUME 3

The Darkness

Accursed vol.3

written by: Phil Hester

pencils by: Michael Broussard, Jorge Lucas, Nelson Blake II and Michael Avon Oeming.

Collects issues #76-79 plus the stand alone Tales of The Darkness story entitled "Lodbrok's Hand." Features art by regular series artist Michael Broussard (*Unholy Union, Artifacts*), Nelson Blake II (*Magdalena, Broken Trinity: Witchblade*), Jorge Lucas (*Broken Trinity: Aftermath, Wolverine*), and Michael Avon Oeming (*Mice Templar, Powers*).

(ISBN: 978-1-58240-100-7) $12.99

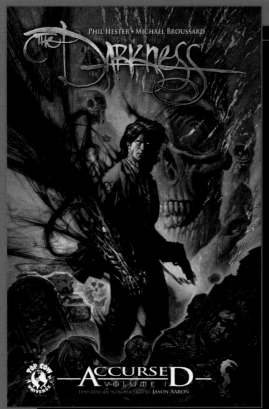

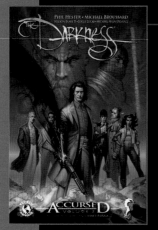

Ready for more? Learn more about the Top Cow Universe with *Witchblade*!

RON MARZ • MIKE CHOI
WITCHBLADE
VOLUME 1
FEATURING AN INTRODUCTION BY
RON MARZ

Witchblade

volume 1 - volume 8

written by:
Ron Marz
art by:
Mike Choi, Stephen Sadowski,
Keu Cha, Chris Bachalo,
Stjepan Sejic and more!

Get in on the ground floor of Top Cow's flagship title with these affordable trade paperback collections from Ron Marz's series-redefining run on Witchblade! Each volume collects a key story arc in the continuing adventures of Sara Pezzini and the Witchblade, culminating in the epic 'War of the Witchblades' storyline!

Book Market Edtion, **volume 1**
collects issues #80-#85
(ISBN: 978-1-58240-906-1) $9.99

WITCHBLADE
VOLUME 2

volume 2
collects issues #86-#92
(ISBN: 978-1-58240-886-6)
U.S.D. $14.99

WITCHBLADE
VOLUME 3

volume 3
collects issues #93-#100
(ISBN: 978-1-58240-887-3)
U.S.D. $14.99

WITCHBLADE
VOLUME 4

volume 4
collects issues #101-109
(ISBN: 978-1-58240-898-9)
U.S.D. $17.99

WITCHBLADE
VOLUME 5

volume 5
collects issues #110-115,
First Born issues #1-3
(ISBN: 978-1-58240-899-6)
U.S.D. $17.99

WITCHBLADE

volume 6
collects issues #116-#120
(ISBN: 978-1-60706-041-3)
U.S.D. $14.99

RON MARZ • STJEPAN SEJIC
WITCHBLADE
VOLUME 7

volume 7
collects issues #121-#124 &
Witchblade Annual #1
(ISBN: 978-1-60706-058-1)
U.S.D. $14.99

RON MARZ • STJEPAN SEJIC
WITCHBLADE

volume 8
collects issues #125-#130
(ISBN: 978-1-60706-102-1)
U.S.D. $14.99

Collected works by William Harms from Top Cow Productions, Inc..

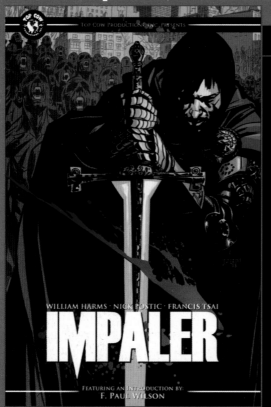

Impaler
volume 1

written by:
William Harms

art by:
Nick Marinkovich, Nick Postic
& Francis Tsai

Acclaimed horror writer William Harms (*Bad Mojo, Abel*) teams with Nick Marinkovich (*Nightwolf*), Nick Postic (*Underworld*) and award-winning artist Francis Tsai (*Marvel Comics Presents*) to breath new, horrifying life into the classic vampire myth.

The brilliant reimaging of the vampire myth is collected in this deluxe trade paperback for the first time and includes *Impaler* #1-3 as well as the final three chapters of the initial storyline not available anywhere else. This volume also includes a collection of bonus materials that sinks its teeth into what it took to make this instant horror classic.

(ISBN: 978-1-58240-757-9) $14.99

Impaler
volume 2

written by:
William Harms

art by:
Matt Timson

Millions of vampires have descended upon America. In a desperate attempt to defeat them the US military nuked New York City. Unfortunately, it was too little, too late. The legendary vampire hunter Vlad the Impaler has returned to stop them and NYC Detective Victor Dailey has become his unwilling companion.

International Horror Guild Award finalist William Harms (*Wolverine: The Anniversary*) returns to his bold new re-imagining of the vampire mythos with this second volume! Joining Harms for this volume is up-and-coming painter Matt Timson (*Popgun*). Collects Impaler Volume 2 #1-6, plus a cover gallery and bonus material.

(ISBN: 978-1-60706-101-4) $14.99